THE CHURCH LIBRARIAN'S HANDBOOK

THE CHURCH LIBRARIAN'S HANDBOOK

A Complete Guide
for the Library
and Resource Center
in Christian Education

Betty McMichael

BAKER BOOK HOUSE

Grand Rapids, Michigan 49506

To
Mac

CONTENTS

TABLES

FOREWORD

We live in a day when many resources are available to communicate Christian truth. But we often lack in ability to make these materials available in an organized and systematic fashion, and unless we do, utilization will be minimal.

Here is a book that will help solve this problem. It is an invaluable resource guide for pastors, Christian education workers, and any person interested in promoting the cause of Jesus Christ.

We owe a real debt of gratitude to Betty McMichael for her efforts in preparing this material for publication. Her research has been superb! And her practical experience over the years as a church librarian has added an obvious touch of reality that is often missing in practical, how-to-do-it books.

As a professor, pastor, and fellow author, I highly recommend this book! Put it in the right hands, and your service for Jesus Christ will be greatly multiplied.

GENE A. GETZ

PREFACE TO THE FIRST EDITION

HAVING WORKED SEVERAL YEARS for a man who often reminded me, "When you write anything, keep your reader in mind," I have repeatedly asked myself as I worked on this book who my readers might be. Ever since I helped start our own church library about fifteen years ago, people from other churches have asked me how to start a library. So my first thought was that this book should help answer that question.

Even more people have asked, "How can we get people to use our library?" Others say, "We have outgrown the classification system we started with. What do you suggest?"; "We are building a new church. Where should we put the library?"; "We have very limited financial support. How can we best use it?" It became clear to me that this book should deal with problems and needs of established libraries as well as with the starting of new libraries.

As I began my research, I became aware of another group in need of information about church libraries. People we classify as full-time Christian workers often are woefully ignorant of the operation and potential value of church libraries. While they are very dependent on their personal libraries, many have little vision of what Christian reading, viewing, and listening can mean in the lives and homes of church members.

When pastors, Christian education directors, and other staff members recognize the potential ministry of an active church library or resource center and understand something of its operation and needs, they can do a great deal to encourage the development of such a facility. For this reason, I am also writing for them. I hope that church librarians will point this out to their church staff and that Bible schools, colleges, and seminaries will find the book a helpful tool in the training of church workers.

My main purpose, however, is to help church librarians develop and expand their library's ministry into that of an effective resource center which will serve the entire church. In order to learn what methods are being used successfully, as well as what problems are being encountered, I mailed the questionnaire found in Appendix 1 to over four hundred church librarians throughout the United States and Canada. Results of this survey are scattered throughout the book.

Some of my survey respondents said they had heard enough about the ideal library, but not enough about how to work in a less-than-ideal situation. In case you are so fortunate as to need them, I have included suggestions for ideal location, equipment, staffing, and funding. But I realize you may have an inconvenient location, very limited financial support, and little or no help as you scrounge for shelving and other supplies. If this describes your situation, you are not as alone as you might think. But never despair! In spite of these obstacles, you have an important ministry to perform. And I know from experience that it is possible to have an effective church library in spite of many handicaps.

"But just a minute," you say. "You keep talking about the church library. What about the resource center?" While the resource center is a relatively new concept for churches, it is an important one, so let's move from the traditional idea of a church library to the newer, more exciting and purposeful concept of a resource center. The terms are often used interchangeably, but there is growing emphasis on replacing libraries with resource centers.

Use of the *resource center* name and idea implies a central location, or at least a coordinated service for providing print and nonprint materials. Not only are such things as audiovisual equipment and teaching supplies included, but the library workers themselves are human resources available for help and guidance of many kinds. *Media center* is another name often used to indicate inclusion of nonprint materials.

The name isn't the important thing. Some church libraries function as resource or media centers but prefer to keep the name *church library* because their people are used to it. One danger of using the newer names is that members who are not active in the Christian education program of the church tend to think a resource or media center exists only to serve that program, and they may not recognize the benefits available to them as individuals unless they are constantly reminded of them.

I have chosen to use the more familiar term, *church library,* most often in this book. However, I strongly endorse the broader concept and encourage forward-looking churches and librarians to be developing a ministry larger than the traditional one, regardless of what name they give it. Such a ministry will serve both the needs of individuals and the needs of church groups.

I wish to acknowledge the contributions of many people to the completion of this book. My thanks to Ruth Skanse and Nancy Dick of the Evangelical Church Library Association, editor Leslie Stobbe of Moody Press, authors Bernard and Marjorie Palmer for suggestions on writing techniques, librarians Sarah Lyons of the Conservative Baptist Seminary in Denver and Joseph Mapes of the University of Colorado for professional advice, pastor William Robert (Bob) Culbertson for inspiration and encouragement, my family for patiently tolerating stacks of questionnaires and other papers around the house, and hundreds of church librarians from all over America and Canada who responded to my survey not only willingly, but even enthusiastically.

Special thanks also go to my friend and fellow church librarian, Janice Mullet, for an excellent typing job combined with a personal interest in the project; to my son David McMichael for taking pictures of libraries wherever we went; and to our pastor's son, David Culbertson, for contributing his drafting skills.

PREFACE TO THE SECOND EDITION

CHURCH LIBRARIANS need and deserve all the help they can get. Although it has its rewards, their task is not easy, for recent years have brought changes that affect both the holdings and the administration of church libraries. To keep up with these changes, therefore, this book has been updated and expanded.

In order to gather information and ideas for the second edition of this book, I visited as many church librarians as I could. Most of these visits left me encouraged about the work that has been recently accomplished and hopeful that librarians will take advantage of new opportunities.

For example, who would have thought a few years ago that we would be giving any serious thought to having computers in our church libraries? Yet that is one of the subjects treated in chapter 12, a new chapter written to inform librarians about recent developments and new technologies that are having an impact on church libraries and can be expected to enlarge their opportunities for outreach even more in the future.

In addition to adding the new chapter, called "Looking to the Future," we have also updated the directory of suppliers found in Appendix 2, the bibliography, and the index. Even though some of the information in the suppliers' directory will become obsolete rather quickly, we expect most of the information to remain of value for some time to come.

I am indebted to Nancy Dick of the Evangelical Church Library Association for her insistence that this book be kept in print. I am grateful to Baker Book House for agreeing with Nancy and making this new edition possible. I also thank my good friend Arlene Culbertson, who has given so generously of herself to help prepare the manuscript for publication.

It is our desire that this book encourage, inspire, and inform both prospective and experienced church librarians as they seek ways to best serve the Lord through this important ministry.

1

RECOGNIZING THE FUNCTION OF THE CHURCH LIBRARY AS A RESOURCE CENTER

Finally, brethren, whatever is true, whatever is honorable, whatever is right, whatever is pure, whatever is lovely, whatever is of good repute, if there is any excellence and if anything worthy of praise, let your mind dwell on these things (Philippians 4:8).

THERE ARE TWO THINGS of which anyone promoting the work of church libraries must be convinced. The first is that there is value in reading, viewing, and listening to Christian material. The second is that the church library can actively promote such activities. If you are already thoroughly convinced on both of these points, just scan the first part of this chapter for ideas to use in convincing others and then go on to portions more applicable to your needs.

THE VALUE OF CHRISTIAN READING, VIEWING, AND LISTENING MATERIALS

"Wouldn't it be better," someone asks, "to just encourage people to read the Bible? After all, that is the Christian's guide to salvation and his road map for the Christian life. Why should we encourage anyone to spend time on something less worthy?" Certainly, there should be no thought of taking time from Bible reading when we encourage use of other materials. Reading newspapers, magazines, and secular books and watching television have their place, but might not our lives be even richer if we replaced some less worthwhile activities with use of Christian materials, while giving Bible reading top priority? Just as a preacher uses explanations and illustrations with Bible quotations, so a Christian writer uses various literary forms to impress Bible truths on our minds and lives.

Books can be friends to bring us companionship and inspiration, teachers to instruct us, missionaries to help us give the Gospel to others, building blocks in developing character, bridges from one mind to another, windows to let light in and open up new worlds, gates through which we enter new adventures, paths to lead us upward, wings to help us fly, links with past generations, storehouses for knowledge, tools to help us with our tasks, exercise for our minds, and food for our spirits.

Communists and other disseminators of false teachings have been quick to recognize the power of the printed word. They are often the first to provide reading materials to newly literate nations. As Christians we need to recognize the powerful weapon for good that God has placed in our hands with the "tweny-six lead soldiers" of the printed alphabet.[1]

Daniel Webster warned us more than one hundred years ago: "If religious books are not widely circulated among the masses in this country I do not know what is to become of us as a nation. . . . If truth is not diffused, error will be."[2] Bishop Quayle once said, "Authors are God's generous gifts to help us to the wider life; use them."[3]

Books are especially important in child development. Most children read, but need guidance in selection of what to read. Without guidance they tend to gravitate toward the worst rather than the best literature. What they read will influence their thoughts, actions, and characters the rest of their lives. A story is told of two brothers growing up in the same home, but having very different goals in life. One aspired to be a robber operating from a mountain hideout. The other hoped to become a medical missionary in Africa. It was discovered that the first boy had been reading a steady stream of comic books about mountain bandits, while the other boy was finding inspiration in the *Jungle Doctor* missionary stories. Their book heroes caused these brothers to develop entirely different ideals and personalities.[4]

When we recognize "the potential of books to build a whole, healthy, spiritually alert child who has the capacity to enjoy God and be useful to Him,"[5] we will look for ways to put the right books into the hands of the child. Books shared through family reading bring a wonderful family closeness. Annis Duff, in her book *"Bequest of Wings,"* quotes an eight-year-old as saying, "I wonder what families do that don't read books together? It's like not knowing each other's friends."[6] We need to read the Bible in our homes

1. Edwin L. Groenhoff, *The Quiet Prince—A Biography of Dr. Melvin G. Larson, Christian Journalist* (Minneapolis: His International Service, 1974), p. 94.
2. J. H. Hunter, "The Ministry of the Printed Page," *Evangelical Beacon* 39 (September 27, 1966): 7.
3. William Alfred Quayle, "The One Book," *Decision* 10 (October 1969): 2.
4. Martin P. Simon, "Miles Apart in the Same Home," *United Evangelical Action* 19 (October 1960): 263.
5. Gladys Hunt, *Honey for a Child's Heart,* pp. 17-18.
6. Annis Duff, *"Bequest of Wings,"* p. 23.

and use other books to supplement and support its teachings. Christian values are learned gradually, reinforced by experiences both from life and from literature.

What are some of the other benefits of good reading, listening, and viewing materials? For one thing, they provide wholesome and needed relaxation and recreation. They help us develop ideals and values, bringing lessons from the past, hopes for the future, and helps for living in the present. They give us understanding of other people and insight into our own needs as we learn how God has worked in other lives and what He can do in ours. They provide us with information to share with others. They bring comfort to the bereaved, as many a lonely widow or widower can testify. The sharing of common interests strengthens ties of friendship. Reading has been demonstrated to have a strong effect on behavior. A study of one group of readers showed that reading definitely changed behavior.[7]

Many Christian leaders have testified of the influence of Christian books in their lives. George Whitefield attributes his conversion to the reading of a book borrowed from Charles Wesley.[8] J. Hudson Taylor, whose own books have challenged and inspired so many, tells that a little leaflet brought him to a place of decision for Christ.[9]

A pastor tells that three books from his church library influenced him to "surrender his life to preach."[10] I know a young man who decided to enter missionary aviation after reading *Jungle Pilot* from our church library. I have another friend whose life as an army colonel's wife was transformed by reading one of Isobel Kuhn's books. Her enthusiasm for that book led her to begin a ministry of giving and loaning books which has borne fruit in many parts of the world, some of them places where open preaching of the Gospel is not allowed.[11]

THE CHURCH LIBRARY OR RESOURCE CENTER AS PROMOTER OF CHRISTIAN MATERIALS

"All right," you say, "I am convinced that reading Christian literature and listening to Christian tapes are important. How can we be sure that a church library will promote these activities? The church I grew up in had a library, but hardly anyone ever used it. Aren't there better ways to spend the Lord's money than to tie it up in shelves and books that are seldom used?"

7. Sister Mary Corde Lorang, *Burning Ice: The Moral and Emotional Effects of Reading* (New York: Scribner, 1968).
8. Onva K. Boshears, Jr., "Books An Asset or Liability," *The Christian Librarian* 10 (November 1966): 12.
9. J. Hudson Taylor, *A Retrospect*, 6th ed. (New York: Gospel Publishing House, n.d.), pp. 4-5.
10. Ed Orberson, "What Are Books That God's People Should Be Mindful of Them?" *The Church Library Magazine* 9 (January, February, March 1967): 9.
11. Dorothy I. Meaders, "Hooked on Books?" *Command* (Spring 1969), p. 16.

"Yes, I'm sure there are," I would answer. "Tell me something about that library."

"Well," you tell me, "I remember there were some shelves in one corner of the junior department. The Sunday school superintendent appointed someone each year to take charge of the library. That person's main duty was to put a notice in the church bulletin a couple times a year to ask people to bring to the library any books they no longer needed. These were put on the shelves, with a sheet of paper tacked up on the wall nearby so people could sign their names when they took books out."

I can see why that library wasn't used much. It probably wasn't even good use of the small amount of space it took. And there are all too many libraries around the country like that—and others that aren't that bad but come too close for comfort.

I wish you could have traveled with me as I visited many libraries that are doing a great job. They exist in every size church, with every size room and budget. The one thing they have in common is enthusiasm and optimism about what a church library can accomplish.

My mail survey of church libraries indicated that, in the nearly two hundred responding churches, an average of twenty books is checked out each week. While this isn't as large a number as we would like to see, it is that many Christian books that may not otherwise have been read. In some churches as many as six hundred books are checked out each week. In addition, many good tapes and other materials are being used.

When you try to promote the need for strong, active church libraries, some will point out how many people are buying Christian books now. And isn't it better for them to own them, have them in their homes, circulate them among friends, and give them as gifts, than to have them stored in a church library? We can only rejoice at the increase in both production and consumption of Christian literature and tapes. It is a healthy sign, indeed, and in many places accompanies a spirit of renewal and revival. If the choice is between privately owned materials being circulated and church library materials being stored, we're all for the former. But that doesn't have to be the choice. Many church librarians have assured me that their most avid library users are people who also buy and give books. There is no conflict. Those who really enjoy reading can seldom buy all the books they want to read. Nor will the availability of books to borrow keep them from purchasing those they want or from encouraging others to read. If anything, it seems to stimulate these activities.

Christian bookstores, sometimes afraid that people will stop buying books if their churches start libraries, have been pleasantly surprised to find that libraries stimulate sales rather than hinder them. We can expect such stores to take an even more active part in working with church libraries in the future as they realize more fully the mutual benefits of a good relationship between them.[12]

Church libraries are nothing new. While tradition alone is not sufficient reason to keep anything, the fact that something has survived the test of time is good reason to consider its value. The Dead Sea Scrolls have been called "the oldest religious library." Many early temples and synagogues had libraries. Paul considered books a necessary part of his ministry. He told Timothy to bring his "books, especially the parchments" (2 Tim 4:13). He undoubtedly shared them with those around him. It is said that in the early Christian churches the Scriptures and related books were kept to the immediate right of the altar. We know that Bishop Alexander founded a Christian library in Jerusalem before A.D. 250. Many churches and cathedrals in England had libraries in the seventeenth and eighteenth centuries.[13]

In 1699 Dr. Thomas Bray proposed establishment of parochial libraries in "all the English colonies in America" as well as in market towns of England, stating that "it is the only Knowledge which can conduct us safe through the Mazes and Labyrinths of this World, to our Rest and Happiness in the other." Libraries established in America by Dr. Bray and his associates were among the best cared for of those in the eighteenth century.[14]

Many of the first libraries in America were established by and for Sunday schools. One of the earliest was established in Boston in 1812.[15] The United States census of 1860 reported six thousand Sunday school libraries with over two million volumes. By 1870 the census reported over thirty-three thousand such libraries with more than eight million volumes. By the end of the nineteenth century, however, church libraries had declined in number and size.[16]

The Southern Baptist Convention, probably the most active single denomination in promotion of church libraries, dates its Sunday school libraries to the 1820s. In 1927 they appointed one member of their Sunday school board to be responsible for church libraries. He began a library page in their *Sunday School Builder* magazine, and from this page has grown a complete magazine called *Media: Library Services Journal.*[17]

Other denominations and associations have promoted church library work

12. Betty McMichael, "The Church Library and the Christian Bookstore," pp. 48-50.
13. E. Anne Read, *The Cathedral Libraries of England;* Neil Ker, ed., *The Parochial Libraries of the Church of England.*
14. Thomas Bray, *An Essay Towards Promoting All Necessary and Useful Knowledge Both Divine and Human, In All the Parts of His Majesty's Dominions, Both at Home and Abroad* (London: E. Holt, 1697, reproduced by G. K. Hill & Co., 1967); Richard Copley Christie, *The Old Church and School Libraries of Lancashire* (Manchester, England: Chetham Society, 1885).
15. Wayne E. Todd, *Library Services in the Church,* p. 1.
16. Arthur W. Swarthout, "The Church Library Movement in Historical Perspective," *Drexel Library Quarterly* (April 1970), p. 117.
17. "From 1820's to 1970's," *The Quarterly Review* 31 (April, May, June 1971), pp. 19-20.

in recent years, with an estimate of more than thirty thousand church libraries operating today.[18] The Evangelical Church Library Association has done a great deal to promote and coordinate church libraries in evangelical churches. The Church and Synagogue Library Association is an active nondenominational, ecumenical organization made up primarily of libraries from the mainline denominations. Other regional associations and denominations have special promotional efforts and agencies to help church libraries.

Whereas early libraries were looked on as storehouses of knowledge, the emphasis today is on circulation. We are no longer impressed with large, beautiful, undisturbed collections. We want good literature that is reaching into homes and changing lives. Think of your library as an arm of the church extending the church's influence into many lives and homes throughout the week. When you see someone leave on Sunday with library material in hand, you know the help received during the short time spent in church will be multiplied many times as library material is used during the week. An editor once said, "The reading of a book can turn a person's life around—for good or for bad."[19] Wouldn't you rather help turn a life around for good than let others turn it around for bad?

THE CHURCH LIBRARY AS A RESOURCE CENTER FOR THE ENTIRE CHRISTIAN EDUCATION PROGRAM OF THE CHURCH

In addition to providing and promoting aids to spiritual development for individuals and families, the library serves the very important function of a resource center for all the Christian education programs of the church. And can you think of any church programs that are not in some way involved in Christian education? Isn't Christian education, considered in its broadest sense, what a church's ministry and outreach is all about?

Just how does the library serve the various Christian education needs of the church? The library provides a centralized, integrated place for materials used in conducting various church programs. In addition to storing and organizing materials, library workers should be prepared to help leaders find materials best suited to their needs. In the case of a youth worker, for example, the library should be able to provide and encourage use of appropriate Bible study and devotional helps for the leader and his young people, cassettes for both group and individual use, visual aids of all kinds, and the equipment necessary for their use. The librarian should let youth workers know about program idea materials and such supplies as maps and pictures.

Other church workers should also be able to obtain similar help from a

18. Merrill Haegi, "The Nature of Contemporary Church and Synagogue Libraries," *Drexel Library Quarterly* 6 (April 1970), p. 119.
19. Donald E. Anderson, "The Pastor Needs Books!" *The Standard* 64 (February 15, 1974): 32.

church library that is serving as a coordinated resource center. The ladies' missionary society could check out curios from a country they are studying; a weekday girls' club could get craft ideas and supplies; an adult training class could obtain an overhead projector with map transparencies.

The church library should serve as a learning center as well as a resource center. Users should not only leave with helpful materials, but they should be able to use such materials in the library. A picture of an ideal church library might show a child on the floor looking at a Bible picture book, an adult looking up some references in a large concordance placed on a dictionary stand, a teenager using headphones for listening to a cassette, and a Sunday school teacher viewing a filmstrip designed to help her understand the age group she works with. It is possible that none of these people will check any materials out of the library, but all will have been helped.

Those mentioned are just a few of the ways a library supports the total ministry of the church. You will find other suggestions in other parts of the book. There are no limits to the library's potential for service in the local church.

SUMMARY

The church library is a valuable resource center for the entire church. There is ample evidence that the use of church library materials promotes spiritual development of individuals, families, and church groups. Because of its valuable services, the church library should be recognized as worthy of adequate support in terms of prayer, space, personnel, and finances. It is time that the library ministry be given its rightful place as an essential service organization to the entire church.

2

STARTING A NEW CHURCH LIBRARY

Whatever you do, do your work heartily, as for the Lord rather than for men (Colossians 3:23).

IT IS HOPED that information found in all parts of this book will be useful for the beginning library. But what about the church with no plans at all for a library? How does one get started?

The fact that you are reading this book indicates some interest. Is it possible that the Lord wants to use you to get a library started in your church? Not that you must do it all yourself, but, like a revival, it must start somewhere.

What steps can one person take to interest his church in this ministry and then see it accomplished? Perhaps you'll find some answers as you follow a lady we call Gladys through the initial steps of one church library.

The Lord seems to be convincing Gladys of the need for such a ministry in her church, along with the possibility that she should do something about it. What can Gladys do?

First, Gladys prays that the Lord will lead her and her church in what He would have them do. Then, as He opens doors, she shares her concern with others. In doing so, she gets some idea of who else is interested and who might be willing to help.

After talking to a few close friends about the idea of starting a church library and finding some interest, Gladys decides to talk to various church officials. Armed with testimonies and figures confirming the value of a library ministry, she talks with her pastor, Sunday school superintendent, Christian education director, and various church board members. She later asks to present the need at a Sunday school teachers' meeting.

Gladys discovers that several people are interested in seeing something of the sort done, as long as someone else does it. She is told that it's a fine idea, but—there's no space available; no extra money just now; no workers who can

20

be spared; no one to build shelves; people are buying their own books, so there's really no need for a library, after all.

What does Gladys do next? Give up the whole idea? She is tempted to do just that, but first, she again takes it to the Lord in prayer. Did she misunderstand His leading? No, the concern is still there. She's just as convinced as ever of the need and of God's leading in her interest. So she begins to work on a plan. Perhaps if she can go to the church board with a definite proposal, they will be more willing to provide support. After all, they haven't said no. They just haven't taken any action.

Gladys found Helen to be the most interested of the friends she had talked with about the idea. Even though she is busy with a Sunday school class, Helen agrees to help Gladys formulate some plans. They go together to the church to look over the space situation. Each of the ladies has worked in various capacities and knows pretty well how the various rooms are used.

First, they look at a large storage closet that the ladies feel could be cleaned out and used for a starter library. But they would so like to see the library start in a better location. Once started, who knows how long it will stay there? So they decide to look at more ideal locations and see how they are being used.

The ladies have noticed, when visiting other churches on vacation trips, that the most active, prospering libraries are usually near the sanctuary. In their own church, the church offices are just off the foyer on one side and the nursery on the other. The church has no other satisfactory location for the nursery. The offices include a study for the pastor, one for the assistant pastor, an office and mimeograph room for the church secretary, and a room for the Sunday school superintendent and secretary to use for meetings and storage of materials.

After this inspection of available space, Helen joins Gladys in praying for the Lord's leading. They don't want to be selfish. They could start some kind of a library in the storage closet downstairs. But they are sure that much more could be accomplished in a better location.

Finally, they feel led to talk to the Sunday school superintendent and Sunday school secretary about the room assigned for their use. Would there be some way they could share it? Perhaps if bulky orders of papers and quarterlies could be stored in the storage closet in the basement until needed and another place found for current Sunday school records, many materials kept for teachers' use could be incorporated into the library. The room could then be kept free for library use on Sunday, but would still be available for departmental teacher meetings during the week. Teachers could continue to get current teaching materials from the same room, with library staff, instead of Sunday school staff, checking them out.

The more they discuss this possibility, the more everyone can see the advantages of using the room in this way. But there still remains the problem of a place for the Sunday school records and a place for the work of the Sunday school to be coordinated Sunday mornings.

While Gladys and Helen are talking these problems over with the Sunday school officers, the assistant pastor drops in from his office next door. Having attended the Sunday school staff meeting when Gladys spoke on what a church library could do for the church, he is already impressed with its potential. He remembers how much his own interest in the Lord's work was influenced by books he borrowed from his home church library as a boy. But his duties in this new position haven't left him time to do anything about starting a library. Now he sees something he can do.

"How would it be," he asks, "if we put the Sunday school desk and files in my office? There's room, and the superintendent and secretary can use my office on Sunday morning; I'm not there then, anyway. That would free their room for a library."

Since the assistant pastor is willing to sacrifice some of his own space and convenience to help initiate a program he thoroughly believes in, the rest of the small group heartily endorse the idea.

Gladys and Helen enlist the assistant pastor's help in preparing a proposal for the church board. When completed, their written proposal includes a brief statement of the value of a church library and a request for use of the preferred room, with statements of approval from those involved in the reallocation of space. The proposal suggests that the board appoint a library committee, approve use of the requested room, and authorize the committee to proceed with establishment of a church library in the near future.

The board is pleased with the proposal and the careful planning that has gone into it. They appoint Gladys, Helen, and Dick—a local sixth-grade teacher who is on the Christian education council—to form the library committee. Permission is given to use the room requested. While no funds are provided, the committee is given authority to proceed and to raise support, subject to board approval.

At their first meeting as a library committee, Dick explains that he won't be able to help in the week-by-week operation of the library; but he will meet in planning sessions and will represent their interests on the Christian education council and the church board. It is agreed that Gladys will serve as chairman of the library committee and as head librarian. Helen is willing to serve as assistant librarian, with primary responsibility for promotion. Dick agrees to submit the need for other library workers to the Christian education council.

Soon the Sunday school furniture and materials that aren't to be incorporated into the library are moved out. The committee decides to use the shelves that had been holding Sunday school supplies as a start, noting gratefully that there is room for more shelves to be added later. Pooling funds donated by committee members and a few other interested individuals, they buy a good used desk for a checkout facility. Helen's husband builds window seats under the room's two outside windows and a small table to put in front of one of them, forming a small reading center for children. The ladies upholster the window seats and make a couple of large floor cushions and some drapes for the outside windows and door window.

They are fortunate to have that door window and will probably leave the drapes open most of the time. The window will allow those passing the room on their way to the sanctuary or classes to look into the library. This serves as good advertising and a constant reminder of library services.

With the space problem solved, at least for a time, the library committee turns its attention to the question of what to put in the library. The board hasn't offered any funds for books, and the ladies don't want to ask for any just now, while the church is making a special effort to get its missions budget out of the red. So they decide to get a starting library without requesting money from the general fund.

First, the committee members and some of their friends look through their own books for ones to donate. They choose only needed books of current interest, in good condition, to place in the library. Then Gladys and Helen look around the church and, after getting permission from appropriate people, gather books from various groups.

The young people have a collection of program helps and teen books that they are willing to put in the library. The women's missionary society has been circulating several books of missionary biography. The men's Bible class, the Sunday school teachers, and the Pioneer Girls all have collections which they are happy to turn over to a central library. It is surprising how many books the church already owns.

Next, the committee makes an appointment with the manager of the local Christian bookstore. He is anxious to cooperate and suggests a helpful plan. Christmas is coming soon. He is willing to provide books on consignment if they will display them, giving people a chance to select books as Christmas gifts for their church library. Any that aren't selected can be returned. The board approves this plan, which works very well. Another two hundred books, all brand new, are made available for the library in this way, bringing the total to nearly five hundred.

Now the fun really starts. No one on the committee has any library experience. They begin to wonder what they have let themselves in for. Gladys visits some other church librarians and learns how they do things. One of them suggests a handbook that has been helpful. Gladys goes back to the bookstore once more for a church library handbook and a kit of supplies for processing books. Then she and Helen are invited to attend a church library workshop in a neighboring town. The workshop leaves them a bit overwhelmed but fired with enthusiasm to get on with the job.

The first task, they find, is to classify the books and prepare them for circulation. Following the instructions in the handbook they have purchased, Gladys assigns Dewey class numbers and Helen pastes in book pockets and date-due slips and goes through the other steps required to properly prepare books for library use. It takes lots of time, but the ladies enjoy the work and the fellowship they have while working. After working their way through the procedures once, they invite a few other people to help with the rest. They are pleasantly surprised at the enthusiasm generated as various ones stamp the church name in the book, type book cards, or prepare labels. Even those who claim they never read find something they can hardly wait to check out.

After the initial collection is ready, except for catalog cards, which will have to wait for more time and help, Gladys goes back to the bookstore for a library record book and set of library posters. Next, she stops at an office supply store for pencils, pens, transparent tape, date stamp, stamp pad, note paper, and other desk supplies. She also buys a label-maker and tape so they can make their own shelf labels. These minimal supplies she has permission to charge to the church account.

During the weeks of preparing the library and the books, the two librarians meet several times with the third member of the library committee—the man who is also on the Christian education council. Together the committee members determine operating policies. They decide to have the library open for one-half hour before and after all regularly scheduled services. In addition, it will remain open through Sunday school and through the Wednesday evening meetings, since teacher training groups meet Wednesday evenings.

The committee also discusses the need to incorporate the audiovisuals into a central media center. Because their assigned space is limited and the Sunday school has someone caring for these materials in another area of the church, they decide to plan toward a combined resource center when the church's proposed building program becomes a reality, but not try to include them just yet.

These policy matters are referred to the Christian education council, which concurs in the committee's decisions. The council suggests two possible helpers whom Gladys and Helen are happy to recruit. The four meet together to set up schedules and assignments of responsibilities.

One of the helpers, a retired secretary, agrees to be responsible for book care, covering book jackets with plastic and repairing books as needed. The other, a high school boy, will come in once a week to shelve books.

In addition, each of the workers will learn the various procedures needed for checking books in and out. Gladys plans to be there as much as possible, but she is glad to know others can take over when necessary.

Even though Gladys has had to learn library procedures from scratch herself, she realizes how important it is that all workers do things the same way. She sets up four evening training sessions for discussing procedures and policies, as well as information about library materials, with all the library helpers. She plans to hold further training sessions about every six months, bringing in new workers as needed and available.

With the first well-chosen and prepared books neatly arranged according to Dewey class numbers, shelves labeled with subject headings and Dewey numbers, desk stocked with necessary supplies, the room given a thorough cleaning, and promotional material distributed throughout the church, all is ready for the grand opening of the new church library.

Plans for this day have been made carefully, knowing it is a one-time opportunity to get the library off to a good start. Working with the Sunday school staff, the library committee has helped prepare promotion for each Sunday school department. The pastor cooperates fully, basing his morning sermon on a theme that brings out the importance of reading Christian literature. At the close of his message, which is briefer than usual to free time for an added feature, he calls for the library committee and workers, chairman of the Christian education council, chairman of the church board, and assistant pastor to come forward and stand together as he leads the congregation in a prayer of dedication of the church library and its workers.

As people leave the sanctuary after the library dedication, they are ushered past the library door, where each one pauses a moment to view the new library and receive a specially prepared folder of welcome and information. In addition to commemorating opening day, the folder describes library contents and procedures, letting the congregation know what is available, when the library is open, how to use it, and what services the library plans to provide.

The regular church bulletin has issued an invitation to attend the library open house anytime that afternoon and evening from three to seven o'clock. At that time coffee, punch, and cookies are served, and people can inspect the library more closely, as well as check out books to take with them. Souvenir bookmarks are given each visitor, and guests are asked to sign a guest book, providing names of interested people for further contacts later on.

The library committee has been asked to plan part of the evening service for this special day. In turn, the committee has asked the young people to prepare and present a skit in which they demonstrate, in a humorous yet effective way, how the library can serve everyone in the church.

After the evening service, any who have not yet attended open house are encouraged to follow carpeted footprints, set out for the occasion, to the library for a first visit.

The initial open house is supplemented in the weeks that follow by group visits to the library in accordance with a prearranged schedule. As each Sunday school class is brought in during its regular class time, the librarian displays books appropriate for the age group, explains checkout and return procedures, and gives opportunity for checking out books.

The months that follow are sometimes discouraging but often encouraging as little by little people begin availing themselves of the library's services.

When one child, on returning a book, tells Gladys he has decided to give his heart to Jesus like the boy in the book did, Gladys's heart leaps with joy, knowing her efforts have been abundantly rewarded. Later, a recent high school graduate confides to her that a book from the library helped him decide to go to Bible school and prepare for the mission field. A young couple finds help in repairing a damaged marriage. A discouraged older lady learns from a library book how she can still make a useful contribution to the Lord's work. A blind lady rejoices to learn she can soon get the Bible on cassettes from the library.

By the beginning of the next church year, the board is convinced of the value of the church library and provides regular budgeted support to assure its continued and expanded ministry. When the church is ready to build a new building, they give serious consideration to the best possible facilities for a complete resource center.

We'll leave Gladys and her helpers at this point, but remember this is really just the beginning, not the end of their story. They will continue to face problems and decisions, but they will grow in size and service, thankful for the opportunity to serve the Lord through a ministry of Christian literature and, eventually, through audiovisual materials as well.

The foregoing example illustrates only one way that a new library might come into being. In another case a librarian might be chosen to head a library committee after the Christian education council has first recognized the need for a library and gone looking for the right person to be put in charge.

The operation of a resource center should be considered an important responsibility of a Christian education council or board. In the absence of such a body, the general governing board of the church should accept this responsibility. The first step in meeting this obligation is the appointment of a library committee. Having done this, the supervising board will leave most decisions up to this committee, but will provide necessary support and will check on progress at regular intervals.

The library committee, preferably a standing committee provided for in the church constitution, should consist of three to eight members chosen for their interest in the work of a resource center and its relationship to the entire Christian education program of the church. It is best to have a representative from each of the major programs of the church on this committee to ensure the library's function in serving their needs.

While at least the head librarian should be on the library committee, and possibly all the library workers in a small church, the committee as such does not carry out the actual operating procedures of the library. Instead, it determines policies, supervises library operation, and provides support for the library. Its responsibilities, guidelines for which are discussed in more detail in later chapters, include the following:

1. Select and secure a location for the library
2. Arrange for library furniture, equipment, and supplies
3. Appoint one or more librarians and helpers
4. Assign and coordinate individual responsibilities of library workers
5. Determine basic library policies
6. Seek adequate financial support
7. Advise the librarian in the selection of library materials
8. Promote the library's ministry to the entire church membership
9. Arrange training opportunities for library workers
10. Coordinate library activities with other church programs
11. Hold regular meetings to discuss problems and evaluate library work
12. Prepare periodic reports of library activities
13. Plan for future growth and expanded services

Summary

Dr. Joseph Wong, in an article on starting a church library, states that "the church library must begin with people—interested people who envision its possibilities and are willing to work to make it a reality." He goes on to state that individuals must then define the church's needs and set goals; select location, workers, and materials; establish procedures and programs; operate the library; and evaluate its effectiveness.[1]

The following chart shows one way to organize a church library or resource center. Variations can be made to fit your church's organizational structure, size, and available workers. Details regarding duties of various workers are given in the next chapter.

1. Joseph Y. Wong, "But How Do I Start a Church Library?" pp. 9-13.

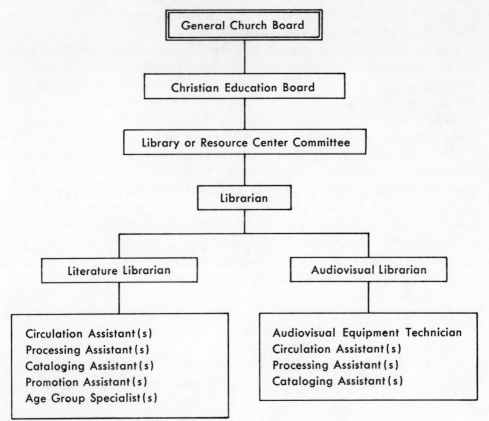

Organizational Chart for a Church Library or Resource Center

3

CHOOSING THE LIBRARY STAFF

As each one has received a special gift, employ it in serving one another, as good stewards of the manifold grace of God. . . . Whoever serves, let him do so as by the strength which God supplies; so that in all things God may be glorified through Jesus Christ (1 Peter 4:10-11) .

GAINES S. DOBBINS once said that "the call to leadership is a call to servant-ship."[1] Nowhere is this more true than in church library work. It is a wonderful truth that each member of the body of Christ has some spiritual gift to be used in "serving one another." The church library is just one of many ministries needing willing workers whom God has equipped for His service.

The library committee, whose duties are discussed in the previous chapter, should appoint the librarian. The committee also has a responsibility to provide her with helpers, although she should be consulted about their choice. Since the librarian is usually a member, and often the chairman, of the library committee, she will be fully aware of all discussions and decisions about library staff.

THE LIBRARIAN

The librarian not only carries the key, she *is* the key to a successful church library. A fine location, good selection of material, and adequate financial support will not in themselves make a library successful. But a good librarian can make a library worthwhile in spite of poor facilities and limited financial support. We must acknowledge, however, that she could do an even more effective job with better support.

I recall feeling a bit envious when I first stepped into the library of a large midwestern church and saw their lovely carpeted, oak-paneled library with its beautiful hardwood shelving, reading tables, and desk. The room was the

---

1. Gaines S. Dobbins, *Learning to Lead,* p. 37.

dream of every church librarian. Then I asked the staff member who showed me the room if it was used much. She replied, "Oh, those few people who really want to read seem to manage to find it." No longer did I consider it an ideal library.

When I thought of the hallways and closets that some dedicated librarians have turned into places of vital spiritual ministry, I wondered about the justice of it all. But then visits to churches that have caught a vision of the importance of a well-supported and well-run library staffed by some of their most able workers restored my confidence in the future of the church library.

DUTIES OF A CHURCH LIBRARIAN

There was a time when the chief function of a librarian was to see that books were guarded from damage or loss. The story is told of the college librarian who was asked how everything was at his library. He replied that one book was out, but he was on his way to the professor's home to pick it up and return it to its proper place on the library shelf.[2] Today we recognize the librarian's job as one of achieving maximum use of library materials rather than that of providing custodial care of the library's holdings.

We need some idea of what the librarian's duties are before we can properly consider what sort of person she should be. Her duties are described in more detail as we consider actual operational procedures in later chapters. It will suffice here just to list the main duties, recognizing that the librarian should have both help and supervision in performance of them. It is the librarian's responsibility, along with her co-workers, to:

1. Pray for the ministry of the library
2. Keep informed about books and other resource center materials
3. Select books and other library materials
4. Purchase library supplies
5. Process material for circulation
6. Oversee the operation of the library
7. Promote library use
8. Coordinate library services with other church activities
9. Plan for future needs and services of the library

QUALIFICATIONS OF A CHURCH LIBRARIAN

I am convinced that sex, age, and marital status have little to do with the best choice of librarian. Charles Dickens did us no favor when he described his fictitious librarian, Tom Pinch, as "an ungainly awkward-looking man, extremely shortsighted, and prematurely bald . . . far from handsome . . .

2. Elgin S. Moyer, *The Pastor and His Library*, p. 7.

dressed in a snuff-colored suit, of an uncouth make."[3] And Jan Struthers described the common concept of a librarian as a "quiet, helpful member of society, not very heroic, probably more than a little short-sighted, living in a dim, pleasant world that smelt faintly of dust and printer's ink and old leather, a world that seemed to us far removed from what we used to call the realities of life."[4]

Many church members have some such idea of what a church librarian is like. They expect to find a little old lady fussing over books being out of place or children making too much noise. I have yet to meet this type of church librarian, but the stereotype idea is still around. I can just hear some church board or council carrying on a discussion like the following when looking for a person to fill this position:

"Edith Webster might be a good choice for librarian. She isn't doing much in the church and should have plenty of time in spite of her job in the courthouse. After all, her mother still keeps house for her. Edith is too shy to teach, but she reads a lot and surely could sit at the desk and check out books. She seems a little ill at ease around children, but that shouldn't make much difference in the library. If Edith won't do it, we might consider Penelope Prentice. They've been wanting to get her out of the junior high school department. She's getting pretty old and set in her ways, and those kids just make fun of her behind her back. She doesn't get along too well with the other teachers, either, but she couldn't do much harm in the library since she'd be working all alone there."

If this book accomplishes nothing else, I hope it can help destroy that sort of picture of a church librarian. In visiting and corresponding with hundreds of church librarians, I've been pleased to find busy libraries staffed with young, active mothers, outgoing and busy working women, dedicated men with a keen interest in both books and their readers, young people, old people, singles, and married people. An eighteen-year-old is doing a fine job as librarian of one church, and a retired couple work together in another.

Let me pause here to apologize to some fine men librarians for my constant references in this book to church librarians as women. Some of the best church libraries I have visited have been operated by male librarians; about a dozen of the librarians responding to the survey were men. But since women far outnumber men in this work, and since it is awkward to keep referring to the librarian as "he or she," I have chosen the easy way in using the female gender. Principles stated are meant to apply to either sex. The possibility of men serving in this capacity should never be overlooked. Here again we are too bound by tradition. One male librarian whose wife occa-

3. Harry C. Bauer, *Seasoned to Taste*, p. 173.
4. William Hugh Carlson, *In a Grand and Awful Time*, p. 38.

sionally helped him was understandably a bit irked by the visitor who commented one day, "How nice of you to help your wife out in the library."[5]

Aware, then, of the need to avoid stereotype ideas and desiring the best possible choice, just what should we look for in selecting a librarian?

Calling. First and foremost, the librarian should be called of God to this ministry, just as the pastor and the Sunday school teacher and other workers are called to theirs. A prospective librarian must be convinced of the value of the church library, recognizing it as a spiritual ministry. The appropriate church officials should feel led, after prayerful consideration, to contact a specific person for this work. That individual should accept only after being convinced that this is the place of service the Lord has for her, and that it is a service she can perform joyfully for Him. With this assurance, other qualifications seem unimportant. But since the Lord often leads through the workings of God-given intellects, it is still a good idea to look for certain traits.

Dedication. It should go without saying that the librarian must be a dedicated, sincere Christian. If you think hers is just a mechanical job without much spiritual impact, you haven't spent much time around a healthy church library. People come to the librarian not only for help in selecting material, but they often come for spiritual help as well. She is in an exceptionally good position to counsel those who drop in and want to talk about spiritual needs without formally requesting help. Combining knowledge of Scripture, personal experience acquired in her own walk with the Lord, and suggestions of helpful literature have enabled librarians to bring spiritual blessings to many.

The librarian should be a mature Christian whose life is consistent with her profession. Young people and children will look to her as an example just as they do their Sunday school teachers. Any inconsistency in her life outside the church will be a hindrance and stumbling block to those younger and weaker in the faith who look to her for guidance.

Training, skills, and experience. There are no specific educational requirements for the church librarian. It would be good for her to have broad interests and a fair knowledge of what is going on in the world. Various experiences are helpful. The Lord has a way of preparing us for His chosen work for us in ways we usually recognize and appreciate only much later, if at all. A church librarian should know as much as possible about the operation of all phases of church life, such as Sunday school, preaching services, youth work, weekday activities, missionary outreach, visitation and evangelistic efforts, women's and men's groups, and camping programs. Any prior experience in these fields will help.

Churches sometimes make the mistake of thinking they can't have a church

5. Gomer Lesch, "You've Come a Long Way, Maybe!" *The Church Library Magazine* (April, May, June, 1970), pp. 14-15.

library unless they have someone with library training or experience. While professional librarians contribute a great deal to many church libraries, they are not essential to their successful operation. As a matter of fact, the following comment one seminary librarian made to me is probably typical of their feelings on the subject: "I'm interested in our church library and am glad to give advice when asked, but after working in a library all week, I don't feel like working in the church library on Sunday."

Some professional librarians are too concerned with proper technical aspects of the work to make the best church librarians. I would rather see an enthusiastic nonprofessional head a church library than a professional librarian who accepts the assignment out of a sense of duty. Those rare individuals who so love library work and the Lord that they really want to work in more than one library should certainly be considered, as well as the person with library experience who is not currently employed. Twenty-eight churches responding to our survey have professional librarians; seven of the churches pay their librarians a salary.

It would be pretty hard to conceive of a librarian who didn't like to read. A church librarian must be familiar with Christian literature and eager to learn more about it. She may need to expand her initial interests to enable her to give useful advice about children's books, youth material, fiction, biography, missionary stories, doctrinal books, teaching aids, and every other kind of material found in the library. In contrast to bartending, "library work is the one field of endeavor in which the practitioner is well advised to sample his own wares and to dose himself liberally from the inexhaustible quartos that are ever at hand."[6]

Rapid reading skills are useful for acquainting oneself with as much literature as possible. A librarian should consider taking some training in speed reading if this is available to her. Artistic ability is useful in producing promotional materials, but it is usually possible to draw on the talents of others in the church for this. It is a handicap for a librarian not to be able to type, but it may be possible to call on others for help in this area, too. While a church librarian doesn't need prior library experience, she does need a reasonable aptitude and willingness to learn basic library skills and procedures.

Personality characteristics. It is not enough that a librarian enjoy reading. As an article in *Library Journal* put it, "Ya Gotta Love People, Too."[7] The librarian must have a desire to infect others with her own enthusiasm for books. In a sense, she is a salesman who must not only be sold on the product for herself, but on its value for others. One writer put it this way: "The

6. Bauer, p. ix.
7. Anne V. Osborn, "It's Not Enough to Love Books, Ya Gotta Love People, Too," *Library Journal* 98 (March 15, 1973): 974.

Photographs by David McMichael

The Right Book to the Right Person at the Right Time

librarian must have a gift for exciting people through all the media at her fingertips."[8]

A good librarian will consider her primary task to be getting the right material to the right person at the right time. Not only must she know the material, but she must know and understand people, including people of all types and ages. She must also be able to exercise a sense of discernment as to the proper time to make suggestions and the proper time just to listen. For example, librarians can often help recently bereaved individuals by suggesting just the right book at the right time. But she must realize that what might be the right book or the right time for one might be resented or misunderstood intrusion for another.

In contrast to the stereotype image of a shy introvert as librarian, a church librarian should be friendly and outgoing. She serves as something of a hostess in the library, putting people at ease and helping them without being overbearing. She must also be able to work well with others, as she will find there is more work than she can or should do alone.

It helps if the librarian enjoys working with details, since there are many such in library work. However, if she is willing to tolerate some of the technical aspects of library work in spite of not enjoying them, she can be a success. Just as the housewife who doesn't really like to scrub floors or do dishes

8. Alice Straughan, *How to Organize Your Church Library*, p. 21.

can still do these things cheerfully and thankfully as an expression of love to her family, so the librarian who doesn't really love to type cards or straighten shelves can still find joy in this service for the Lord.

The ideal librarian is neat by nature, but not compulsively so. Carefully arranged materials make for an attractive, appealing library. But temporary disarray can be a healthy sign of library use. Just so a condition of clutter and disorder are not allowed to become permanent.

I recommend that a librarian have both a good amount of patience and a ready sense of humor. Surely the librarian who told me about her mistake in sending a children's filmstrip to an adult class needed to be able to laugh along with friends who wouldn't let her forget that mistake. It helps to be creative, imaginative, and inventive, as there will be many times that necessity will have to be the "mother of invention" for the librarian. She should also be a person of vision, able to plan and then work toward the fulfillment of her plans.

Even as personality factors have a great deal to do with the success of a salesman, so they contribute much to the success of a church librarian. In reading all I could on church library work, I found the following adjectives, covering much of the alphabet, used in one place or another to describe ideal church librarians: accurate, alert, appreciative, aware, cheerful, consecrated, courageous, courteous, creative, dedicated, dependable, determined, energetic, enthusiastic, friendly, helpful, humble, imaginative, industrious, intelligent, inventive, kind, loving, neat, open, patient, persistent, radiant, responsive, spiritual, tactful, willing, and wise.

"Wait a minute," you say. "Where can we find anyone with all these attributes?"

I doubt that you can. But they can be kept in mind as goals—something to work toward—just the same. Didn't Jesus say, "You are to be perfect, as your heavenly Father is perfect" (Mt 5:48)? And yet each of us must acknowledge with Paul, "Not that I . . . have already become perfect, but I press on in order that I may lay hold of that for which also I was laid hold of by Christ Jesus" (Phil 3:12). Remembering that "I can do all things through Him who strengthens me" (Phil 4:13), we can look to Him for help in developing those characteristics needed in a good librarian.

Time and energy. When you ask someone to be a librarian, don't make the mistake of saying that it won't take much time. That just isn't true. There is no use asking someone who is already too busy unless you have reason to believe she might be able and willing to drop some other activity in order to work in the library. Then again, you aren't looking for someone with nothing to do, for such a person may continue to do nothing. Usually you find your best prospects already busy, but with activities that might be adjusted in response to a new challenge. Remember the Lord knows the need, and His timing is always best. The library shouldn't be supported at the expense of other church activities, nor should it be neglected because of them. There is no need to apologize for wanting the best possible person to head the library even though that person may also be very capable in some other position, as long as the final decision is reached with the Lord's guidance.

One writer sums up her advice to those who work in church libraries this way: "Dedicate your own enthusiasm, energies, and resources toward its success. When God is your helper, heights and horizons are limitless and you can accomplish miracles."[9]

OTHER LIBRARY WORKERS

Hopefully, the librarian will not be working alone. Sometimes it falls the lot of one person to get the ball rolling pretty much alone. But the time soon comes when she must have help. It has been said of F. W. Woolworth that he began his business performing every job himself. An illness forced him to get help. He became really successful only after he learned that he couldn't do the whole job himself. A librarian with lots of time might feel she can handle the work of a small library alone, and sometimes that is the only way it gets done. But she could be more successful with help, so she should keep trying to involve others. Even in a small library, provision must be made for possible illness, vacations, and other absences of the main librarian.

A library serving as a complete resource center will need a head librarian or director of library services to coordinate all library activities. While serving under one director and one library committee, the audiovisual services should have a separate librarian or director. Depending on location and size, the audiovisual portion may need several workers. Someone familiar with operation and care of equipment should either be in charge of or available to the audiovisual library.

It is not necessary that every library worker have the same qualifications as the librarian. Diversity of abilities and interests will be an advantage. Each worker should be an enthusiastic library booster, but each should serve in a unique way, having a specific responsibility appropriate to the individual's time and talent. While one person might accomplish several tasks in a small church and several people might be needed for one task in a large church, the following classifications of workers are needed to assist both the literature librarian and the audiovisual librarian.

CIRCULATION WORKERS

One person should be assigned responsibility for circulation of literature

9. Ruth S. Smith, *Publicity for a Church Library*, p. 42.

Photograph by David McMichael

A Young Circulation Assistant at Work

and another for circulation of non-print materials, unless the two functions are housed together and small enough for one person to handle. The person in charge of circulation will schedule the times that various workers are on duty in the library. She will either be there herself or make sure that someone is at the checkout desk at all times the library is open. She will keep records and acknowledge gifts to the library. She will supervise shelving and filing of all library materials. She will also see that overdue notices are sent out and personal contacts made when needed to encourage return of overdue materials. These responsibilities can be divided among several people, but one person should coordinate them and train new workers in these tasks.

A circulation worker will also prepare and use scheduling sheets for audiovisual equipment. She takes care of reserving the use of materials and equipment in advance.

Taking annual inventory of all holdings and equipment is another responsibility of circulation workers.

PROCESSING WORKERS

Everyone available may be called in to help when there is a new batch of library material to process. However, one person must be in charge, and it helps to have several experienced workers in this area. It will be most efficient if the same person carries out a certain operation each time.

One person can classify all materials; another can open new books properly and check for defects; someone can attach book pockets and date-due slips; one might do all the typing; others can carry out other processes. Details for these procedures are given in later portions of the book. One worker should keep an inventory of processing supplies and be sure replacements are obtained when needed.

Mending of torn or otherwise damaged material is another task for processing workers. Sometimes a person with no other library duties will agree to do book repair work.

CATALOGING WORKERS

Cataloging can be considered part of the processing of materials, but it is sometimes done separately. It is best to have the same person catalog both books and audiovisual material to assure uniformity in choice of classification numbers and subject headings. Cataloging includes typing shelf-list and catalog cards for each entry, as explained in a later chapter, and filing such cards in the proper card file. One volunteer worker might be willing to keep the card catalog up to date. Her duties should include removal of cards for materials no longer in the library, as well as addition of cards for new material.

PROMOTION WORKERS

While every library worker is expected to promote the library, one person should be given leadership responsibilities in the area of promotional activities, with other workers assigned to help as needed. Some of these promotional methods, explained in some detail later, are: use of bulletin boards, displays, newsletters, book and media lists, book talks, special library events, and reading programs and contests.

AGE GROUP SPECIALISTS

Some libraries are large enough to have separate children's, youth, and adult sections, each with its own librarian. Sometimes space arrangements are such that these must be in separate areas of the church. In any case, it is good to have among your workers those who are familiar with the special library needs of various age groups and those who have special rapport in communicating with such groups. These workers should help select material appropriate for the various age groups and work with the promotion director in promoting library use among them.

OTHER WORKERS

An equipment technician is needed to keep audiovisual equipment in proper working order. That individual or another person could deliver audiovisuals to groups that have scheduled their use. It is best if this person or someone familiar with the equipment can stay to operate it.

A carpenter in the church can make a valuable contribution by building shelves and furniture for the library. The more people you can involve in helping with various aspects of library work the more interest you will generate in library use.

THE STAFF AS A TEAM

There are several functions that the library staff should work together on.

Policies that affect all of them should be worked out together, under supervision of the library committee. Each worker should contribute to plans and decisions regarding selection of library materials. The workers should meet to decide on the best use of space and to plan library equipment purchases. They will decide together on services their library should offer, on division of duties, and special assignments. Each person will be a user and promoter of the library and will help acquire useful materials, such as pictures for the vertical file. Staff members will participate together in training opportunities available to them.

Survey Results

Seventy percent of the libraries responding to our survey report having one or more library workers in addition to a head librarian. Table 1 shows that some churches have more than twenty people involved in the work of the church library.

Table 1
Number of Library Workers in Addition to Head Librarian

Number of Workers	Number of Churches	Percentage of Churches
None or no response	50	27%
1	26	14
2	35	19
3	15	8
4	13	7
5	10	5
6 - 9	18	10
10 - 14	11	6
15 - 19	3	2
20 - 24	4	2
25 and up	1	1
Total	186	100%*

*While the sum of the percentages as shown is 101 per cent, their sum before rounding is 100 per cent.

Training Opportunities

Church librarians get most of their training on the job, learning procedures from predecessors, fellow workers, and library manuals. It is hoped that this book will be a helpful tool for training librarians and their helpers.

WORKSHOPS

Library workers should attend any workshops held in their area on the church library. Such workshops are often included in Sunday school association and denominational conferences. If they are not, try suggesting to the proper officials that they be added to the program. I tried this once and was pleased with the well-attended workshop that came about as a result of that request. With a little encouragement, Christian bookstores often will sponsor library workshops. You will come away from such sessions with useful information and contagious enthusiasm.

CHURCH LIBRARY ASSOCIATIONS

Subscribe to and use material published by church library organizations. If at all possible, attend a conference of an association of church libraries. Your region or denomination may have one. The Evangelical Church Library Association has a very worthwhile conference each fall. Instead of an hour or two at a workshop, you can spend a day or more at a conference talking with other church librarians, listening to expert advice, meeting authors, and examining displays of new materials. You will come away full of inspiration and ideas for strengthening and expanding your library ministry.

OTHER LIBRARIES

Visit other libraries. Observe how they do things. Get acquainted with other librarians in your community and discuss mutual problems and possible solutions. Public and school librarians, as well as church librarians, are usually very willing to supply helpful information and advice. When you travel, stop to visit libraries. Many are open during the week. If a church is unlocked, there is usually someone there who will be willing to show you the library and answer questions about it. You will get many ideas for your own library this way.

EVENING CLASSES

A few Bible schools and colleges, seminaries, and Christian publishers offer classes, usually in the evening, for church librarians. These can be very helpful and should be attended by as many church library workers as possible. Inquire about such opportunities in your area.

LOCAL CHURCH TRAINING

If your pastor or director of Christian education has had seminary or college training in church library work or library experience in another church, he can help train library workers. Once the librarian has received her own training, she should begin to schedule training sessions for her helpers, passing along "how-to" information of the type suggested in later chapters of this book and matters of policy and philosophy regarding their particular church library's ministry.

SUMMARY

Paul's instructions to the Corinthians include a good description of qualities that those who work together in a church library or resource center should have. Such a person, demonstrating Christian love, "is patient . . . kind, and is not jealous . . . does not brag and is not arrogant, does not act unbecomingly . . . does not seek its own, is not provoked, does not take into account a wrong suffered, does not rejoice in unrighteousness, but rejoices with the truth; bears all things, believes all things, hopes all things, endures all things" (1 Co 13:4-7).

4

SELECTING BOOKS AND OTHER PRINTED MATERIAL

Wise men store up knowledge (Proverbs 10:14).

IT USED TO BE that the church library was just a depository for books and magazines that people wanted to get rid of. We hope that time is past. Everything in the library should be there for a specific reason.

OBJECTIVES

Those responsible for the library's ministry should have their objectives clearly in mind, and preferably in writing as well. Materials should be selected in keeping with those objectives.

One of the first things a church library should determine is whether or not it will include books considered secular rather than sacred. In other words, will you have copies of *Little Women* and *Alice in Wonderland?* If so, why? If not, why not?

In most areas, city and school libraries are accessible to the church constituency. When this is the case, it seems best for churches to use their resources for materials in keeping with the spiritual goals of the church. If the church is so located that its members do not have convenient access to at least one public library, the church may want to provide a greater variety of materials.

In most cases, the library collection should be a reflection and extension of the entire church's goals and objectives. For example, if those goals are the conversion of unbelievers, strengthening of believers, and training of members for Christian service, then everything in the library should serve in some way to promote those goals. The library's mission is too important and its funds, space, and personnel usually too limited to try to serve members' com-

42

plete library needs. Encourage them to use public and school libraries, reserving your church library for a truly spiritual ministry.

BOOKS

The first things people think of in libraries are books. Actually, the first libraries consisted of stone tablets, and only later did scrolls and then books as we know them come into existence. The library that wants to really function as a resource center today will contain a great many items in addition to books. However, books continue to be basic ingredients of a library.

The listing that follows, while not exhaustive, can serve as a checklist of types of books to be put in a church library. Policies, subject to change as needed, should determine the approximate proportion of funds to be used in each area, depending on the needs and ministry of the individual church.

GENERAL REFERENCES

Any library needs reference tools. They are expensive, so the extent of your reference section will depend on your budget and the way your library is used. If people actually study in the library, such reference tools as a good dictionary, general encyclopedia, and almanac are helpful.

BIBLE STUDY HELPS

These should include the following types of books:

    Bibles in several translations and paraphrases
    Bible dictionaries
    Bible encyclopedias
    Bible handbooks
    Concordances
    Commentaries
    Bible history
    Bible geography, atlases
    Bible biographies
    Bible customs
    Archeology as related to Bible study
    Bible studies of various types, including surveys, book-by-book studies, and topical studies

DOCTRINAL STUDIES

This category includes books dealing with the functions of each Person of the Trinity—Father, Son, and Holy Spirit. It should also include works on such topics as salvation, angels and demons, Satan, heaven and hell, prophecy, death, and resurrection.

DENOMINATIONAL MATERIALS

Your library should contain books that explain the beliefs of your church. These include catechisms, creeds, or simple statements of belief. They may include books written by denominational leaders about doctrinal beliefs. Yearbooks and annual reports describing the workings of your church at the local, district, national, and international levels should be included.

Don't overlook authors from your own church and denomination when choosing books for all parts of the library; but don't limit your collection to your denominational authors, either.

CHRISTIAN LIVING AND DEVOTIONAL BOOKS

One of the big thrills of church library work comes from seeing evidence of Christian growth that can be at least partially attributed to reading Christian literature. The church library that exists only to provide helps for the Christian education workers is missing a big part of its potential ministry. The library should serve everyone. No one is so advanced in his Christian life that there is no room for further growth and development. Dedicated Christian writers are producing a wealth of material to be used along with the all-important reading of Scripture to help individuals relate Bible principles to their everyday lives.

We think primarily of this category as including the many very readable small books found in both hardbound and paperback covers in recent years, written out of personal experiences of various Christian authors. However, there are several other types of books that can also be included here. Devotional books written by church leaders down through the centuries, books of devotional poems and hymns, daily devotional helps, idea books for devotional talks, guidebooks for the development of Christian character, and collections of inspirational messages all have their place in this category.

HELPS FOR ESTABLISHING AND MAINTAINING A CHRISTIAN HOME

The church library has a tremendous opportunity and responsibility to minister in this area. The library should have carefully selected books on marriage and preparation for marriage, divorce, sex education, child training, and family devotions.

CHRISTIAN WITNESS AND EVANGELISM TOOLS

Include books on personal witness and soul-winning and books to help with church evangelism and outreach. Also include some good books explaining other religious beliefs and suggesting ways to communicate the Christian message to those of other faiths. The library should also have books that explain the way of salvation clearly. Members should be encouraged to loan these to unsaved friends.

CHRISTIAN EDUCATION HELPS

There should be books of helps for Sunday school teachers. In addition to Bible study materials, teachers need books that help them understand the age group they work with and teaching methods that will help them present lessons effectively.

The library should work closely with all the church programs, supplying material needed for youth groups, weekday club programs, women's groups, teacher training classes, visitation workers, board members, vacation Bible schools, released time classes, small Bible study and prayer groups, and other special groups and programs of the church.

BOOKS FOR YOUTH

Many fine books have been written for young people. Getting them read may be one of your biggest challenges. Encourage your young people to read from adult areas, but have special selections for them as well. When they discover there are authors who really are interested in their needs and problems, they'll take a look at what they have to say. If they find them helpful, they'll be back for more. So do have a section for them, not just for leaders working with them.

However, be careful not to overdo isolation of youth and their problems. Young people want to be and should be treated as individuals first and as teenagers secondarily. They resent being lumped together as a homogeneous body of troublemakers, and who can blame them? Each is an individual loved by God and in need of respect and understanding.

STORIES FOR CHILDREN

Getting Bible stories and books on Christian living into the hands and homes of small children is one of the library's greatest opportunities. Look for sturdy cloth and board books for the nursery set, well-illustrated books for all the preschoolers, books designed for early readers to read themselves, books to challenge the more able readers, and books that can be read to children of all ages. I think we'd be surprised if we really knew how much these Christian books for children contribute to the development of Christian character. Many adults whose Christian lives have had great impact on others testify to this influence during their early formative years.

BIOGRAPHY

The lives of believers gone before and those living today have inspired countless Christians to closer walks with their Lord and lives of greater usefulness for Him. To read of the way God has used another human being challenges us to let Him use us in similar ways. Have a good section of books of individual and collective biography of missionaries, church leaders, and Christians from all walks of life.

MISSION BOOKS

The church library should be a primary source of information and inspirational reading about missions. Many a missionary has testified of having first felt the Lord's leading to the mission field while reading about some missionary faithfully serving in a faraway place.

FICTION

We list this last, without implying that it is least. Christian fiction may have had a greater influence for good than any other form of Christian literature. There is nothing wrong with presenting Christian truths in interesting, easily readable, story form. The average church doesn't contain many scholars. But it does contain many children, youth, and adults who read for recreation, inspiration, and information. They can find all of these in good Christian fiction. Be prepared to guide some readers in their choices, encouraging them to broaden their reading habits as they go. But don't minimize the influence of your fiction section. While most decisions for Christ, be they for salvation or for service, come as a result of several combined influences, testimonies reveal that Christian fiction has been a strong factor in bringing many to such decisions.

OTHER CATEGORIES

The categories listed above are not all-inclusive, but are enough to suggest types of books to be included. Some other types of books that may not fit neatly into categories already mentioned, but should be included in a church library are books on psychology for Christians, church growth, church organizations, the occult, ecology, apologetics, games and activities, recipes, crafts, music, local church history, humor, comfort for the bereaved, stewardship, temperance, camping, drama, and church recreation programs of various types.

Table 2 shows that the number of books contained in reporting libraries varies from a few books to over ten thousand.

PAPERBACK BOOKS

Many worthwhile books are available only in paperback and should definitely be included in the library. Sometimes the librarian can choose between

TABLE 2

Size of Book Collection

Number of Books	Number of Churches	Percentage of Churches
1 - 399	20	11%
400 - 799	43	24
800 - 1,199	37	21
1,200 - 1,599	16	9
1,600 - 1,999	11	6
2,000 - 3,999	31	17
4,000 - 5,999	11	6
6,000 - 7,999	5	3
8,000 - 9,999	4	2
10,000 and up	1	1
Total	179	100%

paperback and hardbound books. Each has advantages that should be weighed in making such decisions. Hardbound books, while costing more initially, last longer and require less time spent on repair. Books of lasting importance should usually be purchased in cloth editions.

However, there is some economy and popular appeal inherent in paperback books, especially those of particular current interest. Some books are available only in hardcover at first, with paper editions coming out later. Paper editions sometimes have quite small print, which may be a handicap for some readers. Each decision must be based on the material available and the relative importance of various factors such as cost, print size, durability, and potential reader interest and preference.

BOOKS FOR EACH AGE LEVEL

If your library is to serve the entire church, it will need to contain balanced reading material for all ages. The ideal church library will serve the entire constituency. However, a church will sometimes start with just a children's library or just an adult library.

In spite of your holdings, you may find one age group using the library the most. While you don't want to neglect the needs of other age groups, you may decide to concentrate initially on those showing the most interest. The location of your church may result in a congregational makeup concentrated in one age group. These factors should be considered in deciding what to put in your library.

If your church is well supplied with families with small children, be sure

Something for Every Age

you have plenty of Bible story picture books and rhyming books. Early readers enjoy Bible story books, fiction, and missionary stories. Juniors especially like true-to-life biography and adventure. Young people like fiction, but also books on developing personality, grooming, dating, testimonies of famous people, and Bible study helps.

When we asked our survey churches who used their libraries most, the

TABLE 3

Library Use by Age Group

Age Group	Number of Churches	Percentage of Churches
Children	48	27%
Young people	10	6
Adults	52	29
Children and young people	4	2
Children and adults	41	23
Young people and adults	5	3
Children, young people, and adults	17	10
Total	177	100%

number that reported children as the most frequent users was about the same as the number that reported adults as the most frequent (see Table 3). Many churches reported that children and adults use the library equally, but only ten churches considered young people as the age group to use the library most.

CRITERIA FOR BOOK SELECTION

A church library should not be just a collection of books, but rather a selection of carefully chosen books. What criteria should be used in choosing books? Let the questions below serve as a guide in evaluating a particular book as a possible selection for your library.

1. Does the book meet a particular need in our library?
2. Is the book true to biblical teachings and the doctrinal position of our church?
3. Is the subject matter treated accurately, clearly, fairly, and interestingly?
4. Is the book appropriate for the age or interest group for which it is intended?
5. Is the author qualified to write on this subject?
6. Does the publisher have a good reputation in this field?
7. Is the book's physical makeup—binding, paper quality, print size, margins—satisfactory?
8. Are the illustrations well done and appropriate to the text and age level?
9. Are the vocabulary and writing style effective for the intended reader?
10. Are the contents up-to-date?
11. Does the book have current appeal?
12. Does the book have lasting value?
13. Does it contribute to an overall balance of subject material?
14. Has it received good reviews?
15. Is the book included on a recommended book list such as those published annually by several Christian magazines?
16. Does the cost allow its purchase without eliminating something needed even more?
17. Is the book the best choice we can make in the field?
18. Will the people who use our library read it?

Children's books deserve special care in selection, because of the impact they have in the child's development of reading habits, attitudes, and beliefs. Look for books with good literary quality and artistic, appropriate illustrations. Be sure the experiences presented are true-to-life ones children can identify with and not ones they are psychologically unable to deal with. The vocabulary should be appropriate, but not necessarily restricted to words the children already know. The chief purpose of the book should be "to help the young reader develop a biblical concept of God which will color all his life."[1]

CRITERIA FOR GIFT BOOKS

Gift books should be accepted only on condition that the librarian may make other disposition of them if they don't meet a current need. Then the donor will not be offended if the book is not to be found on the shelves later. Gift books accepted for use should be subjected to the same criteria as books purchased. They should be in usable condition and should not contribute to a serious imbalance in types of books in the library's holdings.

BOOK DELETIONS

"Do church libraries ever get rid of books? " one of our survey respondents asked. A problem that churches seldom deal with, but should, is that of maximum size. A related problem is that of periodically weeding out un-needed books. Whether there is need to set a maximum figure on number of holdings or not, the books should be screened periodically for items not being used, items that are outdated or inappropriate, and items too badly worn for continued use. It is better to discard most such books than to clutter shelves with them.

SCRAPBOOKS

The library should have a church history scrapbook, keeping it current with pictures and clippings of church events. One person, not necessarily from the library committtee, should have the responsibility of keeping this scrapbook up-to-date. This should be processed with reference material, for use in the library only, since its contents are usually irreplaceable.

Some of your missionary material will be more useful if made up into scrapbooks, arranged according to fields, organizations, families, or other categories useful to your users.

PERIODICALS

If your library provides a reading room with comfortable seating, many people will spend time there, perhaps while waiting to meet another member of the family. They will enjoy looking at current Christian periodicals. Some who feel they can't afford individual subscriptions will appreciate access to recent information on varied subjects. Christian education workers should be able to use periodicals containing helps for them. Titles and addresses of some recommended periodicals are given in the suppliers' directory in the appendix.

1. Dorothy Martin, "How to Choose the Best Books for Your Children," p. 60.

Back issues of periodicals are very useful to anyone working on programs or researching a particular topic. Keep the older periodicals, bound in volumes if at all possible, where they won't take room from materials used more frequently, but where they can be made available to those with real use for them. A subscription to the *Christian Periodical Index* (address given in Appendix 2) will greatly enhance the value of indexed periodicals.

Convert copies of old magazines that are not needed in their entirety into clippings for the vertical file. This service will save your library users a great deal of time when looking for material on certain subjects and will save shelf space for more useful materials.

VERTICAL FILE

While it may not be the first order of business in establishing a library, somewhere along the line you'll find the need to organize and make available a number of printed materials that aren't books or periodicals. These are usually kept in a filing cabinet in the library. Librarians refer to such a collection of printed and visual material, filed alphabetically in folders by subject content, as a vertical file. The following are some of the items you'll want to consider keeping in such a file, assigning them to the same subject headings as those used for other library materials: annual reports; bulletins and newsletters; career information; catalogs of church supplies; charts; church constitution; clippings from newspapers and magazines; college, Bible school, and seminary catalogs; committee and board records; craft materials and instructions; curriculum materials; directory of church members and officers; flannelgraph materials; missions information and letters; music; pamphlets and booklets; photographs; pictures; prayer reminders and calendars; programs and program ideas; sample Christian education materials; scripts to accompany filmstrips, slides and films, if not stored with those materials; sermon typescripts; Sunday school papers; tracts; vacation Bible school materials; and yearbooks. (See chapter 7 for suggested headings.)

Let church members know about your vertical file, encouraging them to use it as a source of information and as an opportunity for service by contributing items for the file.

SUMMARY

The care with which books, periodicals, and vertical file materials are selected will determine to a large measure the spiritual impact of your library. It is tempting for a librarian to load the library heavily with material in line with her interests. Instead, she should be concerned with selecting materials that promote the overall objectives of the church, maintaining a balanced collection to meet needs of varied ages and interests.

5

SELECTING AUDIOVISUAL MATERIAL

Incline your ear and hear the words of the wise, And apply your mind to my knowledge (Proverbs 22:17).

EVERY CHURCH should consider the advantages of making its library a complete resource center, with all teaching materials, including audiovisual supplies, handled through the library. Even if space arrangements make separate locations and personnel necessary, all units of resource center activities should be coordinated under one library committee.

With so many people accustomed to using nonprint media such as television and cassettes, the church library should be providing material that appeals to interests and habits already developed. Even if a church has a separate audiovisual media center for church workers, the regular library should have nonprint materials for individual and family use. If the church library is a complete resource center, it will also provide for the teaching needs of the church. There are many different types of audiovisual materials appropriate for a church resource center. Some suggestions are made here, with procedures for preparing such materials for library use given in chapter 7.

CASSETTES

Many church libraries are just entering into a vital ministry through cassettes. As with books, there are many types of cassettes a library should consider having.

PASTOR'S SERMONS

A cassette ministry usually begins with taping the pastor's sermons and making copies available through the church library. Deacons or deaconesses, "sunshine committee" members, library workers, pastors, and others (how about young people?) can take cassettes and players to the sick and shut-in members and friends of the church. Doing this early in the week does a great deal to let such people feel a continuing part of the church. Include some of the church music, as that will be especially appreciated.

People who have been gone on vacation or business trips, those home a Sunday with a cold or caring for a sick child, and those taking a turn in the nursery can also enjoy the pastor's sermons by cassette.

It isn't necessary to spend a great deal of money to start this type of cassette ministry. We started by placing a recorder and microphone on the pulpit. Then, I made copies by using two recorders opposite each other in an improvised studio at home. We later used a patch cord between the two machines, to eliminate outside noises. Now, we can plug right into the church's public address system with two recorders, giving us one copy available for loan immediately after the service and one for making additional copies. There are places that will duplicate tapes for you, if you prefer to have them done commercially.

Many churches use high-speed duplicating equipment so several copies are available immediately after a service. The Johnston Heights Evangelical Free Church in Surrey, British Columbia, mails over one hundred sermon tapes a week to shut-ins, missionaries, former members, and people living in remote areas. Their "Tape Ministry News" keeps the church informed of the impact of this ministry which has become a focal point of the church's outreach.

You notice that I said a cassette ministry usually begins with taping the pastor's sermons. Don't stop there. New things are constantly coming out on tapes that can be a help and blessing to your people. The next time someone responds to your library promotion efforts with an, "I never read," ask that person: "Do you ever listen?" Or perhaps a less blunt, "Then we have just the thing for you" would be a better way to introduce them to the library's cassettes.

Remind people that they can listen to cassettes while driving a car, ironing, washing dishes, tending the baby, sweeping the garage, cooking, washing the car, doing routine bookkeeping work, and dozens of other everyday tasks. Might we even suggest that it could at times replace television watching? Earphones can be used if not everyone in a room wishes to hear the tape.

What types of cassettes other than sermons are recommended for church libraries? Some suggestions are listed below.

BIBLE READING

Many find real blessing in listening to good readers read from the King James or The Living Bible. This is especially helpful for those with failing eyesight, but also valuable as a supplement to personal Scripture reading.

BIBLE STORIES FOR CHILDREN

Portable cassette players are much smaller and more convenient to use than record players. Children can listen to them anywhere. They can be incorporated into family devotions and evening story times. It's surprising how much adults learn from them. Cassettes checked out to children from non-Christian homes will reach parents, too. Bible story cassettes can also be used in Sunday school, children's church, and church weekday activities.

CASSETTES FOR YOUTH

Young people tend to prefer listening over reading. Cassettes for youth are often more popular than books designed for youth. Young people may listen to Bible messages on cassettes when they won't listen to words of witness spoken directly to them by an individual. Cassettes are used effectively in youth group meetings as well as for individual listening. There are cassettes available on such subjects as the relationship between science and the Bible, dating, and other subjects about which they commonly ask questions.

FAMILY COUNSELING

Many cassettes are available on subjects concerning marriage and the home. These are helpful for those preparing for marriage, those already married, those facing marriage problems, and those interested in child training. Counselors find it helpful to send cassettes home with counselees to supplement and reinforce counseling sessions and literature.

TEACHING AIDS

Cassettes can be used for teacher training, either in groups or individually. They can be used as part of classroom instruction at all ages. Some are produced to be used with accompanying textbooks.

DEVOTIONAL CASSETTES

In addition to Scripture readings, one can listen to collections of poems and inspirational thoughts throughout the day. Senior citizens who can no longer read as much as they would like especially appreciate this type of cassette.

CONFERENCES AND MEETINGS

Not everyone who is interested is free to attend all the meetings of the local church, let alone conferences involving travel to other areas. Cassettes bring a form of participation to those unable to attend in person.

Encourage people to check out library recorders, if they don't have their own, to take to conferences, retreats, camps, and vacation visits to other churches. Have them share their recordings with others when they come back. Ask permission to copy tapes of interest to your library users.

INTERVIEWS

Taped interviews with well-known Christians, focused on some subject of Christian faith and growth, are a popular type of cassette. Many such are available for purchase. You might also ask permission to tape interviews with visiting speakers who come to minister in your church or area.

EVANGELISM

Many cassettes carry evangelistic messages which Christians can share by loaning them out, inviting friends to their homes to listen, or playing them in a car pool or small group when appropriate.

MESSAGES AND LECTURES BY SPEAKERS OTHER THAN THE PASTOR

Messages from many noted speakers and writers are available on cassette tapes for individual and group listening. Cassettes have been made from old reel-to-reel tapes of several famous preachers no longer living. Faculty of Bible schools, colleges, and seminaries have taped lectures on a wide variety of interesting subjects.

MUSIC

The resource center can't be expected to cater to everyone's interest in the field of music. It can, however, provide some wholesome Christian music in cassette form. It can make available copies of special music from church services, if copying is not prohibited by copyright law. While inexpensive cassettes usually work quite well for speaking voices, it is best to use high quality tape for reproducing music.

INFORMATION

Cassettes can be used to transmit information on many subjects. One of them is missionary work, with some missionary organizations providing tapes for interested churches. If you send taped greetings to missionaries, they can return the tape with information about their work.

Some of the most popular cassettes explain beliefs of non-Christian religions and suggest ways of sharing the Christian faith with people of other beliefs.

TESTIMONIES

Just as books telling personal conversion stories are popular, so are cassettes with people telling in their own words and with their own voices how the Lord changed their lives.

RADIO PROGRAMS

Some gospel radio programs make cassettes available. These can be distributed in hospitals, nursing homes, jails, and private homes. Both adult and children's broadcasts can be obtained in this form.

Be creative in use of cassettes in your church. Talk to people from other churches about what they are doing. The book *Everything You Need to Know for a Cassette Ministry*, while written primarily for the foreign missionary, has practical information about equipment and methods that can be applied to church cassette ministries.[1]

RECORDS

The church resource center should have records for two major purposes. As long as people have record players in their homes, the library should provide Bible story records for children, sacred music for all ages, and Bible instruction records for home use. You may have prospective missionaries in your church who could benefit from records that teach foreign languages. Some of your members may prefer to borrow Bible readings on records instead of cassettes. Most library records will be 33⅓ rpm speed records, but other speeds should also be available.

There are many ways that records can be used within the church building. Nurseries, children's church, and Sunday school classes can benefit from recorded stories and songs. Some records are produced to correlate with Sunday school curriculum. Many filmstrips and slide sets have accompanying records. Some offer a choice of record or cassette. Records also come with various types of phonoviewer equipment, as mentioned under a discussion of multimedia materials.

Cassettes may largely replace records in time, but there is currently much good material that can be obtained only on records, and this material should be made available to as many people as possible.

REEL-TO-REEL TAPES

While cassettes are replacing both reel-type tapes and records for many purposes, reel tapes still usually have better acoustical quality and are easier to edit than cassettes.

Many reel-to-reel recorders produce stereophonic sound. If two speakers are used in proper locations, the effect of the playback is very realistic.

Tapes may be purchased in several lengths. A resource center should make blank tapes available for church recording needs. Tapes can be erased and used over. Some tapes should be kept as library holdings for others to borrow.

SLIDES

When we refer to slides, we usually mean photographic reproductions in

1. Viggo Sogaard, *Everything You Need to Know for a Cassette Ministry*.

$2'' \times 2''$ mountings. The most common are 35mm double-frame slides. A slide projector and screen make slides visible to a large group. Many sizes and types of viewers are available for individual or small group use.

Slides allow more flexibility in use than many other visual aids. Any number can be used, and they can be rearranged in any order. They can be produced by anyone who likes to take pictures or purchased through catalogs listing thousands of titles.

Encourage members to give duplicates of some of their slides to the library. If someone takes a trip to Bible lands, many individuals and groups could benefit from their pictures. Pictures taken at special church functions such as the Sunday school picnic, vacation Bible school, church camp, a class social, the summer library contest, and Christmas program can be enjoyed later and used to promote similar events in the future. Keep a slide record of the church's pastors and their families.

Ask missionaries and missionary organizations for slides depicting their work. Be sure your church's visitors to mission fields let you obtain library copies of some of their pictures when they come back. Get as complete information about the pictures as you can.

There are many ways slides can be used in the church's Christian education program. One slide might be projected on a screen as a focal point during a worship service.

Slides depicting Bible times are good teaching devices. Just a few shown during each class session will hold attention and reinforce instruction. Our pastor used slides of pictures he and his father had taken in Israel and other Bible-related countries to illustrate a series of lessons on Bible geography.

Let your young people try their hand at producing a slide program. They can take their own pictures, use "write-on" slides for titles and printed messages, and write a script to accompany the showing of the slides. Then ask permission to preserve these materials in your library or resource center for future use.

FILMSTRIPS

Filmstrips are probably the most commonly used projected visual aids in Christian education programs. They are a series of still pictures placed on 35mm film. They can be obtained both in color and black and white. Each picture is called a frame. Captions often are put directly on the filmstrip.

Narration in script or manual form is usually provided with filmstrip, unless a coordinated cassette or record is with it. Filmstrips can be stopped to allow for discussion, backed up for review, or advanced to skip some portions. They are relatively inexpensive, so churches can usually afford to buy rather than rent them.

There are many types of filmstrips available for various uses. Sets are often produced by publishers of Sunday school material to correlate with their lessons.

Leadership training filmstrips are especially effective. They include instruction for teachers, music leaders, camping personnel, youth leaders, and various other church workers.

Filmstrips are available on just about every subject and for every age group. Just about any Bible story can be taught with filmstrip. Parables from nature and lessons about Christian living are popular. Other subjects include salvation, witnessing, prayer, dating, manners, marriage, worship, church growth, sex education, and drug education.

Missionary lessons can be taught well with filmstrip. Actual pictures of natives of other lands, living conditions, and missionaries at work on various fields will do much more than spoken words alone to promote interest in missions.

Library users should be encouraged to consider using filmstrips in their homes with their own families, in witnessing to neighbors, and in home Bible study groups.

Even though many good filmstrips are available, there will be times when your workers will want to make their own. Colored pencils, felt-tip markers, ink, and typewriter all can be used on the film used for making filmstrips. Kits are available from Sunday school and public school supply houses. The library should have these supplies available.

Be sure to preview filmstrips before purchasing. The library should have a filmstrip viewer so borrowers can view those they are interested in without leaving the resource center.

Courtesy of Demco Educational Corp.

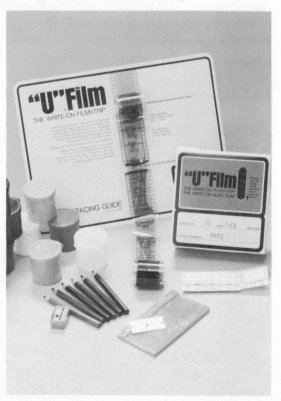

Filmstrip and Slide Do-it-Yourself Kit

Transparencies for the Overhead Projector

The overhead projector is one of the most useful tools available for the Christian education worker. Size and cost made its use prohibitive for many churches until recently. But now lightweight, reasonably priced projectors are available for every budget. Commercially prepared materials to use with them are also increasingly available.

The overhead projector has many advantages. A leader can use it while facing his audience, with the screen a short distance behind him. He can draw or write on the surface to display the types of things he might otherwise put on a chalkboard. Since he doesn't need to turn away from his listeners, he will find it much easier to hold their attention, and no time is wasted erasing full chalkboards.

The overhead projector works well in a fully lighted room. It can be used in small or large rooms, allowing pastors to use it from the pulpit and discussion leaders to use it with small groups. It is easy to operate, requiring no special skill or training. In addition to being able to project material as it is drawn, one can prepare materials in advance.

The plastic sheet from which material is projected by the overhead projector is called a transparency. It is usually an $8\frac{1}{2}'' \times 11''$ sheet of clear acetate, serving much like a large slide. The sheets can be mounted in cardboard frames, and overlays can be designed to fold down over the base transparency. Some projectors use rolls of acetate which can be unrolled during use.

To make your own transparencies, purchase clear, transparent acetate in sheets or rolls and special pens and pencils in various colors. These materials are available in stationery and art supply stores, in college bookstores, in engineering supply stores, and in some Christian bookstores and supply houses. Sometimes an ordinary grease pencil or felt-tip pen will work, but these should be tested on the particular type of acetate to be used, as some combinations do not work well. Some pens leave permanent marks and some leave marks that can be wiped off easily with a damp cloth. Blue, green, red, and purple marks show up the best. Yellow and orange are hard to see. Black is not usually a satisfactory color.

Acetate also can be obtained in colors for special effects. Transfer letters, symbols, and color tapes can be purchased for neat, professional-looking designs. Typed letters are usually too small to project clearly.

Teachers can prepare lesson outlines, charts, drawings, graphs, and other visual aids to illustrate specific lessons. Lessons often can be developed point by point through the use of overlays. Each part is put on a separate sheet of acetate and added as called for in the lesson.

Several makes of copiers can produce transparencies from material prepared on paper. This opens up the possibility of using clippings of various kinds, if you have access to such a copy machine.

A growing number of commercially prepared transparencies are available for Bible teaching. Bible maps are especially useful. Several Bible story sets have been developed. Other sets show archaeological findings and samples of early writings. Library care of these sets will assure maximum availability for all church groups.

The church's resource center should include one or more overhead projectors, acetate, pen and pencil supplies, some commercial transparencies, and an individual qualified to help Christian education workers make maximum use of these supplies. When individual teachers prepare their own transparencies, they should turn them in to the library if they might have further use in any church group.

OPAQUE MATERIALS

An opaque projector will project most printed materials that are less than ten inches square. Maps, pictures, drawings, and books can be used. The library's vertical file should contain much material for use with this type of projector. Transparencies prepared for use with overhead projectors cannot be used with opaque projectors.

The opaque projector is expensive and bulky. It requires some darkening of the room in which it is operated. Once acquired, there is practically no limit to the low-cost and free items available to use with it.

MOTION PICTURES

Since motion pictures are considerably more expensive than most other audiovisual materials, church groups usually rent them rather than purchasing them. It is still the function of a church resource center to order them, check to be sure they are in usable condition, and return them promptly after use. If the church owns some films, the resource center will care for these as well.

The 16mm motion picture film has proven its value over many years of use in church programs. Excellent films are available for children, youth, and adults. They are appropriate for church services and group meetings. They are very effective in attracting visitors and building attendance.

Some of the general subjects on which good Christian films are available are: Bible stories such as the life of Christ, science and creation, Christian life, evangelism, missions, family living, prophecy, and youth problems.

The 16mm film is by far the most popular for church use, but there is some use of 8mm and Super 8 films, which can be produced locally.

Since it is not convenient to stop the showing of motion pictures for discussion, it is best to introduce them carefully and then allow time for discussion after their completion.

VIDEOTAPES, VIDEO CASSETTES, AND VIDEO DISCS

VIDEOTAPES

Churches are finding many uses for videotapes. Taping of sounds alone is inadequate for many purposes. As videotape equipment is becoming available at more reasonable prices, an increasing number of church resource centers have such equipment. They can arrange for rental of videotape recording and playback equipment when purchase is not feasible.

Videotaping has been proved a very effective aid in teacher training. Teachers can learn from master teachers in action. They can see their own mistakes. Parents can observe their children's participation in church activities.

Showing videotapes of church services to nursing home residents lets shut-in church members maintain a more active interest than is possible from just listening to cassette tapes of services. The videotapes also provide a ministry to unchurched nursing home residents.

Videotape adapters for television sets may soon make home use of videotapes more prevalent.

Church libraries and resource centers should have all the supplies needed for videotaping. They should provide library storage and checkout procedures for any videotapes appropriate for repeated use.

VIDEO CASSETTES

There are some Bible stories and gospel messages available on video cassettes to be used with special adapters for television sets. While quite expensive, these cassettes are very convenient to use.

VIDEO DISCS

Discs carrying recordings of both sound and picture are being produced at less cost than video cassettes. The discs are used with a high speed turntable hooked up to a regular color television set. The potential for both church and home use is unlimited. Church libraries should plan to have Bible stories and gospel programs of all kinds available for loan to those with appropriate attachments for their television sets. The library should plan to have such equipment available for loan, as well as the discs.

MICROFORMS

Microforms are miniature reproductions that require magnification to read. Some churches use them to store quantities of material with limited use.

Magazines and church documents could be photographed and produced on microfilm, which comes in the form of a roll of transparent film.

A microfiche is a 3″ × 5″ or 4″ × 6″ sheet of film which can contain photographic reproductions of many pages of printed material. An ultramicrofiche can hold as many as 1,000 pages from a book, reproduced onto a 3″ × 5″ card. Microcards are 3″ × 5″ cards produced from microfilm. Microprints are 6″ × 9″ cards reproduced from microfilm.

Microforms are not in general use in churches, but should be considered by the large resource center. They require special equipment for magnifying and printing portions to be examined.

MULTIMEDIA MATERIALS

More and more suppliers are packaging items of more than one type of audiovisual together, for both home and church use. This creates some classifying and storing problems for the librarian, as you will find discussed in a later chapter, but it greatly increases the effectiveness of the material.

Books and records and books and cassettes are useful multimedia packages. Children enjoy looking at pictures while listening to recorded stories, so these are quite popular. Manuals for pupils, a teacher's guide, and one or more lesson cassettes provide supplies for an interesting study group.

As mentioned earlier, slides and filmstrips often come with narrated script or music supplied by records or cassettes. They may also have study guides. Some transparency sets for use with an overhead projector are packaged with manuals or masters for duplicating worksheets to distribute to viewers.

A very popular use of multimedia with small children is possible with a phonoviewer such as the *Show 'N Tell Phono-Viewer*. David C. Cook Publishing Company offers a package deal that includes a complete set of their excellent *Canon Bible Programs* with a General Electric Phonoviewer. Using these, a small group of children can watch a Bible story on a TV-like screen while listening to the coordinated record played on top of the unit.

NONPROJECTED VISUAL AIDS

A complete resource center will have many visual aids in addition to those already mentioned. Most are produced primarily as teaching aids, but an innovative librarian will think of ways to encourage individual use of many of these items, using the library as a learning center or encouraging home use.

Some of the visual aids listed here might be kept in the vertical file, described in the previous chapter. In some cases, size will be the determining factor. While small pictures, maps, and charts can be kept in a vertical file, larger ones will need separate facilities.

VISUAL BOARDS

Flannelgraph is a convenient and effective teaching device. Flannel or flannel-backed figures of all kinds can be placed on a flannel-covered board to illustrate many lessons. Felt, suede, and flocking-backed paper can be used instead of flannel. Many Bible lesson sets are available commercially. Much material can be prepared by your own workers and preserved by the library staff for wider use.

Chalkboards have never become obsolete, and should be used in Christian education more than they are. White and colored chalk, chalkboards, and suggestions for their use should be available in the church's resource center.

Bulletin boards carry information and promotional material for many church programs. Lettering supplies, thumb tacks, extra boards, and bulletin board ideas should be available in the library. Boards can be made of cork or composition material. Magnetic boards can be purchased with sets of letters to be used with them. Hook-and-loop boards, using synthetic materials that hook together, can display three-dimensional items.

MAPS AND GLOBES

Every resource center should have a good supply of maps that can be hung on the wall or placed on easels. Maps of Bible lands are important for any Bible teaching. Maps should also be used in connection with instruction about missionary endeavors. Globes are often more helpful than maps in developing concepts about our relationships to other parts of the world.

PICTURES

In addition to small pictures in the vertical file, the resource center should care for large framed and unframed art prints, photographs, and original drawings.

OBJECTS

A good librarian will be aware of the possibilities of using everyday objects to illustrate lessons and will have a supply of such objects available. Coordinating them with suggestions found in the library's object lesson books makes them especially useful. Objects such as scrolls and coins that represent things used in Bible times should also be kept.

DISPLAYS

Many types of displays built by individuals or groups should be preserved for repeated use. Models of such things as the tabernacle or a dwelling from Bible times are very useful teaching aids. Dioramas of Bible scenes should be kept in the library. Posters of general interest should be available for various uses. Mobile displays can be stored for later use.

GAMES

Bible games provide an enjoyable way of learning Bible facts. Games should be available for either home or church use.

CHARTS AND GRAPHS

The library should have large wall charts of such things as the books of the Bible and prophecies concerning end times. Any graphs or diagrams of general interest should be kept in the library. Flip charts often have good teaching value.

FLASH CARDS

Flash card sets are available to teach Bible songs, verses, and stories. Others could be made locally.

MISSIONARY CURIOS

Flags, dolls, art work, souvenirs, and items connected with worship in other countries all can be used in missions education programs.

PUPPETS

Regular puppets, hand puppets, and finger puppets are useful as attention-getters and storytellers. Try to get someone in your church to make puppets and demonstrate their use.

COSTUMES

Why make new angel wings every Christmas if the resource center can store them from year to year? Any costumes that can be used again should be stored in the resource center. If the resource center does not have storage room, a record should be kept there of such items and where they are stored.

CRAFT AND DRAWING SUPPLIES

A complete, efficient resource center is the logical place for storing various craft, drawing, and teaching supplies. Instead of being scattered around the church, they can be available in one central location. Duplication can thus be avoided, and supplies can be replenished as needed.

WORSHIP CENTER MATERIALS

Such items as crosses, candles, candle holders, plastic flowers, large Bibles, and various decorative items should be stored in the resource center, if storage space allows this.

CRITERIA FOR SELECTING AUDIOVISUAL MATERIALS

Just as for printed material, it is important that the library have standards for quality in selecting audiovisual material and equipment. Seek out one or more persons with experience in these areas for advice before making any large investments.

The content of filmstrip, movies, cassettes, and other nonprint media is just as important as the content of books on the library shelves. Several of the magazines listed in Appendix 2, as well as many denominational periodicals, review audiovisuals as well as books. Make use of these helps in deciding on purchases. Your Christian bookstore or regional audiovisual center can also be counted on for valuable advice.

Be sure any audiovisual material chosen is accurate and interesting, appropriate for the age or interests of those expected to use it, and educationally effective. They should be technically satisfactory, easy to use, and easy to maintain. Costs should be reasonable and within budget allowances. Where pertinent, check for good tone, color, and synchronization of sound with picture.

AUDIOVISUAL EQUIPMENT

It is not our purpose in this book to go into detail regarding audiovisual equipment. For more information on selecting, using, and maintaining such equipment we recommend that each library obtain the latest edition of *Audiovisual Media in Christian Education.*[2]

A centralized resource center will house the audiovisual equipment used in church programs, as well as equipment available for individual use outside the church. The library that is separate from the audiovisual center will at least have cassette players and possibly slide and filmstrip projectors available for home use.

TYPES OF EQUIPMENT

Specific equipment is necessary for the use of each type of audiovisual material referred to earlier in the chapter. Sources of supply for such equipment are given in Appendix 2.

Cassette ministry equipment. The resource center will need recording equipment for recording church services. It should have duplicating equipment unless other arrangements are made for producing multiple copies. Several cassette player/recorders should be available for home use, for taking to shut-ins, and for use in church programs. The library should also have earphones, microphones, a supply of blank tapes, head cleaners, and tape splicing equipment.

2. Gene A. Getz, *Audiovisual Media in Christian Education.*

Record players. Sufficient record players, allowing for use of records of all speeds, should be available for use in the library, in various departments of the church, and for loan outside the church where this is considered appropriate. If any players are kept in nonlibrary locations, their locations should be recorded in the library. Supplies for cleaning records and caring for players should be kept in the library.

Reel-to-reel recorders. With increasing use of cassettes, most churches will only need one reel-type recorder. The resource center will also have blank reels and repair equipment.

Projection equipment. It is a good idea to have small viewers for slides and filmstrips in the resource center for checking and previewing these materials. Portable screens, extension cords, and flashlights can be checked out with projectors, projector stands, and carrying cases. The types of projectors needed for use with projected teaching aids mentioned earlier are the following: slide and filmstrip projectors, separate and/or combined; overhead projector; opaque projector; and 16mm, and possibly 8mm, movie projectors. Film inspectors and splicers, bulbs, batteries, and other maintenance equipment should be available, along with supplies for making slides, filmstrips, and transparencies.

Filmstrip projectors with coordinated cassette players, phonoviewers, and other equipment combining visual and sound projection are needed for use with multimedia teaching aids.

Churches with adequate financial resources should consider having videotaping recorders, cameras, and projectors; television sets with adapters for using video cassettes and/or video discs. Churches may also have use for television sets without such adapters. While such sets may not be housed in the library, their location and use should be recorded there.

Microform equipment. Some churches will have use for photographing equipment capable of producing microforms, readers to enlarge and project them on a screen, and printers to reproduce the enlarged images on paper. Separate types of equipment are required for use with microfilm, microfiche, and microcards.

Nonprojected visual aid equipment. Some equipment is needed for using the simpler, less expensive visual aids. Easels and boards covered with flannel, suede, or felt are needed for giving flannelgraph lessons. Easels also can be used with such items as large pictures, maps, and chalkboards.

Sand tables have many uses, including holding some of the types of displays mentioned earlier. Puppets can be used most effectively with some background equipment such as folding cardboard stages.

Other audiovisual equipment. Churches should also consider including portable public address systems, photocopy machines, laminating machines, and even teaching machines in resource center equipment. Even though some of this equipment may be permanently located in other parts of the church, its selection and care should be arranged through the audiovisual department of the church library/resource center.

CRITERIA FOR SELECTING AUDIOVISUAL EQUIPMENT

It is not possible to discuss here everything that should be considered in buying the equipment necessary for use with audiovisual materials. However, the following general guidelines should be followed in selecting such equipment:

1. It should be the right equipment for the material the church uses or has reason to anticipate using. Be careful not to invest in something there is no need for or interest in using.
2. It should be well made. Equipment for use in a church by many people needs to be sturdier than something one might use infrequently at home. Choose equipment from a respected manufacturer.
3. It should be easy to operate. Check for ease of such things as threading film, focusing, and controlling speed and volume. Be sure the equipment is sufficiently lightweight to be readily portable.

TABLE 4

Types of Audiovisual Equipment in the Church

Item of Equipment	Number of Churches	Percentage of Churches
Overhead projector	33	16%
Flannelgraph equipment	31	15
Movie projector	30	15
Filmstrip projector	23	11
Slide projector	19	9
Unspecified type of projector	18	9
Record player	17	8
Cassette recorder and/or player	13	6
Screen	8	4
Reel-to-reel tape recorder	4	2
Combined projector and player	4	2
Phonoviewer	3	1
Opaque projector	1	1
Videotape recorder	1	1
Total	205	100%

4. It should be easy to maintain. It is false economy to purchase a low-priced item whose upkeep is costly. Check on the ease of repair, including availability of parts and of service.

5. Its cost should be reasonable in comparison with similar items and in relationship to funds available for the purpose.

SURVEY RESULTS

Libraries responding to our survey report items of audiovisual equipment in their church, whether cared for in the church library or not, as indicated in Table 4.

In our survey we asked churches to report on the number of holdings of certain types of materials found most frequently in church libraries. Table 5 shows the average number of the most common nonprint materials in these libraries, compared with book and periodical holdings. The fact that some churches did not report any nonprint items simply because they are not kept in the library must be taken into consideration when interpreting these figures.

TABLE 5

Library Holdings by Type of Material

Type of Material	Average Number	Lowest Number Reported	Highest Number Reported	Number of Churches Reporting
Books	1,120	100	10,187	188
Periodicals titles	7	1	86	100
Cassettes	48	1	1,000	89
Records	20	1	625	96
Filmstrips	50	4	1,199	85
Slides	75	2	4,000	33

SUMMARY

There are two types of users to be considered in choosing nonprint materials for the church resource center: (1) individuals using these materials for their own spiritual growth and personal witness to others, and (2) church groups for whom audiovisuals are essential teaching tools. The most effective and efficient church libraries will provide resources to meet the needs of both types of users, combining nonprint materials with printed materials in one centralized location.

6

DETERMINING LIBRARY POLICIES

But let all things be done properly and in an orderly manner (1 Corinthians 14:40).

SOMEONE MUST DETERMINE operating policies and have authority to change them as needed. Policies are usually the responsibility of the library committee, under the supervision of a board of Christian education or general church board, working with the library workers. The library committee should discuss and make recommendations regarding the general operating policies, acquisition policies, and extension ministry policies of the library.

LIBRARY OPERATING POLICIES

Operating policies should be determined when the church library is first established and reviewed regularly, making changes when the situation calls for change.

LIBRARY HOURS

Many libraries are open anytime the building is open, with individuals free to check out what they want on a self-serve basis. If this is done, clear instructions must be posted for users. While this system has the advantage of easy accessibility at almost any time, it has several disadvantages.

There is always some risk that people will borrow things without properly checking them out; then it becomes difficult to track down missing items. Church people usually mean well, but often misplace and forget library material. There is greater danger of vandalism and theft in an unlocked library. Unsupervised children playing in the library can cause real problems. Unscheduled meetings in an unlocked library may tie the room up when it is needed for library use. Some people hesitate to use a library if no one is available to help them.

There was a time when I would have said that a room that could be locked whenever a librarian wasn't on duty was an absolute essential for a successful church library; we held out for such a location before starting ours. But more recently I have seen many churches with good library programs conducted from open spaces and unlocked rooms. If someone can get in during the week to shelve returned books, check up on past-due material, and generally take care of essential library duties, but no one is available to be on duty to check materials out on a regular basis, then it is better to have a self-serve library than none at all.

Librarians in our survey were asked whether books were "always," "sometimes," or "never" checked out on a self-serve basis. Table 6 shows that most libraries allow books to be checked out this way sometimes, but not always. About one-fourth of the responding libraries never allow books to be checked out when a librarian is not on duty.

TABLE 6

Use of Self-Service in the Library Checkout System

Self-Service Basis	Number of Churches	Percentage of Churches
Always	45	27%
Sometimes	78	47
Never	42	25
Total	165	100%*

*While the sum of the percentages as shown is 99 per cent, their sum before rounding is 100 per cent.

Churches sometimes adopt a combination system, with scheduled hours when a librarian is on duty and self-serve arrangements at other times. In spite of the risks mentioned, this combination has worked quite well in many places. One church I visited has a buzzer system by which a person can be admitted to the church after stating his business. Once in the building, he is free to use the library, checking out his own material.

It is best to announce hours when the library is open, with one or more persons on duty to check out materials. Arrangements can often be made for a staff member such as the church secretary or director of Christian education to check out materials during the week on request. Individuals in various church groups can be trained in library procedures so they can make library materials available at times their groups meet. This should include individuals from youth groups, weekday club programs, vacation Bible school, choir, women's groups, men's fellowships, board members, and any other special interest groups using the church.

All paid staff members should be trained in the basics of helping people who come to the church during the week for library materials. In spite of the temptation to just borrow things for a short time, staff members should be asked to check things out just like anyone else.

The church library should be officially open, with a librarian on duty, at least fifteen minutes before and after regularly scheduled church services. It is best to remain open during Sunday school to take care of unexpected teacher needs and early church arrivals. Library hours should be posted outside the library, printed regularly in the church bulletin, and announced from time to time in various services and meetings. The library should always be open at the scheduled times. It should also be open whenever special congregation-wide meetings are held, such as missionary and Bible conferences and evangelistic meetings. Consistency and regularity of library hours will do much to promote library use.

Our survey showed the most common times for a library to be open are Sunday morning and evening and Wednesday evening, with 40% of the reporting churches open at these times only. Some stay open through services, and some are open only before and after services. Another 28% reported being open just on Sunday, usually both morning and evening. About 17% reported that the library is open whenever the church is open. This includes those with complete or partial self-serve systems. The other 15% combine various hours other than or in addition to Wednesday evening with Sunday hours. A few from this last group are open from 8:30 or 9:00 A.M. to 4.00 or 5:00 P.M. each weekday, with others open selected days or evenings on a regular basis.

One very successful church library has a librarian on duty five days a week in addition to Sunday hours. Their library is near a public high school and attracts young people who study there and find reference materials for some of their school work. Having earned a reputation in the area for their friendly welcome, this library is also used quite a bit by people from other churches.

KEYS

All regularly scheduled library workers need a key to the library. The librarian also needs a key to the church building, as she will need to get or deliver library material and work on displays and other library business at times when the church is locked. A library key should be kept in the church office for use by staff and other authorized users. Other use of keys should be by special arrangement with the librarian and other church officials. It is not wise to have indiscriminate and extensive distribution of keys.

WORKER SCHEDULE

There should be a definite schedule showing who will be on duty in the library at particular times each week. Even if one person handles the library work alone most of the time, arrangements should be made for someone to replace her in the event of illness, family emergencies, and vacations. No one should be so indispensable that the library must be inoperative when that person is unable to be there.

CHECKOUT PROCEDURES

If you process materials as indicated in chapters 7 and 8, most library items will have a book card to be removed from the book pocket and signed by the borrower. The date the item is due back at the library will be stamped or written on the book card and the date slip. Two to three weeks is usually satisfactory for borrowing time. Check with your nearest public library. It will help your users remember, if your policies match those of other libraries they use.

The book card is then filed in a charging tray. Various systems can be used for this filing. Cards are usually filed by date due. Within each due date, they can be filed by classification number, accession number, or last name of the author. The main objective is to make it easy to match the card to the book or other material when it is returned or renewed. There will also be times when you will need to look in the charging tray to find out who has an item checked out and when it is due back.

One person at the checkout desk can usually take care of everyone, if users

TABLE 7

Average Number of Books Checked Out Each Week

Average Number of Books Checked Out	Number of Churches	Percentage of Churches
1 - 9	38	23%
10 - 19	42	26
20 - 29	32	20
30 - 39	12	7
40 - 49	6	4
50 - 99	18	11
100 - 199	12	7
200 and up	4	2
Total	164	100%

NOTE: The total average number of books checked out per week per church is 20.

are trained to fill in their names on book cards. But this depends on the number of items checked out and the time allotted for this. Church library users tend to congregate in the library during very brief time spans preceding and following church services. You may need help during rush periods and special promotions. We find it helpful to use a folding table for an extra checkout station during our summer reading program.

Libraries in our survey varied a great deal in average number of books checked out each week. They reported figures all the way from 2 to 634, with an average (median) figure 20 as seen in Table 7.

Make it easy for users to renew books as needed. It will help if they bring the book in so the new due date can be entered both on the date-due slip in the book and the book card in your charging tray.

You may want to loan audiovisual materials and equipment for shorter periods of time. And you should be willing to check out materials needed by Christian education workers on a long-term loan basis, keeping their cards in a special section of the charging tray. These cards show no return date, but the librarian may recall the material if someone else needs it.

CIRCULATION POLICIES

Most church libraries will find need for a reference section for books to be used only in the library. This is especially true in libraries with reading space. It is necessary only if you have reference materials that are in sufficient demand, but short supply, that they should be kept in the library at all times. This includes regular dictionaries and encyclopedias as well as such references as Bibles, Bible dictionaries, commentaries, concordances, and atlases. If these are not taken from the library, they need not have book pockets, book cards, and date-due slips. But if users are allowed to take them home or even to other locations in the church, they should have these supplies and be checked out. You may want to let teachers check out some reference books for as long as a quarter.

Keep new books in a special section for a time, with a shorter loan period, possibly one week, until the initial demand for them has decreased.

The library should have a section of books on sex education from a Christian perspective, but you may not want these readily accessible to children. Let it be known that you have them, but that parents or other adults should check them out. This ensures parental supervision and participation in this important phase of their children's education.

Current periodicals will usually be read in the library. Some items in the vertical file should not be checked out, as they may be irreplaceable. Historical church records should be examined only in the library, to prevent their loss.

Much of the audiovisual equipment should be reserved for use only in the church. If permission is granted for other use, it would be reasonable to require payment of deposits.

RETURN PROCEDURES

Urge borrowers to return all materials directly to the library, if at all possible. Provision should be made, however, by the use of book slots and deposit boxes at the library location and at an outside entrance to the church, for people to return material when the library is closed and even when the church is closed. Equipment available for this purpose is described in the last chapter.

If books can be checked out in other areas of the church, some provision should be made for return of books to those areas when this is convenient for the users. It is especially important for the elderly and handicapped to be able to return library materials without going up and down stairs. A return box on the book table will let them know materials can be left there if this is easier for them than going to the library itself.

SHELVING

Books are arranged on shelves in accordance with the classification system adopted. Everyone working in the library should be instructed on how to shelve books properly. No librarian wants to come home from vacation to the surprise one eager librarian spent so much time preparing. "How pleased our dear librarian will be," thought the substitute, "when she sees how attractive the library is with all the red books together, the green ones in another group, and those yellow ones over there shining together in all their glory."

Our recommendation to use the Dewey Decimal System, with only those minor modifications deemed necessary for your library, is explained in chapter 7, along with some description of how it works. An understanding of the basic principles of this system is essential for proper shelving. For example, should a book with a class number of 242.36 be shelved before or after one with a number of 242.4? By understanding that 242.36 is a subdivision of 242.3, you realize that 242.36 comes before 242.4 and that 232.9635 precedes 232.97.

OVERDUE NOTICES

People need to be reminded when library materials are past due. The reminders must be tactful, acknowledging that the library could be in error. No matter how good your instructions are, there are always borrowers who put returned books directly back on shelves or library workers who get the wrong card in a given book. Library errors are possible, and users will appreciate your admitting that possibility.

We have one lady on our library committee who lists overdue materials each Sunday. She carries her list with her and reminds people as she sees them, encouraging them to return or renew books, cassettes, or other material past due. During the week she telephones some she didn't see and sends postcards to others. Form postcards can be purchased from library supply houses, or you can design and duplicate your own.

FINES

To fine or not to fine, that is the question. Feelings are occasionally hurt or children told to stop using the library because of fines. And yet, without them, people tend to become careless about returning materials on time. Most churches charge fines in varying amounts. For many years we charged one cent a day up to limits of ten cents for a paperback and twenty-five cents for hardbound books. However, we became rather lax about enforcing fine rules, usually collecting only when fines were offered or for repeated offenses.

Since our system had become pretty much voluntary anyway, we decided to make it entirely so. We installed a "kitty" bank with a nearby sign saying, "Are your books overdue? Would you like to feed our kitty? Donations will be used to buy more books. Thank you for helping." We have been pleasantly surprised to discover people pay more this way than under the fine system. Posting a "want list" nearby lets donors know how their contributions will be used.

CARD CATALOG

Instructions for preparing cards for a catalog are given in chapters 7 and 8. Each library must determine how complete its cataloging will be, depending on the expected use of a catalog and the personnel and time available for maintaining it.

The card catalog is of little use for the person wanting to browse through open shelves for a book to read. It is very helpful for individuals wanting a specific book, books by a certain author, or material on a specific subject. The catalog of the average church library is probably used more by the library workers themselves than by users, who tend to dash in, asking the librarian to help them. People should be shown how to use the card catalog so they can help themselves more.

The ideal library will have author, title, and subject card catalogs for general use and a catalog of shelf-list cards for library workers' use. Options regarding the amount of information to record in the catalog are discussed in chapters 7 and 8. Church libraries can often settle for less complete catalog information than larger public libraries might require.

In determining cataloging policies, consider future development potential as well as present limitations. If at all possible, it is best to start from the beginning with as complete a catalog as you can anticipate need for. It is much easier to develop a catalog as you go than to try to start or expand one after the library has been in operation for a few years.

Church libraries, for the most part, are just beginning to see the value of a shelf-list catalog. These cards, described in detail in the next chapter, include much of the same information that many church librarians have customarily entered in accession books.

Writers of church library manuals in the past have tended to ignore shelf lists and recommend the use of accession books. Professional librarians now usually recommend eliminating accession books in favor of shelf lists. Some church librarians prefer to use both. In making a policy decision on this matter, consider the following pros and cons of each system.

Accession book. Use of an accession book calls for the entering of each library item as it is acquired into a regular accession book or a notebook ruled for this purpose. A loose-leaf notebook works well, with dividers marking the various types of acquisitions such as books, cassettes, and records. Information recorded usually includes the accession number, date of accession, author, title, publisher, year of publication, cost, and information about how the item was obtained, showing where it was purchased or who gave it and what condition it was in.

This information makes it easy to determine for annual reports the number of items of each kind that have been added during the year, their cost, principal donors, and the total number of holdings of each type on any given date.

From the accession number on a book card, it is easy to find the corresponding entry in an accession book, since everything is listed in numerical order. Without this book, the accession number would have more limited usefulness. Since shelf-list cards are filed in classification number order, items cannot be located there by accession number only.

Shelf list. A shelf list is a file of cards, including one for each title, arranged in the order in which the library holdings are placed on shelves. Each card shows the number of copies of each title, call number, usually an accession number, and cataloging information as indicated in chapters 7 and 8. The shelf list is extremely valuable for taking inventory. It is also the official record for insurance purposes.

Another important use of the shelf list is in the preparation of book and media lists on various subjects. By looking at a section of entries with certain Dewey class numbers, the librarian can easily determine how many and what materials the library has in any category. This helps in deciding what new material is needed, as well as in publicizing material on hand. The shelf list is also a handy tool for the librarian in making classification decisions as she can check in it to see how similar material was classified previously.

Options. A shelf list should be considered a necessity in a church library. An accession book is not essential, but has some desirable features that a church library may not want to give up. A simplified list could be kept, omitting such items as publisher and year of publication, since this information will be available in the card catalog.

If you decide to do without an accession book, there are other ways for you to record some of the information usually kept there. It is still advisable to assign each book or other item an accession number as it is acquired. Numbers and dates of each type of acquisition can be recorded in a library notebook, without listing entries individually. This will provide some information for annual reports.

In lieu of accession book records, include accession number, date of acquisition, cost, and any useful information about the means of acquisition on the shelf-list card. Details for this are given in chapters 7 and 8.

LIBRARY RECORDS

Every church library should have a loose-leaf notebook with tabbed dividers for several sections in which the following information is kept: library hours and other operating policies; a listing of library staff with duties and work schedule for each person; library committee and library staff meeting schedules; training records; selection and gift policies; financial records including annual budget, actual income, and expenditures; "want" lists; circulation records; gift information; and a summary record of acquisitions.

Such a notebook should also include information about special promotions and contests. It should be kept in the checkout desk or other location convenient for the librarian and other library workers.

BOOK REPAIR

When a book appears badly worn, you must decide if it is best to repair it, replace it, or just discard it. You will definitely need to mend books from time to time. Minor repairs can be made when books are returned, before shelving them. More seriously damaged books should be set aside for later repairs.

Try to find some person in your congregation who would accept responsibility for book repair. Furnish that person with needed supplies and instructions. The best source for these will be library supply houses, as they have instruction booklets as well as mending supplies. Public schools with processing centers where books are repaired are sometimes willing to let church librarians observe their methods. It's much easier to learn something like this by watching an experienced worker than by reading directions.

CARE OF NONPRINT MATERIAL

Most repairs to audiovisual material and equipment are quite technical. If no one on your library committee is familiar with repair and upkeep procedures for these items, ask some more mechanically able and knowledgeable person to serve as audiovisual technician.

OTHER OPERATING PROCEDURES AND POLICIES

There are many other operating policies that must be determined in the context of your own church. The following, most of which are discussed in other chapters, are questions a library committee should determine policies about, in cooperation with appropriate church officials: What promotional methods should we use? How will financial needs be met? What training will be provided for new workers? How will we cooperate with other church units and with other librarians?

POLICIES ON OBTAINING LIBRARY MATERIALS

An attractive church library will attract users. It must display new, current material in good condition, along with useful, valuable classics. It won't have much appeal if it is filled with people's castoffs. This means that one way or another you must obtain fresh, new material.

USED BOOKS

Encourage members to give used books as long as they understand that the library committee makes the final decision about their disposition, even if it means passing some things along to the Salvation Army for sale in their thrift shop. Offer to go to people's homes to select books you have real need for from those they plan to dispose of. Families often have good Bible story books they are willing to give the library when their children have outgrown them. And there will be some valuable books you'll be glad to have from estates of pastors and laymen. Just be discriminating about choices and proportion of old to new.

If you can be cautious in your selections, go to auctions, garage sales, used book stores, thrift shops, and similar places where used books are sold. Our city museum collects and sells used books about three times a year. By joining the local historical society, I have been able to be among those allowed to attend the opening hours of each sale. We have added several good current, as well as out-of-print "oldies but goodies," to our collection this way.

Churches vary greatly in their practices regarding used books. Some accept

TABLE 8

Percentage of Books Obtained as Used Books

Percentage Obtained as Used Books	Number of Churches	Percentage of Churches
0 - 9%	43	28%
10 - 19	23	15
20 - 29	18	12
30 - 39	10	7
40 - 49	3	2
50 - 59	25	16
60 - 69	7	5
70 - 79	8	5
80 - 89	6	4
90 - 99	8	5
100	2	1
Total	153	100%

none, and some have nothing else. Table 8 shows that surveyed churches report an average of 25% of their books acquired as used books.

CHRISTIAN BOOKSTORES

I consider a local Bible bookstore the best source of supply. Develop a good relationship with the store's staff, and you'll be surprised how much help they will be. They know their material. Give them a chance to know you and your church library needs. Then, their recommendations will be very helpful.

If you buy in reasonably large quantities at one time, the store will usually give your library a discount. It will also let you return a few books if you find later, before marking them, that they aren't suitable or needed for your particular library. Such a store will usually let you take books on consignment to display at church while appealing for funds to purchase some of them.

If you don't have a Christian bookstore in your community, consider making trips at least twice a year to the nearest city with one. You'll spend most of a day browsing and making choices. Before you go, study catalogs, advertisements, and book reviews. Also check holdings for gaps and needs. Ask your church workers and leaders for suggestions. Go with a "want list," so you won't be unduly subject to impulse buying.

To avoid buying books we already have, we carry notebooks in a special shopping bag when we go to the bookstore. These notebooks have a page, or more if needed, for each author. Books by that author are listed on his page. Before totalling purchases, we check to make sure our selections are not duplications.

BOOK CLUBS

Many church libraries find it convenient to belong to Christian book clubs. They don't rely on these for major purchases, but find it convenient and economical to purchase some books this way. Interest is maintained best when new books are made available from time to time rather than just once or twice a year. Book club purchases can help you keep a steady stream of new books appearing on your shelves.

You can find advertisements of such clubs in Christian periodicals. Write for information before joining. Some cater more to pastors' interests than those of laymen. Some exist more for moving overstocked books than for promoting new books. Book clubs usually include just hardbound books, and you may prefer to get less expensive paperbacks. Postage and handling charges must be considered, too. It may not be necessary for the library as such to belong to book clubs if several church members belong to them and donate books to the library.

MAIL ORDER HOUSES

There are several retail mail order businesses catering to churches, ministers, and individual Christians. Some are primarily Sunday school supply houses. Others combine direct sales business with distributorships serving small retail outlets such as small bookstores, church book tables, inspirational book racks, and camps.

Some mail order houses have good prices on publishers' surplus items. They'll have some things you can use, but be careful not to buy just because prices are low. Be sure you have a need for each item purchased.

DIRECT PURCHASE FROM PUBLISHERS

Most publishers prefer that you purchase through local bookstores, and some insist on it. Denominational publishers usually have a retail outlet you can order from. It will be helpful to have catalogs from several publishers even though you buy from retail stores. Retail catalogs are usually just samplings from several publishers and not complete listings from any. If you can get on mailing lists of publishers, you will have more complete information of their offerings and earlier notice of new items. Addresses of book publishers are included in Appendix 2.

CHURCH BOOK TABLES

As mentioned in another chapter, many churches sell books from a book table or rack, usually on a consignment arrangement with a local bookstore or distributor. Some churches operate bookstores, ordering directly from publishers. The library, which is usually in charge of such sales anyway, will coordinate its buying for the library with purchases for book tables or racks.

BOOK SWAPS

You are sure to acquire duplicate copies of books that you need only one copy of. Why not arrange to trade such books with other libraries for books you need? This can be carried out by personal arrangements between librarians of individual churches within your community or area. It can also be done on a local or area level whenever librarians get together for meetings.

The Evangelical Church Library Association conducts a very successful book swap at each annual meeting. Librarians bring books they don't need and take home books they have use for. This sort of thing could be done at denominational and Sunday school conferences as well as at meetings held just for church librarians.

SURVEY RESULTS REGARDING PURCHASE OF NEW BOOKS

When we asked church libraries to indicate their primary source of new books, the majority gave one source, but many indicated two or more sources. Table 9 shows the percentage giving each response. It is evident that the local Christian bookstore is the main supplier of church library material.

TABLE 9

Sources of New Books

Source	Percentage of Churches Reporting One Primary Source	Percentage of Churches Reporting One or Two or More Primary Sources
Local bookstore	47%	37%
Denominational supplier	8	28
Publisher	1	9
Book club	1	17

SOURCES OF AUDIOVISUAL MATERIALS

Much nonprint library material is available from the same sources as printed materials. In addition, there are regional distributors whose business is to supply audiovisual material and equipment for churches. School supply houses are a help with some items. Your Christian bookstore can usually help you get in touch with the right firm, if they can't meet your needs themselves.

Cassettes can be purchased from a wide variety of places. Cassette clubs operate in a fashion similar to book clubs. Cassettes usually can be purchased at conferences and special meetings of various kinds. Several Christian magazines carry cassette reviews, as well as advertisements for cassettes produced by various organizations.

EXTENSION MINISTRY POLICIES

Don't restrict library activities within the four walls of the church. Encourage readers to loan materials to friends and relatives, but to be responsible for returning them.

Everything that goes out from the library is, in one sense, an extension ministry. Each book and audiovisual is a potential minister to both the borrower and those influenced by him. Church librarians need to look around with dedicated imaginations for new and broader ways to increase circulation of Christian literature and audiovisual materials.

Some of the ways churches have used to expand library ministries are described in the following paragraphs. Your library committee, staff, and supervising board will need to make policy decisions as to which are appropriate for your church.

VISITATION

When you visit friends, try taking along a few books and cassettes that you think may be of interest to them. I have a friend up in the mountains whose car is never without its box of books to loan to friends, old or new. She keeps a small notebook in her purse for jotting down dates and names of borrowers.

Many of the suggestions given elsewhere for taking sermon cassettes to the sick and shut-in also apply to books. Get those active in church visitation to take both books and cassettes with them. First, teach them simple checkout procedures, and be sure they arrange for return of materials promptly. Keep a library record of everything taken out of the building for special purposes.

VACATION BIBLE SCHOOL

Vacation Bible school provides opportunities for library outreach into new homes. Children from unchurched homes often come. They should be introduced to library services during this time. You will need library staff, or people trained especially for this time, on hand, coordinating library hours and activities with the vacation Bible school program. Be sure to get complete address and telephone information for visitors and encourage them to take books that can be replaced fairly easily if necessary. Some churches have discontinued opening their libraries to VBS visitors because of heavy losses, but perhaps a combination of precautionary measures and calculated risk would be better.

CHURCH BUS

Literature racks can be placed on church buses, with opportunity provided riders to check books out while waiting for their bus to be filled and ready to leave the church. Inexpensive paperbacks should be used here because of likelihood of damage and loss.

BRANCH COLLECTIONS

In addition to collections in other parts of the church, some churches have arranged for branch lending libraries in such places as summer camps, nursing homes, and hospitals, with racks of inexpensive books to borrow sometimes placed in stores, shopping centers, large apartment buildings, dormitories, coffee houses, beauty and barber shops, reading rooms, or doctors' offices. Be sure that these collections are checked frequently for needed repairs, replacements, and additions.

REGIONAL COLLECTIONS

You may be able to contribute to, as well as borrow materials from, regional Christian libraries and media centers. Some church libraries have regional audiovisual lending libraries. Others have regional cassette ministries, supplying cassettes for other libraries on a long-term basis.

OVERSEAS LIBRARIES

Some church libraries have had special projects of providing books and cassettes for missionary libraries overseas. You might even sponsor the sending of a librarian on a short-term basis to help set up a library on a mission field.

PUBLIC LIBRARY

Most public libraries have a pathetically small collection of evangelical literature. But they do get requests for it and most would be willing to refer such requests to you, if you provide them with the necessary information. At least give them copies of a listing of your holdings. Ask if you can supply catalog cards of selected books, indicating where the items can be obtained.

If the public library has materials you can use, they may be willing to check them out to your library for longer than usual periods of time. Work at developing a good relationship with your nearest public library, based on mutual interests and benefits.

READING INSTRUCTION

Some church libraries hold tutoring or reading programs for under-privileged children and slow learners. This forms a point of contact from which the church can expand its ministry into many homes.

MINISTRY TO THE BLIND

Your church library can have a ministry to the blind of your community. Offer to read to them. Take cassettes to them, and tape some materials especially for them. Help them get in touch with societies that furnish cassette players for the blind, and then supply them with good cassettes from the church library.

LIBRARY USE BY NONMEMBERS

Encourage church members to let friends and neighbors know that your church library is available for use by nonmembers. Use local advertising media to announce this fact, along with pertinent information about location and hours. If you are near a college, high school, or junior high school, encourage the young people to use your library after school as a resource center and a place to study. You'll be surprised how many more book reviews and term papers will be based on Christian materials, thus extending your influence into the schools.

MAIL AND TELEPHONE SERVICE

Expand your area of ministry by encouraging people to write or telephone for materials which can be mailed at special library rates. Cassettes are especially convenient to send by mail. A former member who has moved away and does not have access to a good church library may continue to benefit from your library in this way.

BOOKMOBILES

If you have a vision for literature needs beyond your immediate area, consider the possibility of a bookmobile ministry. Taking church library books into needy areas provides a gospel witness and serves as a starting point for an expanded ministry by your church. A few churches have ventured into mobile lending libraries similar to those operated by public libraries. There are many rural areas, and crowded city areas as well, that could benefit from convenient access to Christian literature and cassettes brought to their neighborhood or church. Bookmobiles can be equipped with projection and public address systems to add a viewing and/or preaching ministry. You can have a bookmobile designed especially for this purpose; or you can remodel a school bus, van, or recreational vehicle. This is an expensive ministry to be undertaken only by churches with sufficient financial resources.

SUMMARY

It is the responsibility of the library committee to establish policies by which the library will be operated. In the absence of a library committee, the librarian and her helpers, with some supervision from the church board, will set these policies, which should be reexamined from time to time and changed as needed.

Not all policy matters have been included in this chapter—just major ones dealing with library operations, acquisitions, and special ministries. Other portions of the book go into more detail regarding policies that affect classification and processing, choice of workers, promotional policies, facilities, handling of audiovisuals, and financing.

7

PREPARING BOOKS FOR LIBRARY USE

Neither the one who plants nor the one who waters is anything, but God who causes the growth. Now he who plants and he who waters are one; but each will receive his own reward according to his own labor. For we are God's fellow-workers (1 Corinthians 3:7-9).

PROCEDURES INVOLVED in organizing library materials scare many people away from church library work. They may recognize the need for an active library but feel they lack the know-how, the time, or the ability to properly process library materials.

There's no denying that a church library takes time to organize and maintain. A collection of donated books put on a church shelf somewhere is not really a library. But a church library can be effective without following all the accepted practices of library science to the letter. It is possible to learn all you need to know without formal training. We have tried to include in this chapter workable procedures for processing library materials, with options for churches of different sizes and needs.

If you already have methods that work well for you and that you believe will provide adequately for anticipated growth, don't feel you must make them conform to recommended practices. There are definite advantages, though, to some standardization of church library procedures. What would happen, for example, if your present librarian could no longer serve in that capacity? Too often church libraries fade into oblivion when a librarian dies or moves away, mostly because no one else understands the methods she used and developed over a period of many years.

Whatever methods are decided upon should be recorded in a library notebook, so anyone can follow them. Several people should be trained in operating the library, even though you have one faithful, conscientious, capable, and dedicated librarian.

86

CLASSIFICATION SYSTEM

The first thing to decide is what classification system to use. Remember that classification is simply a term used to describe the grouping together in classes of things with certain common characteristics. Library materials are usually classified according to subject material, using numerical or letter symbols to indicate the subject class of each book.

While some will disagree, I consider the choice of a classification system for church libraries a relatively simple decision. After visiting many church libraries and corresponding with hundreds of church librarians, I agree with the overwhelming majority of them in choosing the Dewey decimal system. A few good church libraries use other systems, such as color coding, subject grouping, and various homemade arrangements. To me such systems seem either unnecessarily cumbersome and difficult to communicate to other workers or too simple to serve the necessary functions of a library. Those using such systems usually find a need to reclassify when they grow beyond a few hundred volumes, at which time they face a huge task that could have been avoided by more careful planning initially.

The fact that Melvil Dewey attributes his classification system to an intuitive flash that came to him while sitting in church, supposedly listening to a sermon, may not in itself endear his system to church librarians.[1] The fact that the majority of libraries in America have successfully used his system, with various revisions, since its first publication in 1876, is a more convincing reason for using it.[2]

Libraries that have adopted some modified—or "mutilated," as one librarian said—version of the Dewey system face another difficult decision. Many librarians have complained to me that they have followed a classifying system found in one of several church library handbooks without realizing how much it strayed from the actual Dewey system. Handbook writers tend to include their own adaptations as recommendations, causing some confusion for those not recognizing the difference. If such a system has worked well for you, it's all right to stay with it. But if you're starting fresh, avoid someone else's adaptations.

One reason for staying as close as possible to the authentic Dewey system is the fact that this makes more help available to you in classifying books. Many publishers put Dewey numbers on the back of the title page. Printed catalog cards containing Dewey numbers along with other information can be purchased from the Library of Congress and other sources. Publications that give this information for many books can be found in reference sections of public libraries.

1. Melvil Dewey, *Dewey Decimal Classification and Relative Index*, 18th ed., vol. 1, p. 3.
2. *Guide to Use of Dewey Decimal Classification*, p. 9.

If you have access to any library that is apt to have the same type of books you do, such as a Christian school, seminary, or another church library, you can check its card catalog for Dewey numbers. While many seminaries, colleges, and universities use Library of Congress classifications, their catalog cards usually include Dewey numbers. The Library of Congress classification system works well in college and university libraries, and in some city libraries, but the Dewey decimal classification system is preferable for smaller and special purpose libraries such as the church library.[3]

You need to keep in mind that the Dewey system is revised from time to time, which means that a book classified in a certain way according to the sixteenth edition might not be classified exactly the same way when using the eighteenth edition. It is usually best for a library to continue classifying according to the edition first used rather than trying to change with each edition that comes out. If you take Dewey numbers from any of the sources just mentioned, be sure to check to see that they fit the Dewey edition you are using.

In spite of sources for help just mentioned, most church librarians still find themselves making their own decisions for fitting each book into the Dewey system. At first you do so with fear and trembling. But you grow in confidence as you gain experience. One of the things you will learn from that experience is that you will make mistakes and change your mind as you go along, but the library will survive. A few misclassified books won't completely invalidate your library's ministry.

The publishers of the Dewey system themselves have this to say in their *Guide to the Use of Dewey Decimal Classification:*

> Books are as individual and as diverse as their authors, and no set of principles and rules will cover the classification of all of them. For practical purposes, the classifier must sometimes judiciously ignore the letter . . . while still observing its spirit.[4]

Perhaps you are asking just how this Dewey system works. Most public schools use it, so the children and young people of your church are apt to be familiar with it. As a nonprofessional librarian, let me try to explain the basic idea on which the system is built. While the uninitiated tend to be a bit intimidated at their first encounter with the Dewey decimal classification system, it is basically a simple and adaptable system.

The fundamental concept behind the system is that of dividing all subjects into ten broad categories. Then each category is subdivided into ten subdivisions, and each subdivision is similarly divided, with unlimited capacity for further subdivisions through expansion of decimal places. The ten main classes are the following:

3. Esther J. Piercy, *Commonsense Cataloging*, p. 65.
4. *Guide to Use of Dewey Decimal Classification*, p. 19.

000   Generalities
100   Philosophy & related disciplines
200   Religion
300   The social sciences
400   Language
500   Pure sciences
600   Technology (Applied sciences)
700   The arts
800   Literature (Belles-lettres)
900   General geography & history[5]

The Dewey system is hierarchical, with broad categories broken down into progressively more specific subjects. The following example taken from the complete 200 series illustrates the hierarchical nature of the subject subdivisions in the Dewey system:

200   Religion
  230   Christian doctrinal theology (Christian dogma)
    232   Jesus Christ and his family (Christology)
      232.9   Doctrines on family and life of Jesus
        232.96   Passion and death of Jesus
          232.963   Crucifixion and death
            232.963 5   Seven last words on cross

Librarians must make choices. This is the reason not all librarians will classify a given book the same way, even when using the same system. One library may not want to carry several decimals, but put all books related to the "Doctrines on family and life of Jesus" in 232.9, or even just 232, rather than using expanded decimal indications of further subdivision. The number of books in a given category has a strong bearing on the amount of subdividing to be used. However, remember to consider future plans as well as present holdings.

Most, but usually not all, church library materials are classified in the 200 series. The one hundred main divisions of the 200 series, as shown in the eighteenth edition of the Dewey system, are listed below. An expanded list from the 200 series, including all classifications needed by most church libraries, is given in Appendix 3. If this is not complete enough for your library, a listing of all the 200 series classifications is available in an inexpensive paperback booklet, *200 (Religion) Class, Reprinted from Edition 18 Unabridged Dewey Decimal Classification.*[6]

5. Dewey, *Dewey Decimal Classification*, p. 449.
6. *200 (Religion) Class, Reprinted from Edition 18 Unabridged Dewey Decimal Classification.*

200 Religion
201 Philosophy of Christianity
202 Miscellany of Christianity
203 Dictionaries of Christianity
204 General special
205 Serials on Christianity
206 Organizations of Christianity
207 Study & teaching of Christianity
208 Collections of Christianity
209 History & geography of Christianity

210 Natural religion
211 God
212 Nature of God
213 Creation
214 Theodicy
215 Science & religion
216 Good & Evil
217 Worship & prayer
218 Man
219 Analogy

220 Bible
221 Old Testament
222 Historical books of Old Testament
223 Poetic books of Old Testament
224 Prophetic books of Old Testament
225 New Testament
226 Gospels & Acts
227 Epistles
228 Revelation (Apocalypse)
229 Apocrypha & pseudepigrapha

230 Christian doctrinal theology
231 God, Trinity, Godhead
232 Jesus Christ & His family
233 Man
234 Salvation (Soteriology)
235 Spiritual beings
236 Eschatology
237
238 Creeds & confessions of faith
239 Apologetics & polemics

240 Christian moral & devotional theology
241 Moral theology
242 Devotional literature
243 Evangelistic writings for individuals
244
245 Hymns without music
246 Art in Christianity
247 Church furnishings & related articles
248 Personal religion
249 Worship in family life

250 Local church & religious orders
251 Preaching (Homiletics)
252 Texts of sermons
253 Secular clergymen & duties
254 Parish government & administration
255 Religious congregations & orders
256
257
258
259 Parochial activities

260 Social & ecclesiastical theology
261 Social theology
262 Ecclesiology
263 Times & places of religious observance
264 Public worship
265 Other rites, ceremonies, ordinances
266 Missions
267 Associations for religious work
268 Religious training & instruction
269 Organized spiritual renewal

270 History & geography of church
271 Religious congregations & orders
272 Persecutions
273 Doctrinal controversies & heresies
274 Christian church in Europe
275 Christian church in Asia
276 Christian church in Africa
277 Christian church in North America
278 Christian church in South America
279 Christian church in other areas

280   Christian denominations & sects
281   Primitive & Oriental churches
282   Roman Catholic church
283   Anglican churches
284   Protestants of Continental origin
285   Presbyterian & related churches
286   Baptist, Disciples, Adventist
287   Methodist churches
288   Unitarianism
289   Other denominations & sects

290   Other religions & comparative religion
291   Comparative religion
292   Classical (Greek & Roman) religion
293   Germanic religion
294   Religions of Indic origin
295   Zoroastrianism
296   Judaism
297   Islam & religions derived from it
298
299   Other religions[7]

Church libraries have varying needs for Dewey numbers outside the 200 series. For this reason, the "Second Summary," which lists the 100 divisions of Dewey classification numbers as given in the eighteenth edition, is included in Appendix 3. This summary provides all the numbers that would usually be required for classifying church library materials not covered by the 200 series. If you need more complete subdivisions of non-200 numbers, obtain a copy of the most recent abridged edition of the Dewey system.[8]

You will notice that there are some unassigned numbers in the Dewey system. These can be assigned to appropriate subjects in your library that are not adequately covered in the regular listing. Keep a record of your use of these numbers and any other adaptations you make for your own library.

Two of the auxiliary tables provided in the eighteenth edition of the Dewey system are of special value for church libraries. The numbers shown in them are never used alone, but are used as needed following any number from the regular schedules. Decimal points always follow the third digit. The following is the summary of the main notations used with "Table 1. Standard Subdivisions":

—01   Philosophy and theory

7. Dewey, *Dewey Decimal Classification*, p. 453.
8. Melvil Dewey, *Abridged Dewey Decimal Classification and Relative Index*, 10th ed. rev.

—02   Miscellany
—03   Dictionaries, encyclopedias, concordances
—04   General special
—05   Serial publications
—06   Organizations
—07   Study and teaching
—08   Collections
—09   Historical and geographical treatment[9]

Since church libraries have material on the Christian church and missionary endeavors in many parts of the world, "Table 2. Areas" is very helpful in classifying these materials. For example, a book about Lutheran churches in Africa could be classified 284.14, with 284.1 the classification for Lutheran churches and the final 4 indicating the continent of Africa.

The listing below gives the numbers from the area table that are the most useful for church libraries. Since numbers 4 through 9 are the ones most needed, further subdivisions for them are included in Appendix 3.

—1   Areas, regions, places in general
—2   Persons regardless of area, region, place
—3   The ancient world
—4   Europe
—5   Asia   Orient   Far East
—6   Africa
—7   North America
—8   South America
—9   Other parts of world and extraterrestrial worlds   Pacific
      Ocean islands (Oceania) [10]

In selecting the Dewey classification number for a particular book, the classifier first determines which class the book belongs to (e.g., the 200's), then the division (e.g., 260), the section (e.g., 268), and finally the subsection (e.g., 268.6). Further subdivisions can be used as needed and additional notations can be added from the standard subdivision and area tables.

A rule that is helpful in assigning class numbers is the following: "Class a work in the most specific number that will contain its subject; then, if its subject is limited geographically, and if the number is specifically for that subject, and if the schedules permit, add subdivision for place."[11]

It will not always be easy to choose a class number from the book title alone. A glance at the table of contents will help. Information on the jacket or back

9. Dewey, *Dewey Decimal Classification*, p. 115.
10. Ibid., pp. 123-369.
11. *Guide to Use of Dewey Decimal Classification*, p. 19.

cover may help further. Reading the preface helps you understand the author's purpose and viewpoint. Checking to see how you have classified similar works saves time and avoids inconsistencies. Sometimes a book fits equally well in two places in the classification system. Then, you just have to make a decision as to which one you prefer to place it in.

There are various designations used for books not readily placed under the Dewey system. Church libraries can use the following letters, or others of their own choosing, for the first line of the call letter for fiction and children's books:

F (or Fic)	Adult fiction
SC	Collections of short stories
JF (or Fc)	Juvenile fiction
J	Juvenile nonfiction, used with or without appropriate Dewey numbers, depending on need for subject grouping
E	Easy books for children, including picture books and books that children in grades one through three can read themselves

Some libraries use Y preceding other designations to indicate that a book belongs in a special youth section. Sometimes B is used to designate individual biography, rather than placing such books under the Dewey system.

PROCESSING BOOKS

Having settled on a classification system, just what are the steps involved in processing books for circulation? Let us suggest a set of procedures that you may want to follow or to adapt to your own needs. Make notes of adaptations in this book or in a library notebook so other workers can follow your procedures.

Sometimes one member of the library committee takes book preparation as her responsibility and does this work herself. There are, however, several advantages in making this a cooperative project for several people. Working together will train more people in library procedures. Involving young people will open their eyes to new areas of service. Using various church members will acquaint them with what goes on behind the scenes. Asking your elderly members to help gives them a useful outlet for their desire to serve.

We try, in our church, to get our library committee and two or three other people together about once a month to process new books. We vary the "other people" deliberately to interest more people in the library's ministry. Inevitably, these other people, even though they have never set foot in the library, find something of interest while working on new books and ask to be first to check it out. These helpers often turn into enthusiastic library boosters.

Since preparation procedures are somewhat different for books and other print materials, we will first consider how to prepare books and then deal with preparation of other library materials in the next chapter.

You will usually find it most convenient to work in or near the library, although our group meets in our home because we don't have storage or working space at church. You can set up assembly line procedures around one long table or a few small ones. Assign a specific task to each individual, combining tasks where it makes for more efficiency. The following listing gives the steps required for complete processing of a book.

1. CHECK FOR DUPLICATE BOOKS

Before any actual processing is done, check your card catalog and other books to be processed to be sure you don't already have the book. Unless you need another copy, duplicates should be set aside for return for credit or for giving to some individual with a particular need for that book or to be exchanged with another church library. For example, an extra copy of *Audio-Visual Media in Christian Education* might be given to your minister of Christian education or to your Sunday school superintendent for his personal library.

2. OPEN NEW BOOKS PROPERLY

Care taken in opening new books prolongs their lives and makes them less susceptible to damage at the hands of eager readers. Books should be opened to the center of the book, with the covers resting on a table. Small groups of pages from the front and back, working toward the middle of the book, should

Drawing by David Culbertson

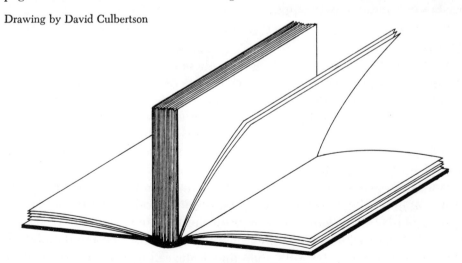

Proper Way to Open a New Book

be pressed back toward the book covers, being careful not to put undue stress on the binding.[12]

At the time a worker is opening new books, she can also cut open any pages that may have been missed and check the book for defects. If defects are found to be serious enough that simple mending procedures won't remedy them satisfactorily, defective material should be returned. Bookstores are very cooperative in exchanging defective books for good ones.

3. ENTER ACCESSION NUMBER

If you decide after considering the pros and cons discussed in the preceding chapter to use an accession book, enter each book acquired in your accession record book, assigning it an accession number, beginning with number 1 for the first book acquired and continuing in numerical progression for each book added. Accession record books can be purchased from Christian bookstores and library supply houses. You can just as easily set up your own looseleaf notebook for this purpose. Information should include: date acquired, accession number, author, title, publisher, year, cost, and notes which might include place of purchase or donor. Most public and many church librarians have found shelf-list cards to provide sufficient record of this information, eliminating need for a separate accession book. Description of these cards is found later in this chapter.

Even if you do not use an accession record book, assign an accession number to each book, and place that number on the title page just above the publisher's name.

4. ENTER THE CALL NUMBER

The call number goes in pencil on the upper left corner of the title page, allowing for tentative entries to be changed later. The person responsible for assigning call numbers may wish to enter these in advance of group work, as she needs to scan some of the books, read parts of others, and possibly check to see how other libraries have classified some of them.

The call number is made up of two parts. The Dewey classification number or letter code, as described earlier in the chapter, indicates the book's subject matter and makes up the first line of the call number. A code to indicate author and possibly title goes on the second line.

While Cutter-Sanborn numbers, based on an alphabetical order table, are still used in some libraries, they are considered by most authorities to be outdated and too cumbersome for the average church library.

A simple procedure that works well is the use of the first three initials of the author's last name for the second line of the call number (e.g., *Get* for a

12. Alice Straughan, *How to Organize Your Church Library*, p. 32.

book by Getz). Another acceptable method combines the first two letters of the author's last name with the first two of the book (e.g., *GEau*). Whichever system is adopted should be used consistently. We recommend the system using just the first three initials of the author's last name, as this is simple and adequate for most church libraries.

Reference books should show an R directly above or preceding the Dewey number to indicate this is a book to be kept in the reference section of the library.

Photograph by David McMichael

Title Page

An exception is made to the practice of using authors' initials for the call number in the case of biography. It is recommended that the initials of the biographee be used instead, to keep all biographies of a given person together, both on the shelf and in the card catalog. It is a good idea to add the name of the subject of the biography, if it is not in the title, on the book's spine. If you use B for biography as the first line of the call letter, the subject's last name can appear on the second line, continuing into a third line if necessary.

5. RUBBER STAMP THE NAME OF THE CHURCH OR CHURCH LIBRARY

The church name and address should be stamped on the title page, underneath the publisher's name, if possible. It should also be stamped near the bottom of book pockets, preferably before pasting them into the book. You can also stamp the church or library name on white edges of books large enough to accommodate the stamp.

6. PASTE BOOK POCKETS NEAR THE BOTTOM OF THE INSIDE COVER OF THE BOOK

If there is material printed on the inside cover or if you plan to use a plastic-covered book jacket, find another place for the book pocket, as near the back as possible, or inside the front cover, if necessary. Be sure the church name is stamped on the pocket. Put the accession number in the upper right corner of the pocket and the classification number in the upper left corner. The author's last name and the book's title can also be included on the pocket, although they aren't essential unless book cards are filed in the charging tray according to author's name. When borrowed books are returned, the information on the book card should be compared with the information on the pocket to eliminate the possibility of putting the wrong card in a given book.

If you prefer to eliminate the task of pasting pockets and are willing to pay a little more, you can get pre-gummed pockets that need just to be moistened with water. Reference books not taken out of the library will not need book pockets, book cards, or date slips.

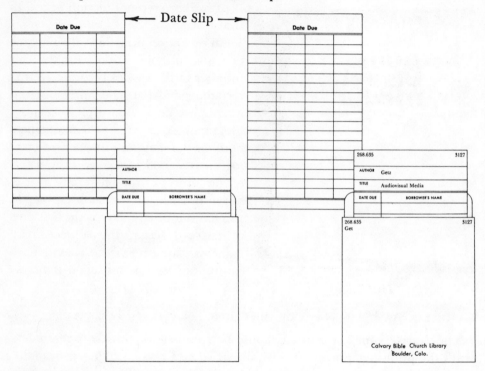

Book Card in Book Pocket

7. ATTACH DATE SLIPS

Date slips, also referred to as date-due slips, should be attached to the center of the page opposite the book pocket. If there is material printed on that page, the slips can be attached to the margin at the top of the page in such a way that readers can lift the slip to read the printing underneath.

When date slips become full, they should be removed and replaced with new ones.

8. LABEL THE SPINE OF THE BOOK

The call number should be placed near the bottom of the book's spine. If the book is too thin to have room for a call number on the spine, put the number on the lower left corner of the outside front cover. This is often necessary with children's picture books. A general rule is to put the call number on the spine if you can read at least three digits.

The call number can be entered in one of two ways:

The call number can be printed directly on the book. Unless you purchase a special electric pencil for this purpose, you will need to use permanent India ink for printing call numbers on books. You can paint a dark strip on the book first, or attach a strip of black tape, and then enter call numbers with white ink. If no strip is painted, use black ink on most books, reserving white for very dark books only. Seal with shellac or a special spray available from library supply houses.

The use of white labels has several advantages. They can be typed instead of hand lettered. They can be placed over book jackets (inside plastic covers), adding a great deal to the library's attractiveness.

The ¾″ by 1″ label is the most convenient size, using the ¾″ side horizontally. Labels should be sealed with library sealer or covered with clear tape such as the Scotch brand magic transparent tape. Avoid the kind of tape that yellows with age.

Placing all call numbers an equal distance from the bottom edge of the book gives a neat appearance; however, I prefer to adjust placement as needed to avoid covering up part of the author's or publisher's name.

9. COVER BOOK JACKETS AND BOOKS WITH PLASTIC

Plastic covers greatly improve the appearance and life of library books. Without them it is not practical to leave book jackets on books. Since book jackets add a great deal to a book's appeal to readers, they are well worth protecting and using.

Plastic jackets can be ordered in various sizes from library supply houses. This is probably the most expensive method for protecting books and book jackets. The least expensive is the purchase of a roll of medium weight clear plastic from a lumber company or fabric store. From such a roll, you can cut a piece of plastic about one inch larger on all sides than the book jacket, fold the overlapping edges over, attach them to the jacket with clear (magic transparent) tape, and then tape the covered jacket to the book in several places.

A simpler, and not much more expensive, method for covering book jackets and books is to use a clear adhesive plastic such as CON-TACT brand transparent plastic. Several other brands are available in discount stores and library supply houses. Directions for their use are included with the material.

Some libraries cover all their books with plastic, not just those with paper jackets. It is especially helpful to cover children's picture books, as they are

Drawing by David Culbertson

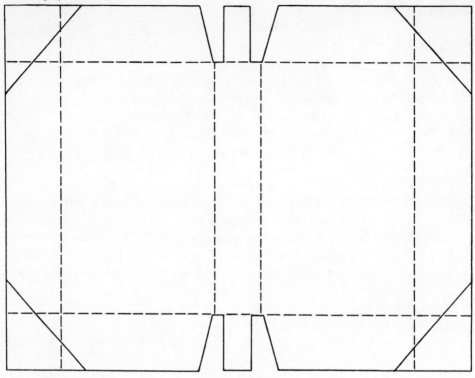

Pattern for a Plastic Book-Jacket Cover

subject to unusually hard wear. You can increase the life of any paperback book by covering it.

You may have some books that you prefer to cover with colored adhesive material to hide the original cover. By choosing attractive material you can make old or damaged books appealing again.

10. ATTACH BOOKPLATES

If a book is given in memory or in honor of someone, or just as a special gift, an appropriate bookplate carrying this information should be placed inside the front cover or on one of the first pages.

11. TYPE BOOK CARDS

The book card to be inserted in the book pocket should contain the following information: classification number, author, title, accession number, and blank lines for entering due date and borrower's name. These cards can be purchased in varying weights from Christian bookstores and library supply houses.

12. TYPE CATALOG CARDS

Having decided earlier, as part of your policy determination, just how complete a catalog to have, you will need to type catalog entries at the time you process books, filing them in their proper places when you enter new books into the library collection.

A complete set of cards includes shelf–list cards for librarians' use and author, title, and subject cards for use by both borrowers and library workers. Cataloging details are given in the next section of this chapter.

If you use notebooks such as we describe in chapter 6 to take along when you shop, enter titles from author cards after the latter have been alphabetized for filing.

Displays of New Books

13. SHELVE THE BOOKS

Put newly acquired books in a special display of new books or mark them with special bookmarks to indicate they are new additions. Have new books listed in a church newsletter, with brief reviews. Mention them to library users when they come in to browse.

After new books have been displayed in a special location for a time, they should be placed in their proper place on the shelf, following the numerical sequence provided by Dewey system. Fiction, children's books, and possibly youth books will be in special sections. Collections of short stories follow fiction books. Books without Dewey numbers are placed in alphabetical order according to the author's last name. Books with the same Dewey numbers are also arranged alphabetically by the author's last name. When there are several books with the same Dewey number by the same author, arrange them according to title.

CATALOGING

"A catalog is a record of the material in a library."[13] While this is a simple definition, the process of cataloging is not very simple. As one author puts it, "Catalogs are not simple, because people and books are not simple. If each book were written by one person, who never changed his name from the way it appeared in the title page of his first book; if each book were published at some plainly designated place and on a date explicitly set forth; if there were but one edition permitted; if there were no societies, clubs, universities, journals, academies, legislatures, governments issuing books; if all reprints, separates, and pre-prints could be prevented, then, and only then, might catalogs become simple—on their author side."[14]

Once your cataloging policy is set, it becomes a part of processing procedures to prepare cards in accordance with this policy. It is best to use regular library catalog cards, with holes at the bottom for inserting the rod in card files. You will also need alphabetical dividers and some blank dividers for entering headings for shelf-list and subject cards.

Every library book should have a card in the author and title catalog, so borrowers can look for an entry under either author or title. Nonfiction books should also be listed on one or more subject cards, depending on the number of subjects treated. Cataloging of nonbook items is described in the next chapter.

Library users should be informed that cards are arranged in alphabetical order by author, title, and subject. Each book's call number is listed in the upper left corner of each card, so borrowers can go from the catalog to the shelves to locate books. When a book is not found on a shelf, this same information can be used for locating it on a sorting shelf or finding its book card in the charging tray.

It is possible to purchase catalog cards for many books, but this is usually too expensive for church libraries. Typing instructions for making your own cards, as illustrated in the samples shown, follow general instructions found in *Commonsense Cataloging*,[15] a standard guide for school and small public libraries.

A complete set of catalog cards should be prepared when a book is first processed for library use. The typing instructions that follow are based on use of elite type. Some adjustment may be needed for larger type. Single

13. Susan Grey Akers, *Simple Library Cataloging*, p. 1.
14. William Warner Bishop, *Cataloging as an Asset* (Baltimore: Waverly/Williams and Wilkins, 1916), p. 10.
15. Esther J. Piercy, *Commonsense Cataloging*.

spacing is used unless otherwise noted. Tabular keys should be set for 10 spaces, 12 spaces, and 14 spaces from the left edge of the card. Titles need not use any capitalization other than that which is needed for normal use of the words found in them.

AUTHOR CARD

The author card is usually considered the main entry card and, as such, it carries the most complete information of any of the cards in the dictionary catalog. Exceptions are explained under the discussion of "Title Card." The author card includes the following information:

1. Call number. As defined earlier in the chapter, the call number starts with the class number on the third line from the top edge of the card and two spaces from the left edge. The second line and any other lines appear as they do on the spine of the book.

2. Author's name. Type the author's name, last name first, on the third line from the top and ten spaces from the left edge of the card. Give complete first name and also middle name, if indicated. Optional for a church library is inclusion following author's name of date of author's birth and date of his death, if deceased. In the case of joint authorship, separate cards should be prepared for the second author, with the second author's name typed above the usual listing and indented twelve spaces. It is not customary to make author cards for more than the first two authors. Cards can also be made for one or two editors, a compiler, illustrator, or translator.

3. Title. Start the title on the line below the author's name, twelve spaces from the left edge of the card. Information about joint authors, editors, edition, illustrations, and similar types of information are included, immediately following the title. If more than one line is needed, align the second line under the first letter of the author's last name.

4. Imprint information. Leave two spaces after title and related information, and then type the imprint information, which includes the publisher's name and the copyright date. Short form is adequate for publisher's name.

5. Collation information. Often this information is omitted from church library catalogs. It includes number of pages or number of volumes, *illus.* notation if illustrated, and series information. This begins on the line below the previous information, twelve spaces from the left. Following lines begin ten spaces from the left.

6. Notes. You may want to add notes in separate paragraphs to explain something about the book. A double space should be allowed between previous information and notes. Notes are used only if there is some information considered important enough to be placed there. This is one area where small church libraries can usually omit information that larger public libraries might include. This space can be used for shelving information, such as "Reference book" or "Ask librarian for location," in cases where books are in unusual locations.

7. *Tracings.* These are notations indicating all other catalog cards on the same subject. They should be typed at least three lines below the information listed previously. Subject headings under which cards are entered are typed in capital letters. Abbreviations are used for such listings as joint author (jt auth) and title (t).

It would be possible to omit tracings on author cards and include them only on shelf-list cards. They are essential information on the shelf list to make possible changes or removal of complete sets of cards when an error is discovered or a book has been removed from the collection. Tracings on the author card have the advantage of referring readers to subject headings under which they can find references to related material.

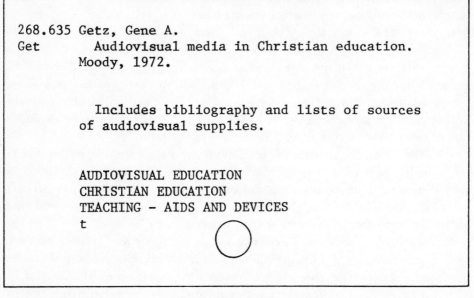

```
268.635 Getz, Gene A.
Get       Audiovisual media in Christian education.
        Moody, 1972.


          Includes bibliography and lists of sources
        of audiovisual supplies.


        AUDIOVISUAL EDUCATION
        CHRISTIAN EDUCATION
        TEACHING - AIDS AND DEVICES
        t
```

Author Card

TITLE CARD

A short-form title card is adequate, except in cases where it is used as the main entry. When the title card is the main entry, as it is for many reference books, the type of additional information usually put on the author card should be included on the title card. The short-form title card has the call number and author as shown on the author card. The title is typed on the line (or lines) above the author's name, indented twelve spaces (two more than the author's name).

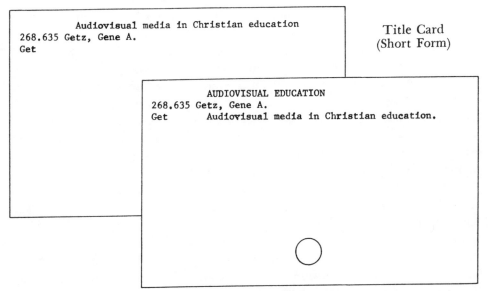

Title Card
(Short Form)

Subject Card

Subject Card

A subject card should be made for every book that deals with a specific subject. If a book deals with more than one subject or fits more than one of your subject headings, a separate subject card should be used for each appropriate subject heading. It is not necessary to prepare subject cards for fiction books. You may also decide to omit them for young childrens' books unless your library users have a real need to be able to locate them according to subject.

Subject cards indicate on the top line the subject treated in the book. Subjects are chosen from a subject heading list, as explained below. The appropriate subject heading is typed in capital letters on the line just above the author's name and indented twelve spaces from the left edge. Call number, author's name, and title are typed exactly as on the author card.

If subdivisions of subject headings are used, they follow the main subject heading. Punctuation separating main headings from subdivisions should be the same as that used in the subject heading list used as a guide.

Subject headings. The most difficult task in typing subject cards is determining the proper subject heading to place a book under. It will help to have the person who chooses the Dewey classification number also select a subject heading for the subject card, as that person will already be familiar with the book's contents.

Subject cataloging. While a subject is the topic treated, a subject heading is restricted to a word or phrase that expresses that topic concisely for cataloging purposes. Subject cataloging involves listing all books on a given subject under one subject heading.

The first task in subject cataloging is determining what subject a book deals with. Then an appropriate subject heading must be chosen. A standard reference to choose such headings from is *Sears List of Subject Headings*.[16] A large church library, especially one that contains many books of a secular nature, should have its own copy of the *Sears List* in the most recent edition available at the time of purchase. For small church libraries preferring not to purchase the *Sears List,* Appendix 4 provides a list of subject headings designed especially for the small- to medium-sized church library.

Whether you use the list in Appendix 4 of this book or a copy of the *Sears List of Subject Headings,* you may want to put a check mark in front of each heading adopted and note any changes made for your own purposes. For example, if you choose to change some wording to make it easier for your library users to understand or to add headings of your own, enter these changes and additions on the list you are using. Subject heading lists do not include names of people, organizations, places, and other types of names. Add those you need to your copy of a subject heading list.

In choosing a subject heading, use the most specific term available if you expect to have enough entries under that heading for a separate category. Use as many subject headings for each book as necessary to properly cover its contents, but don't multiply entries needlessly. Be sure that all material on one subject appears under the same subject head.

Subdivisions. Use subdivisions when necessary to define a subject more specifically than provided for by the main subject heading. Subdivisions allow books with the same major heading to be listed in close proximity, while still allowing for more specific categorization.

Subdivisions are used to describe a particular phase, form, geographical area, or time period within a larger subject heading category. The tenth edition of *Sears* lists subdivisions in general library use.

Various types of cross reference cards are needed with use of subject headings. A *see* reference refers the user from a subject term that he has thought of to the subject heading under which books on the subject are listed in the card catalog. A *see also* card is used at the end of a group of cards with the same subject heading to indicate where a user might locate material on related subjects.

A *see* cross reference card carries the term not used as a catalog subject heading on the third line from the top of the card, indented twelve spaces. Two lines below that and indented fourteen spaces from the left edge is the word "see." Two lines below this and indented ten spaces from the edge is

16. Barbara M. Westby, ed., *Sears List of Subject Headings,* 10th ed.

the subject heading which is used as a catalog listing. All words except "see" should be capitalized.

A *see also* card is typed in similar format, with the subject heading, capitalized, on the first typed line; "see also" on the next typed line; and the subject heading referred to on another line, using the same indentations as for a "see" card. When there are several subject headings referred to, they should be listed alphabetically, one below the other.

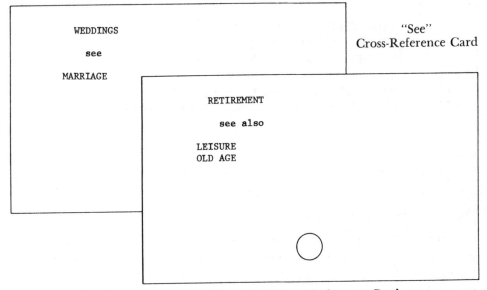

WEDDINGS

see

MARRIAGE

"See" Cross-Reference Card

RETIREMENT

see also

LEISURE
OLD AGE

"See also" Cross-Reference Card

SHELF-LIST CARD

The advantages of a shelf-list card over an accession book are described in the previous chapter. A shelf-list card is needed as an inventory record even when an accession book is used, but less information is required in that case.

The shelf-list card carries the same information as the author card, with some additional information for the librarians' use. The accession number described earlier in the chapter begins on the second space from the left edge of the card on the second line below the last line of the book's description. If the library has more than one copy, the accession numbers are listed in numerical order. All copies are entered on the same card.

If no accession book is kept, the shelf list should carry any information the library needs on the source of the book, date acquired, and cost.

Tracings, as described under author card, could be placed on shelf-list cards instead. They are not needed both places. If left on the author card, the librarian should check there to be sure all related cards are removed when an item is withdrawn.

```
268.635  Getz, Gene A.
Get          Audiovisual media in Christian education.
          Moody, 1972.

             Includes bibliography and lists of sources
          of audiovisual supplies.

          AUDIOVISUAL EDUCATION
          CHRISTIAN EDUCATION
          TEACHING - AIDS AND DEVICES
          t
3127  5.95, Lighthouse Book Store, 3/19/74
4287  6.95, Bible Book            Store, 4/10/76
```

Shelf-List Card

FILING OF CATALOG CARDS

Shelf-list cards are not considered part of the catalog. They are housed separately, usually available to library workers only. Shelf-list cards are filed in numerical order according to classification number first and author or biographee next. This arrangement puts them in the same order that books are arranged on shelves.

While some libraries prefer separate author, title, and subject files, the recommended practice for small libraries is an integrated dictionary catalog in which all these cards are combined in one alphabetical arrangement. A guide card should be placed about every inch to help users find entries. Card trays should be no more than two-thirds full. A sign or poster should be placed on top of the cabinet or on the wall near it, explaining how to use the catalog.

The American Library Association has put out detailed rules for filing catalog cards.[17] *Commonsense Cataloging* and *Simple Library Cataloging* also give filing rules and examples.[18] You can probably look up answers to specific questions in a nearby public library. Since your filing will follow the same order as words in a dictionary, look for similar cases in the dictionary when problems arise. The rules stated below give guidance for handling the most common filing problems, with some examples to illustrate correct filing order.

17. American Library Association, *A. L. A. Rules for Filing Catalog Cards.*
18. Piercy; Akers.

1. Arrange entries in alphabetical order, using words on the top line of the card.

   STORYTELLING
   Strauss, Lehman
   Streams in the desert

2. Arrange word by word, with a one-word entry preceding the same word followed by other words.

   Book
   Book trade
   Booksellers

3. Disregard beginning articles (a, an, the) in filing and go to the next word.

   Before I forget
   The beginning of sorrows
   A biblical theology of missions

4. Names beginning with Mc, Mac, or M' are filed as though spelled out as Mac.

   Macaulay
   McCain
   MacNeil

5. Most abbreviations are arranged as though spelled out. *Mrs.* is one exception which is filed as written.

   St. is filed as saint
   Dr. is filed as doctor
   Mr. is filed as mister

6. Numbers, including dates, are filed as if they were spelled out.

   1976—nineteen hundred seventy-six
   1000—one thousand
   200—two hundred

7. When the same word or name is used for different types of headings, follow this order: author, subject, title.

   Graham, Billy (author)
   GRAHAM, BILLY (subject)

8. A letter, single-letter word, or initial comes before words beginning with that letter.

   A is for angel
   The ABC book of Bible stories
   A CAPELLA SINGING
   AARON

9. Ignore punctuation in filing.
    APPLES
    APPLES, RED
    APPLES—WASHINGTON
    APPLES (WINESAP)

10. Arrange subject entries by main entry first, then in chronological order, and then by alphabetical order of subdivisions. Subdivisions that are part of a larger category follow the larger category.
    ISRAEL—HISTORY—OLD TESTAMENT
    ISRAEL—HISTORY—NEW TESTAMENT
    ISRAEL—HISTORY—RECENT
    ISRAEL—HISTORY—1970-1975
    ISRAEL—HISTORY—BIBLIOGRAPHY

11. The effect of hyphens for filing depends on usage. If a hyphen is used with a prefix, consider the word as one word. If a hyphen is used between two words that retain their meanings without it, treat the words as separate words as though they had no hyphen.
    Non-Christian
    Nondenominational
    Non-European
    Self-understanding
    Selfish

12. Follow the general rule that "nothing comes before something" in applying word by word alphabetizing.
    A
    Air
    Air Mail
    Aircraft
    Benson, C. H.
    Benson, Clarence H.

13. Names with prefixes other than Mc, Mac, or M' are treated as one word.
    Lafayette
    LaFontaine
    Landers
    LaSor

14. *See also* cards are filed after all subject cards for that subject.

15. *See* cards are filed before titles with the same words.

16. In the case of Oriental names where you may not be sure which to con-

sider as last name, enter as given, with a cross reference to any other possible entry.

SUMMARY

The main objective of the church library is getting the right material into the hands of the right person at the right time. Library material should be organized in whatever way will facilitate reaching this objective the most often. Good library procedures for preparing material for circulation will lay the groundwork for future growth without confusion. Not every church library must follow all the steps described in this chapter. But none of the steps should be omitted without careful consideration of the possibility of regretting the omission as library services expand. Count the cost in terms of time and dollars, present and future, in deciding which steps to use and which to omit.

8

PREPARING NONBOOK MATERIALS FOR LIBRARY USE

And the Lord said to him, "What is that in your hand?" And he said, "A staff" (Exodus 4:2).

SOME CHURCH LIBRARIES provide only storage facilities for nonbook materials. Most at least have a system for checking such materials out. Each library must decide, on the basis of the quantity of its holdings in these areas and uses that are made of them, how completely to follow recommended library procedures. You may want to differentiate somewhat between materials checked out for home use and those used only in the building, processing the former more completely for circulation.

Most of the processing steps described in the preceding chapter for preparing books for circulation are commonly accepted practices in small libraries. There is no such uniformity in the preparation of nonbook materials for circulation.

In the absence of generally accepted practices, many libraries have developed their own systems for processing nonbook printed materials and audiovisual materials and equipment. Some of these systems are very workable and should be continued if considered adequate for current and future needs.

The pages that follow give some suggestions for preparing periodicals, vertical file materials, and varied audiovisual materials for circulation.

PERIODICALS

A church library seldom will need to process and catalog periodicals as completely as books. It is usually sufficient to stamp the name of the library on each issue. A catalog card should be prepared for each periodical title, indicating which issues are available in the library.

> Moody monthly. Chicago v. 69, no. 8 (April
> 1969) –

Main Entry Card for a Periodical

The title of a periodical is the main entry and should be typed on the line usually used for author, as described in chapter 7. This will be the third line from the top and the tenth space from the left. Put call number on the card in its usual place, if one is used, give the city and name of publisher, and list volumes and dates of the periodical to be found in the library. Many periodicals include an index of the year's articles in one issue. Include this information on the catalog card.

Enter each issue of a given periodical on your shelf-list card for that periodical when it is received or purchase from a library supply house checking cards that are made for recording receipts of periodicals.

Current issues of magazines should be kept in racks or on reading tables for convenient use. Older ones should be shelved, bound into volumes if use warrants this expense. An index to periodical contents, such as the *Christian Periodical Index* (see address in Appendix 2) is essential for deriving much benefit from a collection of periodicals in the church library. If you do not subscribe to such an index, you may prefer to clip pertinent articles for your vertical file and discard the remainder of older magazines.

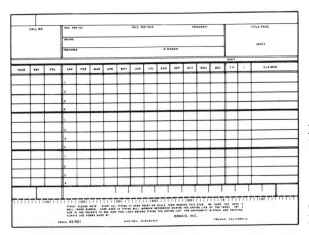

Monthly Periodical Record Checking Card

Courtesy of Demco Educational Corp.

If you have some issues of periodicals that are circulated a great deal, prepare them with book pockets and date-due slips and treat them like books. Put hard covers on them, if possible. Magazines with very limited circulation should be checked out on a checkout slip or sheet at the circulation desk. It is assumed that periodicals will usually be used in the library, but provision should be made for possible use outside the library.

Vertical File Materials

It is possible, but not usually essential, to assign Dewey numbers to vertical file materials. It is more common practice in church libraries to assign subject headings and arrange material, within various categories, alphabetically by subject heading. These subject headings should be chosen from the same list as that used for books, with additions and modifications made as needed.

All related printed material such as pamphlets and clippings should be grouped in file folders, with the subject headings typed on pressure sensitive labels and placed on folder tabs. The church library name should be stamped on each item in the folder. The following additional steps should be taken in preparing clippings for the vertical file:

1. Attach each clipping to a sheet of typing paper with rubber-based cement. Several small clippings on the same subject can be together.
2. Staple two or more pages of an article together.
3. Write the date and source of each clipping vertically in the left margin.
4. Print the subject heading in the upper right corner.
5. Place the clippings with others on the same subject in file folders with appropriate subject labels.

Small pictures to be kept in the vertical file should be mounted on tag board or laminated between two sheets of plastic. If you do not have a laminating press, you can cover pictures with clear adhesive contact plastic. Pictures are then filed according to suitable subject headings.

Large manila envelopes should be available at the checkout desk for use when pictures and vertical file folders are taken out of the library. Checkout slips or sheets can be used to record the borrower's name and date the material is due. The checkout envelope should have the library name on it and a date-due slip.

Flannelgraph materials can be kept as part of the vertical file or in a separate file. They can be processed very much like books, using Dewey classification numbers, accession numbers, book cards, date-due slips, and catalog cards as described in the previous chapter.

Flannelgraph figures should be cut out and placed in the envelope with the lesson text. The call number should be put in the upper left and accession number in the upper right corner of the envelope. The pocket and date-due slip should be attached to the back of the envelope.

The main entry card for flannelgraph will be by title, as with periodicals. The call number should indicate "flannelgraph" on its first line, the Dewey number on the second, and the main entry (title) code on the third. Subject cards should be prepared to refer to the flannelgraph material from either the main catalog or a separate card file for flannelgraph material.

There should be references in the main catalog subject heading cards to indicate when material is available in the vertical file. The card can carry a note saying, "Material on this subject is available in the vertical file."

```
Flannel-  Lessons from Romans.   ABC Flannelgraph Co.,
graph       1976.
227.1
Les


           Located in the vertical file.
```

Main Entry Card for Flannelgraph Material in Vertical File

AUDIOVISUAL MATERIALS

There have been some recent developments that encourage more uniformity in library handling of audiovisual materials. Upon the recommendation of other church librarians, I have chosen to recommend, for the processing of most audiovisuals, procedures suggested in *AV Cataloging and Processing Simplified*.[1] This book has been developed by Audiovisual Catalogers, Inc., and has been used successfully in school libraries. I have made minor adaptations for church library use.

The codes suggested for various media are as follows:

Cassette tapes	CT	Filmstrips	FS
Charts and graphs	CH	Flash cards	FC

1. Jean Thornton Johnson et al., *AV Cataloging and Processing Simplified*.

Games	GMS	Records	REC
Globes	GL	Reel-to-Reel Tapes	TA
Maps	MAP	Slides	SL
Microforms	MF	Transparencies	TR
Motion picture films	FI	Video cassettes	VC
Multimedia kits	K	Video discs	VD
Objects	OBJ	Videotapes	VT
Pictures	PIC		

CASSETTE TAPES

1. Before processing, be sure the tape is one you want to put in the library. Have one or more people listen to it. Check to see that it isn't an unnecessary duplicate of something you already have.
2. Assign an accession number to each tape. This will go in an accession book, if one is kept. Otherwise, it goes on a shelf-list card. The accession number includes the media code and the assigned sequential number: e.g., CT-1 for the first cassette tape acquired.
3. Select a call number for the tape. The call number consists of the word "Cassette" on the first line, the Dewey classification number on the second line, and the code for the speaker or singer on the third line. Use the same rules for determining call numbers as you did for books.
4. Put identifying information on the cassette label. If you are making the label, as for your pastor's sermons, type them as shown in the example.

Drawing by David Culbertson

Cassette Label

If you are marking a cassette that already has a label, add the missing information as near to the recommended position as possible. Put the call number at top left and the accession number at top right of the label. Put speaker (or equivalent) and title in upper center, if not already provided. Put name of your church library across the bottom of the label.

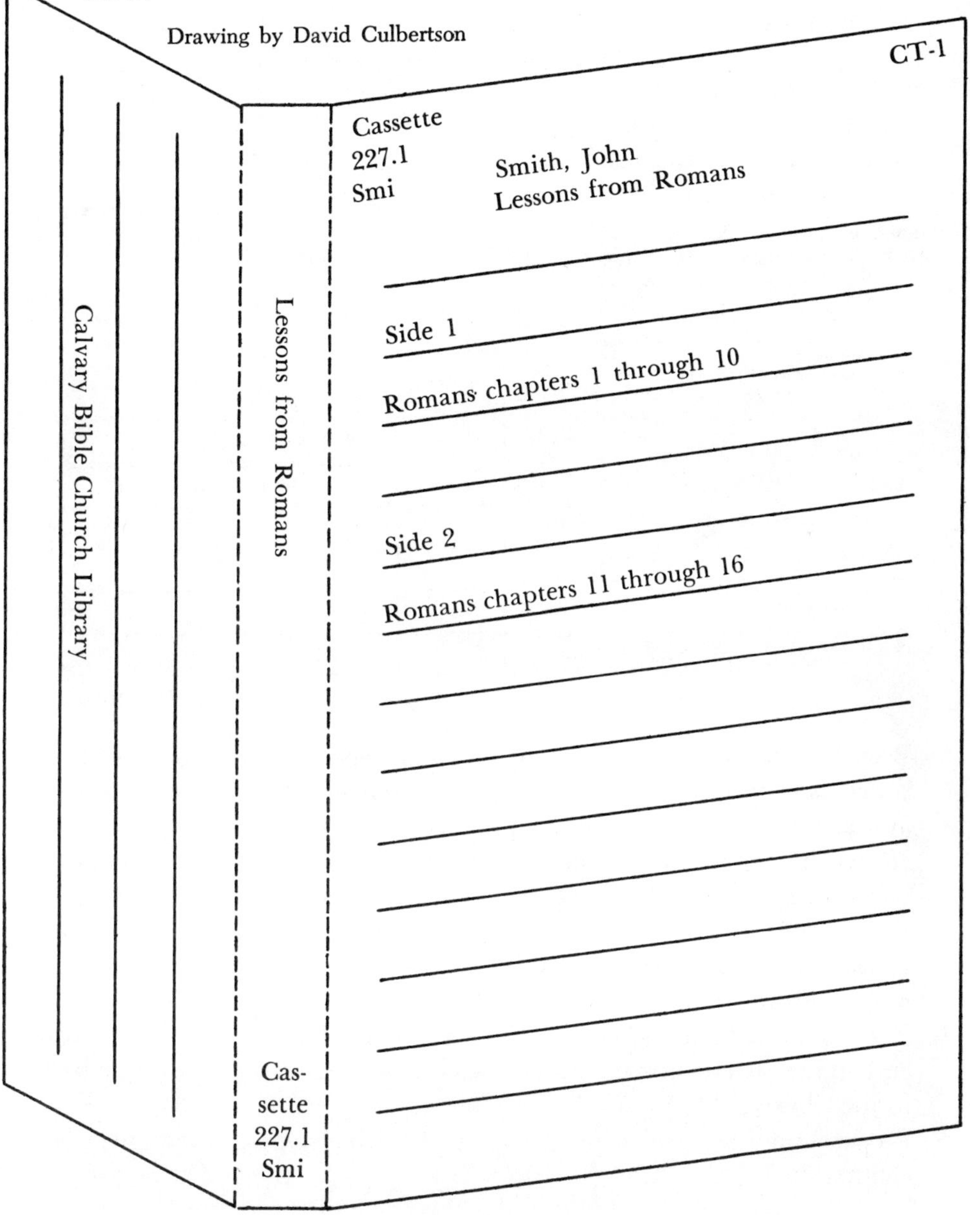

Drawing by David Culbertson

CT-1

Cassette
227.1
Smi

Smith, John
Lessons from Romans

Side 1

Romans chapters 1 through 10

Side 2

Romans chapters 11 through 16

Lessons from Romans

Calvary Bible Church Library

Cas-
sette
227.1
Smi

Cassette Box Label

5. Label the cassette box. Labeling will vary somewhat according to the type of box. Your library may contain several types, if you use the boxes tapes are purchased in. Most boxes have index labels. Some can be made or purchased for those which don't. The box label should include:

Name of library on narrow side of label

Title and call number on spine of label

Call number in upper left, accession number in upper right, with speaker (or equivalent) and title centered near the top of the wide side of the label. The rest of the label can be used for listing contents of side 1 and side 2.

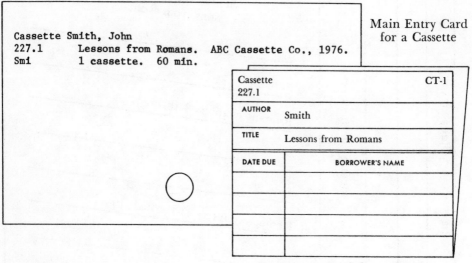

Main Entry Card for a Cassette

Cassette Smith, John
227.1   Lessons from Romans. ABC Cassette Co., 1976.
Sm1   1 cassette. 60 min.

Cassette		CT-1
227.1		
AUTHOR	Smith	
TITLE	Lessons from Romans	
DATE DUE	BORROWER'S NAME	

Borrower's Card for a Cassette

6. Prepare a borrower's card, using the same type cards referred to in the previous chapter as book cards. Put the call number in the upper left and accession number in the upper right. The name of speaker (or equivalent) and title are entered next. This card can be folded and inserted in the cassette box, to be filled out and filed in a special section of the charge tray when the cassette is checked out. Some libraries prefer to leave the borrower's card unfolded and attach it to the cassette box with a rubber band.

7. Put a gummed address label with "Date Due" typed across the narrow end on the cassette box to remind the borrower when the tape is due back in the library.

8. Prepare shelf-list and catalog cards, following typing rules given in chapter 7.

The main entry will be entered under the name of the person responsible for the content, whether this is a speaker, author, composer, or director. The tape title on side 1 is used as the main entry when the tape is a compilation of selections by various people. The main entry card should show producer, copyright date or year purchased, if no copyright date is shown, number of cassettes in set, and running time. The call number, including type of medium, goes at the top left. Notes are added if needed. Tracings are optional on this card.

The title card, unless used as main entry, should give only name of medium ("Cassette"), call number, and speaker (or equivalent), with title typed on the line (or lines) above the latter, spaced as indicated for book cataloging.

Subject cards should be prepared according to the directions given in chapter 7.

The shelf-list card should contain the information given on the main entry card, producer's catalog number or other information about source of the tape, cost, accession number, and tracings.

RECORDS

1. Examine the record to be sure its quality and content are satisfactory for your library.
2. Assign an accession number to each record or album, using REC-1 for the first one. Enter in a special section of your accession book, if you use one.
3. Select a call number, using "Record," Dewey number, and code for the artist's last name.
4. Label the record with a curved, pressure sensitive label. This label should include the call number on the left, accession number on the right, and name of church library in center. The artist and title information should be available on the original label.

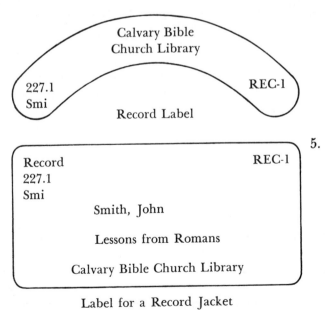

Record Label

Label for a Record Jacket

5. Label the record jacket. Place a pressure sensitive label on the jacket with this information: call number in upper left, accession number in upper right, artist and title in center, and name of church library at the bottom.

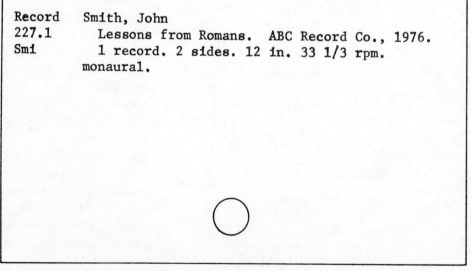

AUTHOR	
TITLE	
DATE DUE	BORRO

Record 227.1		REC-1
AUTHOR	Smith	
TITLE	Lessons from Romans	
DATE DUE	BORROWER'S NAME	

Record 227.1 Smi   REC-1

Borrower's Card and Pocket for a Record

6. Type a borrower's card and pocket, with call number in upper left, accession number in upper right, artist, and title. It may be necessary to attach the pocket to a slick jacket with clear plastic contact paper cut larger than the pocket and slit where the card is to be inserted. Attach pockets in various locations near the bottom of the jacket, so they won't cause a "build-up" storage problem.

```
Record    Smith, John
227.1         Lessons from Romans.  ABC Record Co., 1976.
Smi           1 record. 2 sides. 12 in. 33 1/3 rpm.
          monaural.
```

Main Entry Card for a Record

7. Fasten a date-due slip to the back of the jacket.
8. Prepare shelf-list and catalog cards according to the instructions given for cassette tapes. Main entry information should include number of records if processing an album, size, revolutions per minute (rpm), and stereo or monaural indications.

REEL-TO-REEL TAPES

1. Check the quality of the tape. Make any needed repairs.
2. Assign an accession number, using TA-1 for the first reel-to-reel tape acquired. Enter this number in a separate section of the accession book, if used.
3. Choose a call number, combining "Tape," a Dewey number, and code for the speaker or musician's name.
4. Label the tape on the glossy side of the leader with the following information, from left to right: call number, church library name, and accession number.

| 227.1 Smi | Calvary Bible Church Library | TA-1 |

Reel-to-Reel Tape Label

5. Label the reel with two pressure sensitive labels. The top label should give call number in upper left corner, accession number in upper right, and short title near the center of the label. The lower label gives track number and name of church library.
6. Label the reel box with a pressure sensitive label on the spine of the box, giving tape, title, and call number.

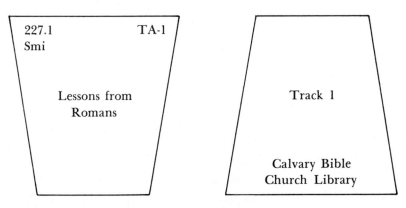

Tape Reel Labels

Drawing by David Culbertson

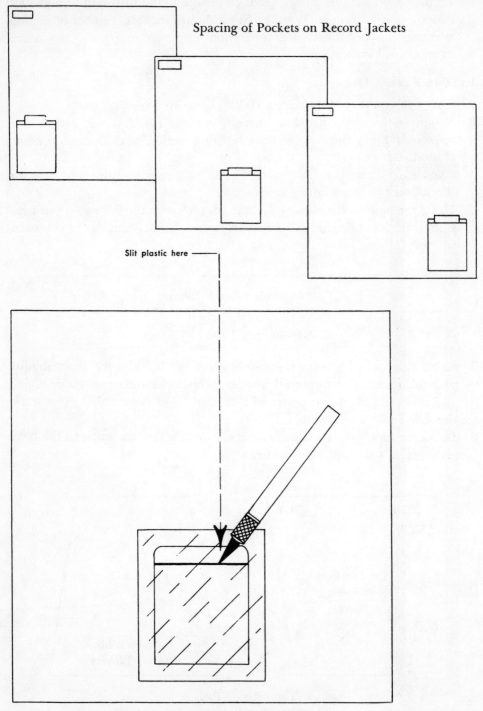

Spacing of Pockets on Record Jackets

Slit plastic here ————

Record Jacket with Plastic-covered Pocket

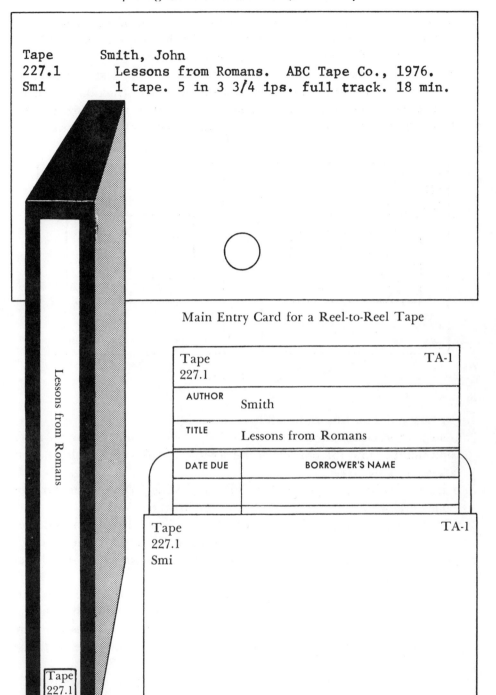

```
Tape        Smith, John
227.1          Lessons from Romans.  ABC Tape Co., 1976.
Smi            1 tape. 5 in 3 3/4 ips. full track. 18 min.
```

Main Entry Card for a Reel-to-Reel Tape

```
Tape                                          TA-1
227.1
    AUTHOR    Smith
    TITLE     Lessons from Romans
    DATE DUE        BORROWER'S NAME


Tape                                          TA-1
227.1
Smi
```

Lessons from Romans

```
Tape
227.1
Smi
```

Label for Tape Reel Box   Borrower's Card and Pocket for a Reel-to-Reel Tape

7. Type a borrower's card and pocket with call number in upper left, accession number in upper right, and artist and title on spaces indicated. Attach the pocket to the inside of the container top.
8. Fasten a date-due slip to the inside of the container top, next to the pocket.
9. Prepare shelf-list and catalog cards according to instructions given for cassette tapes, including information on the number of reels, size of reels, running time, and whether it is single track, dual track, or full track.

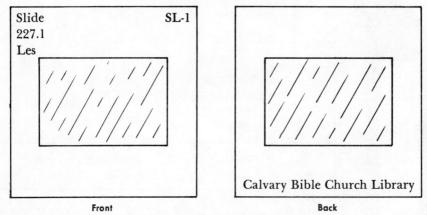

Front   Back

Slide Labels

SLIDES

1. Review slides for library suitability.
2. Assign an accession number, using SL-1 for the first slide. Enter the accession number into the portion of the accession book kept for slides, if an accession book is used.
3. Choose a call number for each slide, using "Slide," Dewey number, and code developed from the first letters of the main entry.
4. Turn the slide so the image appears as it will on the screen and then label the front of the slide with call number at the top left and accession number at top right. On the reverse side, put the name of the church library at the bottom.
5. Place related slides in storage trays. Label each tray with a pressure sensitive label indicating call number, accession number, and title of the series.
6. Type a tray contents label to include call number, accession number, series title, and brief titles of individual slides.

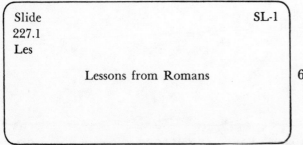

Slide Tray Label

Slide 227.1	
AUTHOR	
TITLE	Lessons from Romans
DATE DUE	**BORROWER'S NAME**

Borrower's Card for a Set of Slides

7. Type a borrower's card for each slide tray, with call number, accession number, and series title. Fold vertically to fit storage tray, and place card inside the tray.
8. Put a pressure sensitive label on the tray of slides that might be checked out for home use, with "Date Due" typed at the top.
9. Prepare shelf-list and catalog cards according to instructions given for cassettes. Include information about number of slides, size, and whether in color or black and white. The main entry card, which gives series title, should include a listing of the complete contents.

Slide   Lessons from Romans. ABC Slide Co., 1976.
227.1   10 slides. 2" x 2". color.
Les

       Contents: stick-figure drawings to illustrate
the book of Romans.

Main Entry Card for a Set of Slides

FILMSTRIPS

1. Check appropriateness and quality of filmstrips and any accompanying sound forms.
2. Assign accession number, using FS-1 for the first one. Enter into separate section of accession book.
3. Select a call number, using "Filmstrip," a Dewey number, and code from the main entry which will usually be the title.
4. Mark the following information on the emulsion (dull) side of the leader: call number (without medium name), name of library, and accession number.

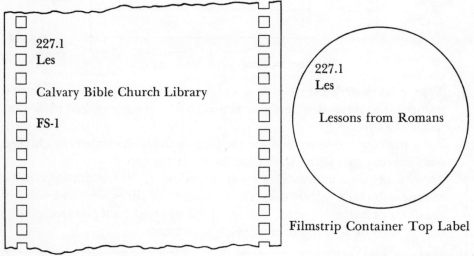

227.1
Les

Calvary Bible Church Library

FS-1

Filmstrip Label

227.1
Les

Lessons from Romans

Filmstrip Container Top Label

5. Label the top of the container with the call number (without medium name). Add title if not using a label already giving that information. Put the accession number inside the lid. To label the side of the container, put the following information on a pressure sensitive label: call number in upper left, accession number in upper right, title in center, with series title in parentheses if not shown on lid, and name of library. Cover labels with plastic adhesive to protect them.

Filmstrip		FS-1
227.1		
Les	Lessons from Romans	
	Calvary Bible Church Library	

Filmstrip Container Side Label

Filmstrip 227.1		FS-1
AUTHOR		
TITLE	Lessons from Romans	
DATE DUE	**BORROWER'S NAME**	

Borrower's Card for a Filmstrip

6. Type a borrower's card with call number in upper left, accession number in upper right, and title on appropriate line. This card is kept in a convenient location at the checkout desk.
7. If a date-due slip is desirable, secure it to a manila envelope to put the filmstrip in at the time it is checked out.
8. Prepare shelf-list and catalog cards as explained for cassettes. The main entry will use the title. Include information on number of frames, size, color, and series title.

```
Film-      Lessons from Romans.  ABC Filmstrip Co., 1976.
strip         43 frames. 35 mm. color. with narration
227.1      booklet.
Les
```

Main Entry Card for a Filmstrip

TRANSPARENCIES

1. Make sure the transparencies to be processed have continuing rather than one-time use, so they are worth processing for library distribution.
2. Accession each transparency, with TR-1 for the first accession number. Enter in a special section of the accession book, if used.
3. Determine a call number, combining "Transparency," Dewey number, and main entry code.
4. If transparency is not mounted, mount it by attaching it to a cardboard frame with magic transparent tape.

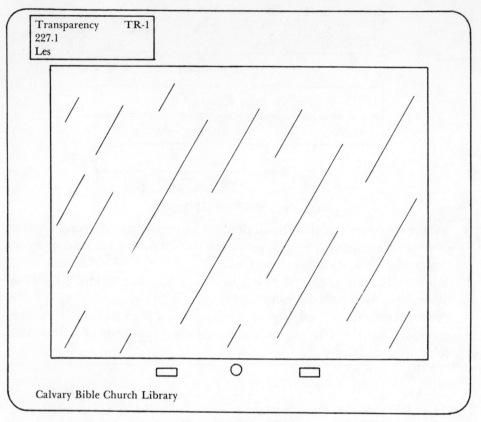

Transparency   TR-1
227.1
Les

Calvary Bible Church Library

Transparency Label

5. Label the frame by placing in the upper left corner a rectangular pressure sensitive label on which you have typed the call number, accession number, and title of transparency, with series title in parentheses if needed. Put the library name at the bottom.

6. Prepare a $10\frac{1}{2}'' \times 12\frac{1}{2}''$ envelope, preferably an open-end, x-ray style envelope, to hold the transparency. Place a rectangular pressure sensitive label with identical information as that described for step 4, on upper left corner. Put accession number in upper right corner.

7. Type borrower's card and pocket with call number in upper left, accession number in upper right, title, and a list of any other items such as an accompanying discussion guide to be kept in the envelope. Paste the pocket near the bottom edge of the envelope, varying locations along the edge to prevent irregular "build-up" in the files. The library name should be stamped on the pocket and on the envelope, along the bottom edge.

8. Attach a date-due slip to the envelope if the transparency might be checked out for a period of time.

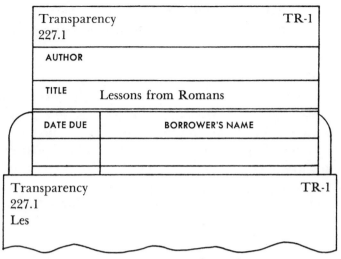

Borrower's Card and Pocket for a Transparency

9. Prepare shelf-list and catalog cards according to instructions given for cassettes, including information about number of overlays, color, series, and whether it is a motion transparency. Add a brief note to explain overlays. Use title for main entry.

OPAQUE MATERIALS

Materials used with the opaque projector are drawn from various media.

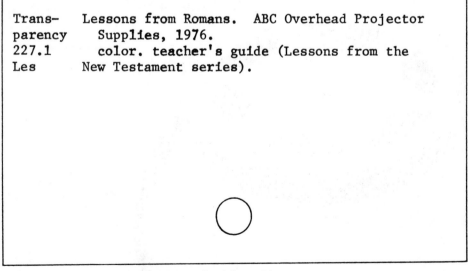

Main Entry Card for a Transparency

Books, periodicals, and vertical file materials are the most commonly used. They will already have been processed for regular library use, so no special treatment is required.

MOTION PICTURES

1. Preview the film for appropriateness and put it into good condition.
2. Assign an accession number, using FI-1 for the first film acquired. Enter into a special section of the accession book if one is used.
3. Select a call number for each film, combining "Film," a Dewey number, and main entry code.
4. Mark the following information on the emulsion (dull) side of the leader: call number (omitting name of medium), library name, and accession number.

| 227.1 | Calvary Bible | FI-1 |
| Les | Church Library | |

Motion Picture Film Label

5. Label the top of the container with a pressure sensitive label giving the call number in upper left, accession number in upper right, title in center, and name of library on the bottom.

Drawing by David Culbertson

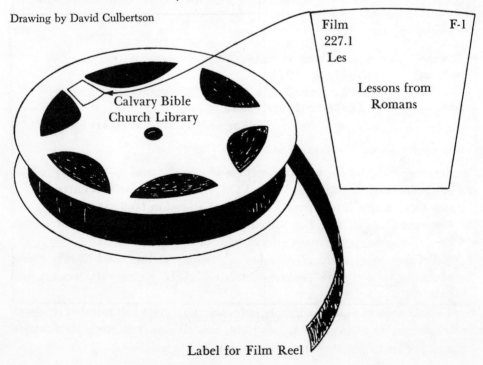

Label for Film Reel

6. Print the call number and accession number on the rim of the container top.
7. Label the reel with a pressure sensitive label cut to fit a portion of the reel, giving call number, accession number, and title.
8. Type borrower's card and pocket for each film, with call number in upper left, accession number in upper right, and title. Attach card and pocket to inside of container top.
9. If you use a date-due slip, attach it to the container top.
10. Prepare shelf-list and catalog cards as explained for cassettes, giving added information on number of reels, size, whether sound or silent, color, and running time. Use title as main entry.

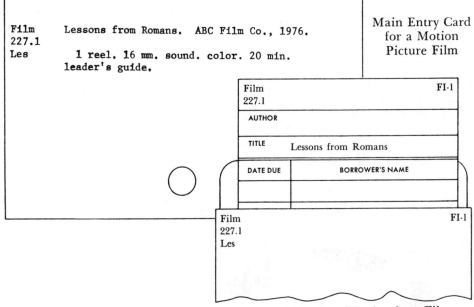

Film 227.1 Les	Lessons from Romans. ABC Film Co., 1976. 1 reel. 16 mm. sound. color. 20 min. leader's guide.

Main Entry Card
for a Motion
Picture Film

Film	FI-1
227.1	

AUTHOR

TITLE   Lessons from Romans

DATE DUE	BORROWER'S NAME

Film	FI-1
227.1	
Les	

Borrower's Card and Pocket for a Film

VIDEOTAPES, VIDEO CASSETTES, AND VIDEO DISCS

1. Preview material for appropriateness of content and quality of product.
2. Accession each item, using VT-1, VC-1, or VD-1 for the first entry in each category. Enter into separate sections of accession book, if used.
3. Determine a call number for each item, indicating the type of media, Dewey number, and main entry code.
4. Label each item with call number, accession number, and library name.
5. Mark containers with pressure sensitive labels, giving call number and title.
6. Type borrower's card and pocket for each item, with call number in upper left, accession number in upper right, and title as indicated. Attach card and pocket to the container top, inside where possible.

Drawing by David Culbertson

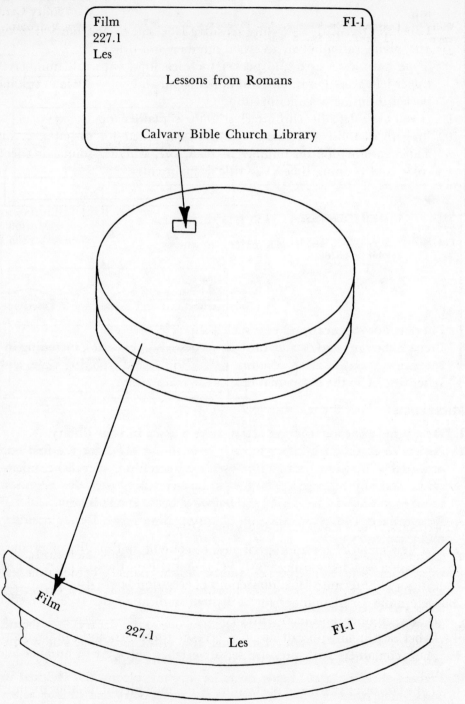

Film Can Labels

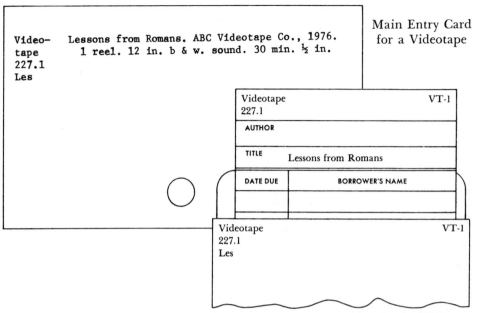

Main Entry Card for a Videotape

Borrower's Card and Pocket for a Videotape

7. Put date-due slip near pocket if such a slip is to be used.
8. Prepare shelf-list and catalog cards as suggested for cassettes, including information about number of units, size, color, sound, running time, and series title. Use the individual title as the main entry.

MICROFORMS

1. Determine what microforms, if any, have a place in your library.
2. Assign an accession number to each item, using MF-1 for the first one acquired. This same code can be used for microfilms, microfiche, microcards, and any other microforms the library has. Enter this accession number in a special section of the accession book, if one is kept.
3. Determine call number, made up of the medium name, Dewey number, and main entry code.
4. Label microfilm, reel, reel boxes, cartridges, microfiche, microcards, and other microforms by placing call number, library name, accession number, and titles, in the most accessible locations. Suggestions given earlier for films and tapes apply here as well.
5. Since microforms will not usually be taken out of the library, they should not need borrower's cards. If someone does check something out, a sign-out sheet or slip can be filled out at the checkout desk.
6. Prepare shelf-list and catalog cards for any microforms not indexed in some other manner. Use the title as the main entry and catalog as for printed material.

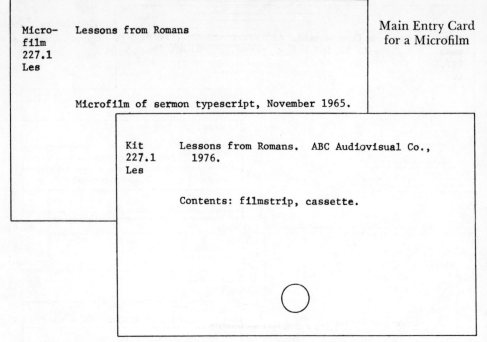

Main Entry Card for a Multimedia Kit

MULTIMEDIA KITS

1. Check for usefulness, completeness, and good quality of all materials in kits before processing them for library use.
2. Assign one accession number to each kit, beginning with K-1 for the first one. Enter this into the designated section of your accession book, if one is used.
3. Determine a call number, showing "Kit" as medium name, Dewey number, and main entry code.
4. Label the items of a kit in accordance with rules given for the appropriate media, using the kit's accession number on each item.
5. Label the kit container with a pressure sensitive label, indicating call number, accession number, kit title, and name of library.
6. Type a borrower's card and pocket with call number, accession number, kit title, and number of items in the kit. List the kit's contents on the pocket. Attach the pocket to the inside of the container's lid.
7. If a date-due slip is needed, put it next to the pocket for the borrower's card.
8. Prepare shelf-list and catalog cards, using the kit title as the main entry and listing complete contents on the title card. Include information about producer and date produced.

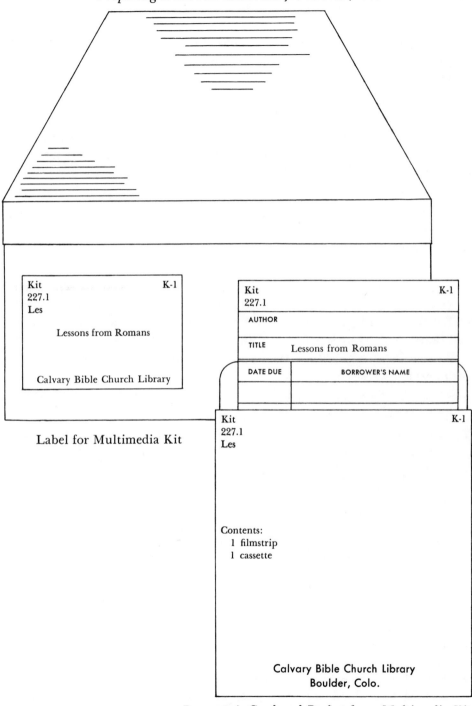

Label for Multimedia Kit

Borrower's Card and Pocket for a Multimedia Kit

NONPROJECTED VISUAL AIDS

Each type of visual aid requires somewhat different processing. However, a basic pattern can be followed, with adaptations used as needed for various media.

1. Check the desirability of each item for library use. Make any necessary repairs.
2. Assign an accession number, using short letter codes for the media, followed by a number beginning with number 1. Suggested codes for those nonprojected visual aids listed in chapter 5 which call for library processing are as follows:

Maps	MAP	Games	GMS
Globes	GL	Charts and Graphs	CH
Pictures	PIC	Flash Cards	FC
Objects	OBJ		

3. Determine a call number for each item, combining the media name, Dewey number, and code for main entry which will usually be a title.
4. Label each item with call number, accession number, title, and name of library. Label any separate containers with this same information.
5. Type a borrower's card, with call number, accession number, and title, for each item and a pocket for those that have a place to put them. Cards for items that don't have a place for pockets should be filed in a special location at the checkout desk.

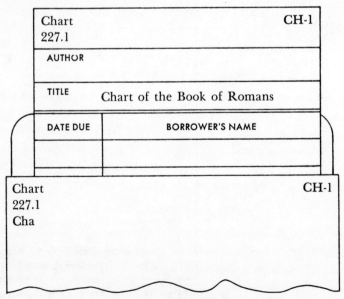

Borrower's Card and Pocket for a Chart

6. Attach date-due slips if used.
7. Prepare shelf-list and catalog cards, as indicated under instructions for processing cassettes. Use the title as the main entry. Include special information pertinent to each medium, with added notes and descriptions to help the catalog user know just what is available.

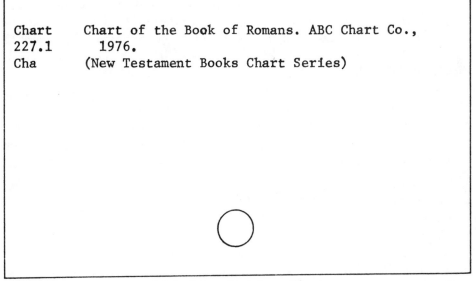

```
Chart      Chart of the Book of Romans. ABC Chart Co.,
227.1        1976.
Cha        (New Testament Books Chart Series)
```

Main Entry Card for a Chart

Audiovisual materials and equipment that do not lend themselves to subject classification should at least be marked with library identification. Borrower's cards can be prepared for each item and kept at the circulation desk.

AUDIOVISUAL EQUIPMENT

A special section in the shelf-list catalog can be used to record all pertinent information about such equipment, including serial, model, and manufacturing numbers; insurance coverage; size and description; cost; source; and date of purchase. Guarantees and instruction on proper care should be filed with library information. Each item should be labeled as to church ownership. Booking cards should be prepared for each unless sign-out sheets are used.

FILING OF CATALOG CARDS

There should be a separate section in the shelf-list file for each medium. However, cards for all media should be integrated into one file in the general catalog. Cards for nonbook materials will indicate the medium as part of the call number. There is no need to use separate colors for each medium, although some libraries prefer to do so.

The filing rules explained in the previous chapter should be followed. Subject cards for books are filed first, then those for audiovisual materials, and then those for vertical file materials, followed by any *see also* cross reference cards.

Summary

Nonbook materials are becoming an increasingly important part of the ministry of a church library or resource center. Proper preparation and care of these materials will increase their usefulness in several ways. The material will be available when needed and easy to locate. It will be kept in good condition and much less likely to be lost or seriously damaged.

It is a recommended practice to assign Dewey classification numbers to most audiovisual materials. However, small libraries can devise more simplified methods, if they choose. This chapter has given fairly complete library procedures for the various media so church libraries and resource centers can be familiar with them and use those that apply to their particular situations.

9

PROMOTING THE LIBRARY'S MINISTRY

*Like apples of gold in settings of silver
Is a word spoken in right circumstances* (Proverbs 25:11)

I WAS CERTAINLY SURPRISED when one unusually successful church librarian told me that she never uses promotional "gimmicks" such as posters and contests. She said that she had found that "the best way to promote a library is to offer something that people need and do a good job of it." Her advice is to "continually try to keep close to current needs of your people and supply those needs; then the people become your promotional material."

I tend to agree with this view more and more as time goes on. But I have also seen posters and contests used successfully, and so I believe they have their place. However, we need to recognize that they are not the most important or most effective means of promotion available to us; we should never rely on them completely.

Keeping in mind that nothing will encourage library use more than a well-run library with informed and enthusiastic workers providing good service, consider with me several promotional ideas that can be tried in various combinations to ensure maximum library effectiveness.

PERSONAL RECOMMENDATIONS

There are two ways by which a librarian or a library user can pass along his or her enthusiasm for library materials. This can be done on a person-to-person basis or in a group sharing situation.

PERSON-TO-PERSON SHARING

Vance Havner tells about finding "a better cup of tea" and sharing his find with friends:

Some time ago a preacher friend of mine gave me a recipe for a better cup of tea. He told me how to mix certain ingredients I had never tried before and the results were revolutionary. Sara and I have been drinking the new tea ever since and like it better all the time. I have been telling people about it and everybody who has tried it is enthusiastic. This week I recommended it to the pastor of the church where I am preaching and to the song leader. Both became ardent "converts." So the word gets around and a new club of tea drinkers forms by passing on the word from one to another. There is no advertising campaign—it is just that we have found a good thing and we share it.[1]

While Vance Havner uses this story to illustrate the way the Gospel is spread, I would like to suggest that it also illustrates the best way for a vital church library ministry to develop. One reader tells another of a need met through a book or cassette from the church library, encouraging a friend to try it, too. Word spreads.

Mrs. Eleanor Matthews, full-time librarian at First Baptist Church in La Crescenta, California, was quoted in an interview with Norman Rohrer as saying: "The best library promotion is one reader who gets excited about the effect of a book on his life and then tells someone else and brings him into the library."[2]

You may have to get the ball rolling with your own recommendations, but let others take it from there. Everyone expects a librarian to be enthusiastic about books, but they really pay attention when others tell of the blessings and help they have found through library materials.

It took a long time for one lady's recommendation to her husband to come to fruition; but eventually it did. A Canadian librarian wrote to tell me the story of one of her favorite readers, a widower in his seventies. While his wife was living, she had often urged him to read something more worthwhile than the newspaper. After her death, he resolved to read a book a week from the church library. In announcing his achievement of this goal at a New Year's Eve service, he testified of a transformation in his own life as he read of the faith of fellow Christians and urged others to read as they had never read before.

GROUP SHARING

Encourage your readers to share such blessings in group sharing times. Many Sunday school classes (including those for children), youth groups, women's meetings, and men's fellowship groups have sharing times that could include this type of testimony. At times, arrange for brief discussions of

1. Vance Havner, *Song at Twilight* (Old Tappan, New Jersey: Revell, 1973), p. 39.
2. Norman Rohrer, "Don't Stop with Books," *Leaders Guidebook* (September, October, November, 1972), reprint of article, p. 4.

"blessings from books" in such groups. Relate discussions to the study emphasis of the group at the time.

One church had a midweek service in which several readers gave testimonies about the value of the church library in their own lives, in their Christian service in the church, and in their homes. Some young mothers "emphasized the value of reading to their small children and encouraging older children to read good books."[3]

PROMOTION BY PASTOR AND STAFF

Pastors with a vision for the potential of library ministry can do much to promote that ministry. Ask your pastor for sermon topics in advance, so you can order coordinated material, displaying and promoting it at the proper time. Ask him to check with you if he plans to mention a book in his sermon, so he can let it be known if that book is available in the library. Encourage him, in his announcements from the pulpit and in his sermons, to periodically stress the value of Christian literature, reminding the congregation of the availability of such material in the library. For example, we noticed a marked increase in library use after a sermon on "The Upward Look," in which our pastor, W. Robert Culbertson, challenged us to "read things that God can approve of and that God can use."

Let pastors and others doing counseling know that they can suggest—or better yet, borrow—helpful literature from the library to put in the hands of those with special needs. Their own ministry will then be reinforced by the printed or recorded words of others.

Encourage Sunday school teachers to give assignments involving use of the library. Let youth leaders know of program materials available for their use. All church workers, paid and unpaid, should be acquainted with library materials and trained in library procedures.

PRINTED PUBLICITY

Remembering that publicity and promotion are not necessarily synonymous, you will still want to use several methods by which the library's ministry can be both publicized and promoted in print.

CHURCH BULLETIN

Keep the work of the library before the congregation through your church bulletin. Many churches include library hours with other regularly printed information. New acquisitions should be listed from time to time and special events announced. Bulletin inserts can be used occasionally for added emphasis.

3. Lucie Anne C. Eldridge, "What National Library Week Did for Us," *The Church Library Magazine* 7 (January, February, March, 1966): 24.

NEWSLETTER

Most churches publish a church newsletter of some type. The church library should be a regular contributor to such a publication. This is a good way to inform members about library activities and services. Get some of your satisfied users to contribute testimonies and brief reviews of books and cassettes that have been a blessing to them.

DIRECT MAIL

Personalized mail is very effective. Try dropping a postcard or letter to someone you know that would be especially interested in a new item the library has just acquired. Your personal interest and attention will be hard to resist.

Send letters, using form letters if you cannot take time for personal letters, to visitors, new members, newlyweds, new parents, and recently bereaved members, letting them know about library services and materials of special interest for them. They are apt to respond because of your personal interest. You might further strengthen their motivation with the offer of some gift such as a bookmark or appropriate booklet if they come into the library.

BOOK LISTS

Get lists of library materials into the hands of the right people. Lists of teaching aids should be given to teachers. Lists of program material should be given to those with program planning responsibilities. Youth workers and leaders should have lists of material for youth. Young married couples should be given lists of books on Christian marriage and child training.

Consider the possibility of preparing a catalog of all—or selected—library titles to give each family of the church. Don't forget to update such listings frequently. Instead of compiling bibliographies, listing books only, make them *mediagraphies,* listing both printed and nonprint materials.

BOOKMARKS

Supplying bookmarks will promote library interest while prolonging the life of books by preventing use of an astonishing array of things people use to mark places in a book—things such as spoons, pens, pencils, paperweights, combs, shoes, carrots, and anything else that happens to be handy. They also help eliminate the destructive practice of laying open books face down to mark one's place.

Bookmarks should have the church name on them to remind borrowers where the books came from. They can also be used to inform people of library hours and rules. Attaching bookmarks to church bulletins will remind and inform people about the library.

Special bookmarks can be prepared to promote special events and contests. New books should be flagged with a bookmark indicating that the book is new. Bookmarks can be handmade, printed to order, or purchased from library and church supply houses.

LOCAL NEWSPAPER

Send library news and pictures to your local newspaper. You will find that your own church people will take more interest in your library if they read of its activities in their local newspaper. They may ignore library announcements in church bulletins and newsletters, but their attention will be captured by interesting write-ups in the local paper.

News items in district or national denominational publications will also bring them scurrying in to see what's so special about *their* library. We were surprised at the number of people who came to visit, and eventually to use, our library because they had read a magazine article about it.

DISPLAYS

Let people see, not just hear and read about, books. Display them attractively and in locations where everyone will see them. If anyone in your church, past or present, has written worthwhile material, feature it in your displays, as there will be built-in interest already.

DISPLAY WINDOW OR CASE

Fortunate is the library with a display window where attractive book displays can be arranged and left for a period of time. If such a display window isn't part of the library itself, see if a display case can be built in a location near the main sanctuary entrance. Change displays at least once a month, using seasonal themes, themes centered around sermon topics or church activities, and themes relating to specific library materials. For example, you might build a diorama depicting an interesting scene from a featured library book.

LIBRARY DISPLAYS

Attractive displays inside the library itself will lure some of those non-readers in. They may surprise themselves and you, too, by leaving with a book. But don't be surprised if they return for more.

Three-dimensional displays are especially effective to draw attention to certain areas of the library. They can be set up on empty shelf or table space or on pegboard fixtures. Dolls from foreign countries can be used near missions books and stuffed animals in the children's section.

Books themselves can be displayed face out on easels which you can make or purchase from library supply houses. For interesting table displays, use remnants of velvet, burlap, or plastic. Using wadded paper and easels under the cloth, display books and other materials on top.

Displays of special Bibles or rare books will interest many. Special displays in connection with missionary, Bible, or prophetic conferences will bring people in and help them get acquainted with the library.

Book Display Rack

MOBILES

Attractive mobiles can be used to call attention to a new book display or a particular area of the library needing special emphasis at the time. You can make these yourself or order them from The Children's Book Council, Inc. (see Appendix 2 for address) . Hanging balloons are good, simple eye-catchers.

BULLETIN BOARDS

Whether you do or don't have a display window, you'll find a library bulletin board a good place to advertise new books, inform people about library activities, and generally attract interest in the library. Book jackets make attractive bulletin board displays. Other ideas are available from church library periodicals and other sources.

Cartoons attract attention, so be on the lookout for appropriate ones for your library bulletin board. Pictures—of church people, of authors, of library activities, and even of interesting scenery—will get people to stop and look. Use printed captions that tie your display to some feature of the library. Post baby or wedding pictures from church families and watch the increased traffic to the library.

An article in *The Christian Librarian* suggests these three sets of three's to remember in using a bulletin board: its purpose is to capture attention, hold attention, and make a forcible impression; boredom is produced by monotony, confusion, and ugliness; its design should include balance, continuity, and emphasis.[4]

BRANCH LOCATIONS

Books displayed in convenient locations will arouse interest. There is no question that a good location for a library makes a tremendous difference in library use. However, many churches don't have libraries in ideal locations; this should not become an excuse for poor circulation, but a challenge to try harder.

Taking books into classes and departmental areas is a time-consuming, but proven method of increasing circulation. Depending on your library's location and your success in getting people trained to go to the library, taking books to other locations may or may not become a permanent arrangement. The central library should be responsible for keeping records on all books, but someone in each location should be in charge of promoting them and checking them in and out. If opportunity isn't given for checking them out on the spot, many potential readers will pass up the opportunity, even though some interest is aroused through posters and displays.

If not done regularly, books should at least be taken to other locations occasionally. This will remind people of your library and encourage them to go there when the temporary service is discontinued.

The Kenosha Bible Church in Kenosha, Wisconsin, reports a tremendous increase in circulation by this method. Their librarian wrote to tell me, "We have a very poor location for the library so for the past year we have brought a few books to the foyer on Sunday nights to be checked out. This has increased the number of books checked out per month from three to sixty."

POSTERS

Now we come to the library promotional method that usually receives the most attention. Posters can be valuable library boosters. Having a willing and talented artist in your midst will help, but it isn't necessary. Several of the library supply companies listed in Appendix 2 have inexpensive library posters. You can get ideas by visiting school and public libraries. Adapt poster ideas from Sunday school materials. Make up a set of felt letters that can be used in various ways, or purchase magnetic letters for use with a metal

4. Miriam Hunter and Elizabeth Dinning, "Bulletin Boards in the Library," *The Christian Librarian* 6 (October 1962): 3.

bulletin board. In lieu of a metal bulletin board, use magnets to hold material to the side of a metal filing cabinet.

Librarian's World, the official publication of the Evangelical Church Library Association which comes with membership in the organization, is an excellent source of poster ideas. *Media: Library Services Journal* often carries poster suggestions, as well as centerfold posters that can be removed and used just as they come. The *Wilson Library Bulletin* also has good poster ideas that can be adapted for church library use. Addresses for these periodicals are found in Appendix 2.

Cartoons by Howard Paris

Library poster contests held at various times for different age groups serve two purposes. They supply posters and inspire library interest in those making them. A Sunday school class or other group with a special concern for the library's ministry might take on the making of posters as a special project.

Try applying your imagination in adapting some of the following themes that have been used for posters in recent years by various libraries:

Book Power
Books for a Rainy Day
Books for Reading while Sitting in the Sun
Crack Open a Good Book or Two This Fall
Dive into Summer—Read
Don't Fall Behind—Use Your Library
Don't Just Stand There—Read
Get Hooked on Books
Go Places with Books
Good Books Like Flowers Can Brighten Your Life
Good Books Make Good Friends
Grow with Books
I'Owl See You in the Library

It's Raining New Titles
Make Reading a Picnic—With Books from the Library
March Winds Blow Good Books Your Way
Put Some Spring in Your Life
Read Christian Books
Read! Look! Listen! . . . in Your Library
Reading Is for Everybody
Reading Is Fun
Reading Is the Key to Unlock Many Worlds
Relax with Books
Searching for Something New to Read? Try our Church Library
Slate of New Books
Some Delicious Titles from Our Library
Summer Reading Is Out of This World
Take a Book on Your Vacation
Treasure Chest of Good Reading
Untangle the Web of Ignorance—Read
Worm Your Way to the Library

While some churches rely too heavily on posters as their only or primary means of library promotion, posters can supplement other methods by adding interesting and attractive eye appeal.

Book Talks and Skits

Take the work of your library to church groups in person, not just in print. Develop interesting presentations of various phases of library ministry.

Book Reviews

Volunteer the services of your library staff and cooperative readers to give book talks. These can be anything from a one-minute promotion of a featured book or cassette to a half-hour feature at a group meeting. When reviewing a book, tell enough to make the listener want to read it rather than summarizing the entire contents. Hold the book in your hand. Read brief excerpts, but no long passages.

At times, instead of reviewing one book, discuss several books on one subject. For example, at an evening meeting of a young couples' class, you might tell a little about several books on marriage and child training. Display the books as you talk about them and make them available for checking out during or after the meeting.

If your book talk is for children, use hand puppets to tell about the books and to invite the boys and girls to visit the library. Let them know the church library is an exciting place, not the "dullsville" some seem to expect a library to be.

Skits

A playlet or skit is a very effective way to remind your audience of the library's ministry and to inform them about its contents and potential outreach. Your library staff can write and give a skit or even ad-lib one as you go, if you have the idea pretty well worked out in advance.

Two of our library workers used a simple dialog presentation, with one acting as librarian and one as a Sunday school superintendent asking for helpful materials for her teachers. In this way, they informed the entire Sunday school staff about materials available for their use. Our librarians had books and audiovisuals with them and teachers checked out several before they left that meeting.

Young people might enjoy preparing a library skit for a youth meeting or for a "library night" church service.

Slide Presentations

Slides can be used to accompany a book talk or to acquaint people with library activities and services. These could be used in a Sunday evening service, a meeting of some particular organization, or a special library function. A taped commentary would add to their usefulness in that it would allow various groups to use the slide and tape presentation without someone from the library being there.

Library Events

In the next chapter, which deals with finances, a number of plans are suggested that incorporate library promotion with raising of funds to support it. There are various events that can be sponsored by or on behalf of the library. Most of them can be held with or without fund-raising objectives.

Open House

Posters, bulletin boards, and displays all around the church will accomplish nothing unless they get people into the library. One method that will bring them in to see for themselves is the open house. It should be used first in connection with the dedication of a new library; but that is just the beginning.

Hold open house in connection with a library anniversary, "Library Sunday," and National Book Week. Celebrate any expansion or remodeling of facilities or acquisition of a sizable group of new materials with an open house.

Have open house for small groups. Bringing just one Sunday school class into the library each week for a period of time is one of the best ways to familiarize young and old alike with the library. Be sure to give them opportunity to check something out. Make the event special with light refreshments or a small gift.

Some churches regularly serve coffee in the library before or after a service. This will get people into the library, but could crowd facilities in a way that would inhibit, rather than promote, its primary purpose.

LIBRARY EMPHASIS DAY OR WEEK

Whether you have a library day, library night, book Sunday, or book week, there should be at least one Sunday a year when special attention is called to the ministry of the church library. It can start with special emphasis in each Sunday school department. The pastor's sermon should be correlated with the theme. If its location makes it possible, let everyone be ushered through the library as they leave church that day. Skits, slides, posters, and displays can all be used in promoting the event.

Many churches plan their church library emphasis to coincide with National Library Week, held each spring, thus capturing interest already aroused through school and public libraries and local newspapers.

BOOK FAIR

A book fair can be used both for raising financial support and for promoting library interest. Booths should be set up to display different types of books. Young people can be dressed as book characters. Missionary displays can be related to books on missions. Skits, slide presentations, and lots of posters can be incorporated into the event.

BOOK TEA, COFFEE, OR BANQUET

Again, these functions which are usually geared for raising financial support should be planned to promote interest in library use, as well. You may even want to have such a function with no appeal for finances. People dressed as book characters can serve refreshments. Bring in an author or good reviewer as speaker. Have interest centers around the room to display books and other library material. Encourage people to check something out before they leave.

STORY HOUR

Holding a story hour for children provides both a service function and a means of promoting interest in the library. Some churches hold such a program on Saturday; some have it Wednesday evening before or during the midweek service. Others have it Sunday afternoon or evening.

If at all possible, have two separate groups—one for preschoolers and one for primary children. Choose books with pictures and vocabulary suitable for the age group. Meet in the library if there is room, letting the children sit on a special rug or on cushions. Discuss the books you read with them. Then give the children a chance to check out books at the close of the story hour.

BOOK DISCUSSIONS

Some churches have had success with reading clubs or discussion groups in which participants all read the same books and get together to discuss them. This serves a social function of bringing people with similar interests together. It is also a good time to promote library material and to recruit helpers and supporters for the library.

PROMOTIONAL USE OF FACILITIES

Don't keep the location of your library a secret. It's appalling how many people don't know where their church library is located. Just try asking when you visit other churches.

Be sure there are adequate signs around the church indicating where the library or resource center is located. On special occasions, use arrows attached to the walls or big footprints on the floor leading from all directions to the library. There should be an attractive permanent sign at the entrance to the library, using whatever name you have decided on, such as "Joe Doe Memorial Library," "Media Center," or "Resource Center."

Offer use of the library room for committee, staff, or other small group meetings at times that won't conflict with regular library use. Before such meetings, prepare displays of materials of special interest to the group using the room. Train someone in the group to check out any library materials people may want to take with them.

CONTESTS AND READING PROGRAMS

Contests tend to produce more lasting results than such promotional methods as posters and displays, because of the active participation of contestants in actual library use.

CONTEST THEMES

There are all kinds of themes that can be used for reading contests. You can adapt ideas from Sunday school contest materials or find suggestions in catalogs, magazines, and library handbooks. Pick a theme, plan tie-in promotional gimmicks, and prepare for an onslaught of new readers. Put on your thinking cap and imagine what you might do with some of the following idea starters:

Animals of all kinds
Baseball
Bees and bee hives
Bookworms
Candyland
Christ our Pilot
Climbing a ladder
Fishing
Flying
Fruit
Glory train
Hawaiian holiday
Holy Land trip
Ice cream cones

Indians with feathers
Kites
Library shelf
Mountain climbing
Races of all kinds—foot,
    horse, sailboat, etc.
Readathon
Readers with Jesus
Reading roundup
Thermometer
Trains
Treasure chest
Trees
Trip around the world
Vacation time

Train Theme for Contest and Party

Most of these themes have been used for library contests, and materials for many of them can be purchased from library supply houses listed in Appendix 2.

There's nothing wrong with using charts and plain gold stars, seals, or colored bars to show progress. Be sure to have each participant's name posted where he can check his own progress and compare it with that of his friends.

Some contests pit boys against girls, one class against another, or one department against another. This appeals to team spirit and may get some started reading who wouldn't otherwise.

SUMMER READING PROGRAMS

We have found a summer reading contest very effective in promoting library use. Children are eager for change-of-pace reading once school is out. Parents are glad to have them doing something quiet and constructive. The following steps, which were developed for our own library and published in *The Evangelical Beacon** have worked well for us:

1. *Define your goals.* Sit down with your library committee and Christian education workers to discuss why you want to promote reading. In these days of stress on "accountability" and "management by objectives," there is no sense putting forth all the effort a contest requires unless worthwhile goals are to be obtained.

2. *Plan the end from the beginning.* The most distinctive feature of our contest is the party at the close. Letting contestants know what their rewards will be increases incentive to win. However, we found that after the first few years our parties had earned a reputation for being fun, and we could just announce a surprise ending.

3. *Have your library in tip-top shape.* We like to purchase whatever new books the budget will allow and have them shelved in time for the beginning of the contest. Line up librarians and helpers, keeping in mind that you may need to extend library hours somewhat during the contest.

4. *Advertise ahead.* See that the contest is mentioned often all spring. Announce it for at least two weeks in the church bulletin. On the Sunday the contest starts, which is the first Sunday after local schools are out, we have a special insert in the church bulletin and handout sheets for all attending Sunday school.

5. *Follow a theme.* Choose an exciting theme and use it on all contest materials. One summer we developed a bee hive theme, using a separate hive for each age group. Another year we made small paper books for each contestant and used gold stars inside to show progress.

6. *Include everyone.* Enroll readers of all ages. By summer's end you'll have three main types of contestants. One group will read just enough to

*Betty McMichael, "Summer Time Is Reading Time," *The Evangelical Beacon*, April 4, 1972, pp. 6-7. Used by permission.

get in on the festivities. Another group will compete for top prizes. The third group are regulars who read regardless of the contest. We have just as many boys as girls, but have to twist arms a little to get men and teenagers to take part. Once they do, they keep coming.

7. *Set rules and stay with them.* We give one point for each page of fiction and two for nonfiction, to encourage readers to enlarge their reading interests. We give first and second prizes to those with the most points in each department and honorable mention to all who meet minimum point requirements. The following scale for minimum points to qualify for the party allows each contestant to compete at his own level:

Beginner department	200 points
Primary department	400 points
Junior department	600 points
Junior high department	800 points
Senior high department	1,000 points
Adult department	1,200 points

8. *Keep interest high.* Keep your congregation aware of the contest all summer. See that summer visitors and other new people feel welcome to take part. Encourage participation by Vacation Bible School students. We find that about half our contestants start at the beginning, with the rest joining in as they catch the spirit of enthusiasm from others.

9. *End well.* The "party's the thing" in this contest. Everyone who qualifies for it is considered a winner. Slower or less highly motivated readers feel just as much sense of accomplishment as the "eager beavers" with more reading skill and enthusiasm. Our party, given the first week of school, always includes a picnic and some special activity such as a visit to a zoo, a boat ride, a trip to the mountains, or miniature golf. One year we had the unlikely combination of an 84-year-old grandmother, a 45-year-old father, a teenage boy, and a preschool girl as a golf foursome. Prizes are awarded during Sunday school or a church service on the Sunday after the party.

10. *Evaluate results.* When the contest is over, it is again time to sit down with your library committee and other workers to evaluate the success of the contest and to begin planning for next year while triumphs and failures are fresh in your mind.

WINTER ADULT READING PROGRAMS

While many adults enjoy participating in a church-wide summer reading program, some prefer a special winter adult contest. January, February, and March are usually the best months. Some who are too busy for much reading in the summer will enjoy participating then. And by making it for adults only you'll avoid making them feel that they're joining in an activity designed primarily for children.

AWARDS AND CERTIFICATES

Awards are an important part of every contest. You might consider adopting the method used in Montgomery, Alabama inner-city schools, where the offer was made that after students had read a certain number of books, they got one to keep.[5] This is a means of getting good literature into homes, while serving as an incentive to read, as well.

Awards or bonus points can also be given those who get other people, such as parents or unchurched friends, to read books from the church library. Trophies make good awards and serve as a reminder of library activity. Books or gift certificates from a Christian bookstore are certainly appropriate prizes for a library contest.

People of all ages like recognition of their accomplishments. Appropriate certificates can be made or purchased for presentation to those participating successfully in reading programs. One church conducts a "book-a-month" reading program, giving each successful participant a certificate at the end of a year of reading.

ESSAY CONTESTS

Perhaps you have some budding writers in your Sunday school. Why not sponsor an essay contest with themes based on Christian reading, some phase of church library ministry, or a specific book or author? The South Side Bible Church of Battle Creek, Michigan gave their contestants the following subjects to choose their essay topic from:

> I Love to Read
> The History of a Book
> Favorite Books I Have Read
> Settle for a Book
> Reading Is for Fun
> My Favorite Place—the Church Library
> Every Church Should Have a Library
> Going Places with Books
> Reading for Adventure
> Around the World with Books
> Reading Roundup
> Happiness Is . . . Books
> Leaders Are Readers

5. James Daniel, "A Reading Program That Works," *Reader's Digest* 104 (February 1974): 46.

EVALUATION OF PROMOTION EFFORTS

Stop now and then to evaluate your promotion efforts. Check circulation statistics during and following times of special emphasis to see if you can detect increases. Ask new library users what was most influential in bringing them in. See what happens if you stop using some method for a time. Then invest your resources in those methods that produce best results.

SURVEY RESULTS

Librarians sent me all kinds of good promotion ideas. Some of their poster and contest ideas have already been mentioned. These are a few of the comments and suggestions that have come from church librarians all across this country and Canada:

"We have started a beginning readers program for the children, with carefully selected books for the parents to start them out on."

"We show new books in opening exercises of Sunday school. We announce circulation for the past month the first Sunday of the month in opening exercises. . . . We have a poster contest for National Library Week."

"Our library, which has been functioning for about six years, really began to grow when we put into operation a reading program with regular awards. Our circulation doubled right away and has continued to climb ever since."

"Our library is large enough now so we can help high school students out by supplying material for term papers. . . . We are talking about opening the library to the neighborhood during the week."

"I tried one year to get a family reading program, to encourage everyone to read. The father had to read one book. One family of four children had read their required number of books and they insisted on Dad's reading his one. Teenage daughter had read one and enjoyed it very much. Dad read it! He liked what he read and said the family would read good material from then on. He came back every week or two for a book, and I was to pick it out. This went on for some years. He always wanted fiction. Gradually he was weaned to nonfiction and now he is reading Torrey, Murray, etc. He has, since starting to read, become involved with youth direction and Sunday school teaching."

"We have book reports come in from the readers and then publish them in the church newspaper."

SUMMARY

Promotion, you'll find, is more an attitude—a frame of mind—than a set of instructions. Anyone can come up with promotional ideas if the enthusiasm is there. It helps to exchange ideas and hear of what has proven successful for others; but our own enthusiasm for the job is the primary tool for library promotion.

Reluctantly I admit that available time and help are very real limiting factors. It is often said that we can do what we really want to, and there is much truth in this statement; but we must also allow for other interests and commitments. I learned this the hard way. For several years I seemed to be the only one interested in carrying on the work of our church library. At the same time I had a husband and four children to care for, a full-time job which required the earning of a Master's degree while working, and other church and family responsibilities. Needless to say, I couldn't spend all the time I would have liked in library promotion. But the Lord knew the desire and the need and brought others in to share the work and the blessings of this ministry.

It helps if you can assign one library committee member to have general responsibility for publicity. Such a person should see that all displays are kept current, interesting, and attractive. She should arrange for book talks and announcements. She will supply copy for church bulletins and newsletters. But don't leave the entire job of promotion to this one person. Remember that enthusiastic workers, convenient location, and satisfied customers of a well-run library do more to increase your library's effectiveness than all the displays and contests you can dream up.

10

FINANCING THE LIBRARY

He who tends the fig tree will eat its fruit (Proverbs 27:18).

PURCHASES OF LIBRARY MATERIAL, supplies, and equipment account for the principal expenditures of a church library. Audiovisuals used in the Christian education programs of the church are usually budgeted separately, even though they are often checked out through the library. Figures used in this chapter will assume this to be the case unless indicated otherwise.

AMOUNT OF EXPENDITURES

The amount spent is not always in proportion to library size, as some fairly large libraries have small expenditures, just maintaining what they already have and adding little new material, while some small libraries spend large amounts in building up their holdings. Expenditures may not be closely related to size, but they do have some bearing on library use. Libraries that are constantly adding new material attract reader interest and have greater circulation than others.

Churches employ varied methods for supporting their libraries. Some rely entirely on donations of used and new books. One church library among those surveyed reports spending $6,000 a year; thirteen report library expenditures of $1,000 or more, and thirty-three have at least $500 a year to work with. Survey results, as seen in table 10, show an average (median) expenditure of $160 a year.

FUND-RAISING METHODS

Church libraries are often supported by a combination of methods. Some of the plans used most frequently in churches visited and surveyed for this book are described in the following pages.

157

TABLE 10

Approximate Annual Expenditures for Library

Number of Dollars	Number of Churches	Percentage of Churches
0	3	2%
1 - 49	13	8
50 - 99	23	14
100 - 149	25	15
150 - 199	21	13
200 - 299	23	14
300 - 399	14	9
400 - 499	6	4
500 - 999	17	11
1,000 - 1,999	13	8
2,000 and up	3	2
Total	161	100%

NOTE: The average number of dollars spent by reporting churches for the library is $160 a year. The highest amount is $6,000 a year.

CHURCH BUDGET

It is the responsibility of the library committee, working with the librarian, to prepare an annual proposed budget. This is needed for consideration by the budget committee or board charged with preparing the church budget; it also helps the library determine its own needs and objectives, even if the necessary funds must be raised apart from the church budget. Careful records must be kept, so a proposed budget can be related to past expenses as well as future needs.

One writer suggests that the library budget be from one-half to one percent of the total church budget, or an amount equal to fifty cents to one dollar for each person enrolled in Sunday school.[1]

Most active libraries are granted funds from the regular church budget. Practically all leading authorities on church libraries recommend this method for the library's main source of income.[2] In addition to providing dependable and predictable amounts of money to work with, a place on the church budget recognizes the library as an important regular program of the church, deserving members' prayerful support and participation.

1. Sunday School Board of the Southern Baptist Convention, *The Church Library Development Plan, Stage 3, Lesson 2: How to Administer a Church Library*, p. 8.
2. Christine Buder, *How to Build a Church Library*, p. 14; Charlotte Newton, *Church Library Manual*, p. 5; LaVose Newton, *Church Library Handbook*, pp. 18-19; Alice Straughan, *How to Organize Your Church Library*, p. 27; Elmer L. Towns and Cyril J. Barber, *Successful Church Libraries*, p. 23.

MEMORIALS

Memorial gifts to libraries are traditional in many churches. Church libraries are sometimes established from the beginning as memorial libraries, usually in memory of one person who may have had a strong interest in books and provided for establishment of a library in a will, or whose family chose this way to honor their loved one.

A New Mexico library was started by a group of Gold Star mothers in memory of a young man who had become a casualty of the Vietnam War. He had worked at odd jobs as a boy to help his mother establish a church library. After his death, one of his former Sunday school teachers built some shelves, and the Gold Star mothers raised funds for eight hundred books.[3]

Individuals frequently place single books in the church library in memory of a loved one. Appropriate memorial plates should be placed on the title page of such books, indicating the donor if desired and always showing whose memory the book is given in. A memorial book is also a good way to record and display memorial gifts.

Our own family decided one year that we would like to place a nice children's Bible story book in the library for Memorial Day, in memory of a grandson who had recently died of cancer. After selecting a book, it occurred to us that there might be others who would like to make similar gifts, as a number of the library's most active supporters had died in recent months. We obtained a good supply of suitable books on consignment from a Christian bookstore, using them for a special display on the two Sundays preceding Memorial Day. We chose books from a wide price range and for various age levels, keeping in mind special interests of those recently deceased. Over fifty books were added to the library's collection as members selected books in memory of specific individuals of their choice. The memorial bookplates remind readers of the faithful service of those who have preceded us into our Lord's presence.

A Sunday school class or other group will sometimes place a book in the library in memory of a deceased member. One denomination placed the books of one of their authors in each church library of the denomination as a memorial soon after his death.[4]

The Israelites were told to "Write this in a book as a memorial" (Ex 17:14). Librarians should keep a memorial album with names of books given, donors, and individuals whose memory is being honored. Memorial books should be displayed in a prominent location, and the congregation kept informed about memorial gifts through church bulletins or newsletters.

3. "Memorial Libraries," *Media—Library Services Journal* 3 (January, February, March, 1973): 7.
4. "Book Memorials for Kent Knutson," *Lutheran Libraries* 15 (Summer 1973): 63.

Church leaders should remind members every now and then that gifts to the library make appropriate memorials. When such gifts are received, prompt acknowledgments should be made to donors and families of the deceased.

Books Given to Express Honor or Appreciation

You have often heard it said, "Why not give flowers while people are living instead of waiting until they are dead?" In the same spirit, some choose to give a book in honor of a living person. For example, you might offer the choice of honoring a living mother or the memory of one who has died by a gift to the church library on Mother's Day. A Sunday school class might express appreciation at Christmas time for its teacher's faithfulness by placing one or more books in the church library, with an appropriate bookplate expressing their sentiments. A pastor who has been a strong supporter of the library could be honored on his birthday or on the occasion of his leaving for another field of service by the placing of books in the library in his honor.

Book Displays

The book display idea can be used in many ways. Christian bookstores are usually very cooperative in making books available for book tables on a consignment basis. From time to time, display books that you would like to have in the library, offering interested members the opportunity to select a book and donate its price. Special envelopes should be provided, assuring tax credit for the gift. Type book cards in advance, so donors can reserve the right to be first to check out the book they have paid for.

Book Lists

Post or distribute lists of wanted books and provide a convenient means for people to respond with money gifts to make their purchase possible. "Want lists" can be displayed in the library or on bulletin boards in other locations. They can be passed around in Sunday school classes and other meetings. Mimeographed copies can be distributed as bulletin inserts or mailed with church newsletters. Let your needs be known, and people will respond.

In addition to responding to your want lists with cash, individuals or groups may purchase listed books at a local store and then donate them. They may find books on your lists that they already have and decide to give the library their copies. Be sure to indicate prices on your list and keep it up to date by indicating when a need has been provided for and by adding new items regularly.

One writer suggests that every librarian have a "dream file," in which she files cards for wanted books in the order in which they should be purchased when funds are available.[5] Information can then be taken from this file for want lists, with details such as publisher and publication date readily available when it comes time to order the books.

Book Fair

The book fair idea, used by many churches at least annually, both promotes library use and provides new books for the library. In addition to tables with books the library hopes to acquire, there should be booths and displays depicting various types of materials found in the library and services performed there.

In response to our survey, Mrs. Ruth Skanse of Evangel Baptist Church in Wheaton, Illinois, described their book fair in these words:

> I sent to the bookstore a list of about 175 books to be ordered for what we call our church library annual book fair. The library committee selects the books. After church service on a Sunday evening, we invite the church family to fellowship hall where we have the books on display. People who wish to look them over and donate one or more of the books to the library. At that time we give them an envelope with the price of the book, and they put the envelope with the correct amount in the church offering within a month's time. We make it a fellowship hour by having light refreshments.
>
> This year the library committee has charge of the complete service the evening of the book fair.

Library Day Offering

Some churches have a special occasion called library day, library night, or book Sunday. Either the pastor gives an appropriate message correlated with a library theme, or a special program is provided by the library committee. The services and needs of the library are made known and a special offering is taken. Suggestions for library day activities are included in the previous chapter, recognizing its value both for increasing interest in the library and for raising financial support for its continued ministry.

Fines

Money collected from fines can supplement other sources of income in supporting the library. If people know their fine money will be used to buy more books, they will pay fines more willingly. You might try having a specific purpose for your fine money. Post the name of a special purchase you will make as soon as fine money makes it possible. Then post a list on the bulletin board of such acquisitions.

We have found voluntary donations in lieu of fines to bring even more

5. "Do You Have a Dream File?" *Librarian's World* 3 (Fall 1972): 2.

generous contributions than our former system of fines did. The volunteer system was inaugurated after several years of scheduled fines. People were used to being fined for late books and now contribute to our library kitty without urging. Along with any system you may use, assure your borrowers that fine money or voluntary donations will be used to improve and expand library services.

DESIGNATED GIFTS

There usually are individuals who can be counted on for designated gifts to the library throughout the year. When the library's needs are made known through church newsletters, bulletins, special mailings, and posted want lists, encourage designated giving for those with special interest in the library.

Designated gifts can be made directly to the library or through regular church offerings, depending on your church's financial policies. If made through regular church channels, it is best for the donor to let the librarian know of the gift so she can plan for its use and can also make sure that the money is directed to its intended purpose.

SMALL GROUP SUPPORT

Within most churches there are a number of small groups that like to undertake special projects. Sunday school classes and departments, women's groups, men's groups, youth groups, and weekday clubs all are potential sources of help. You may have to drop a hint, but there should be at least one such group willing to take a special interest in the library. In addition to financial support, such a group can help with promotion, prayer, and operation of the library.

Financial support should be related to areas of interest. An adult Sunday school class might take on support of one phase of the cassette ministry; a ladies' missionary group could help build up the missions section of the library; and a primary department might support a vertical file collection. A young married couples class could supply funds for books on marriage and child training; a junior high class might choose to help purchase biography or fiction books that interest them; and teenagers could take a special offering to buy books by Christian athletes, beauty contest winners, and other well-known believers. Some group might like to initiate a book-of-the-month program, purchasing one book every month for the library.

One author suggests that the Sunday school provide funds for purchasing teaching aids to be circulated through the library.[6] In our church, we found the deacon board willing to underwrite part of the expenses for taping the pastor's sermons and purchasing cassette players, since these are frequently used for the sick, the elderly, and the shut-ins.

6. Erwin E. John, "A Church Library Needs Good Administration," p. 7.

Book Clubs

Encourage church members to join good Christian book clubs and share their books by giving them to the library. Our church has one lady who gives us her club selections as soon as they arrive, saying she can always check them out when she's ready to read them. That way we have the books to display and circulate when interest in them is at a peak.

Book Tables and Book Racks

Many churches sell books, often using library staff and facilities to handle sales and making profits available for library purchases. While a few churches operate regular bookstores, purchasing directly from publishers, most take books on consignment from local bookstores, usually dividing the profits on a percentage basis. Books may be sold regularly or just occasionally, in connection with special conferences.

The feasibility of such plans depends on church policy, area zoning and regulations, interest, space, and relationship with suppliers. When used, the primary objective should be greater distribution of Christian literature rather than raising of funds.

Bookstore Discounts

Most Christian bookstores give some discount to church libraries, especially if they buy in large quantities. These discounts increase the purchasing power of available funds. Learn what discount policies apply in your area and plan your purchases so as to take the best possible advantage of quantity rates.

However, don't press your bookstore for discounts if they have no such policy. Remember, they can't fulfill their ministry without reasonable profits. In some locations, paying full rate for library purchases may be the price you willingly pay to help a struggling Christian bookstore serve in your community. The store, in turn, will help you by having material available for your inspection and use when needed. Cooperate to achieve your mutual goal of wider distribution of Christian literature.

Library Stamps and Coupons

A number of Christian bookstores and denominational suppliers give stamps or coupons that can be redeemed with books for the church library.[7] Encourage your church people to collect these, both for official church purchases and personal purchases, and turn them in to the library. You'll be surprised how much they will amount to. A librarian in a fairly small church

---

7. Wesley Engstrom, "Building a Church Library Without Money," *Bookstore Journal* 7 (February 1974): 18.

told me she gets about seventy-five dollars in free books each year this way. A bookstore manager whose store gives a five-cent library coupon for each dollar spent points out that this method involves all the members of the church in providing support for their library.[8]

SPECIAL PROJECTS AND PLANS

Some churches raise money for their libraries through special fund-raising projects. Any such project must be in keeping with financial policies of the church and must have prior approval from appropriate church officials.

While a few churches raise funds through car washes or bake sales, most prefer more library-oriented projects, such as used book sales. People donate used books with the understanding that the library can keep any they need and sell others to raise money for book purchases. This gives the library a chance to remove books that are just taking space and replace them with needed material. It also provides a way of getting some benefit from those books donated throughout the year that are not needed in the library.

A librarian in Connecticut wrote to me about an interesting way that she raised book money at Christmas time. She reported: "This Christmas, I set up a small artificial tree, decorated with paper ornaments made from old Christmas cards. On the back of each, I put a title and price—then invited people to choose one and sign their name and pay me!"

You'll find all kinds of interesting fund-raising ideas in library magazines and handbooks. Several of them are described briefly in the following paragraphs.

Some churches charge membership fees for the privilege of using the library; others charge rental fees for use of library material.[9]

You might hold a "bookworld banquet" or other library fellowship dinner.[10] While the main emphasis may not be raising funds, some opportunity to support the library financially can be included.

Some churches use birthday offerings to help the library. One writer suggests that people buy a book to give the library on their birthday, bringing it on the Sunday following the birthday.[11]

Another writer suggests that the librarian organize a reading club, which in turn would purchase a book a month for a member to review for the group. The book can then be donated to the library.[12]

8. James Sabinske, "To Bookstore Managers: Church Libraries—Competitors or Promoters!" *Librarian's World* 3 (Fall 1972): 8.
9. Merrill Kaegi, "The Nature of Contemporary Church and Synagogue Libraries," *Drexel Library Quarterly* (April 1970): 120.
10. Mabel King Beeker, "Bookworld Banquet or Fellowship," *Media* 4 (April, May, June, 1974): 19.
11. LaVose Newton, p. 19.
12. Buder, p. 15.

If you have a large number of interested readers, you might organize a book club so members can buy books—possibly at a discount as members of a club—read, and discuss them, and then donate them to the library.[13]

The entire church, or some subgroup of the church, might hold an annual book shower, with donors supplying books from a recommended list.[14]

A "thanksgiving month for the library" in November, with people expressing thanks for "written words" by giving books to the library, is another good idea.[15]

A Sunday school in Canada voted to give their library a tithe of all Sunday school offerings, with a resulting increase in enthusiasm as well as financial support.[16]

One church gives its library four nights each year in which to promote the library with appropriate programs. Another has an entire church library week, with a special sermon on Sunday, outside speaker on Wednesday, library open house, designation of all loose offerings to the library, and opportunity to provide wanted books.[17]

The idea of a foodless bake sale has a certain appeal to those weary of spending time preparing food for sales to raise money for various clubs and projects. Distribute notices with envelopes, reminding recipients of the work saved and asking them to enclose the price of a pie or cake. Let them know how the library intends to use the funds raised.[18]

A library tea or coffee is a good way to present the work and needs of the library and at the same time raise support for it. You might try a silver tea, with those attending bringing gifts of silver for the library; or a new book tea, with people bringing or buying new books for the library. You might put up an "I love our library" tree at a Valentine tea, with names of donors placed on red hearts hung on the tree.[19]

OUTSIDE SUPPORT

Some church libraries have been started with outside help. Our own church has helped several others get started just by giving them duplicate copies of books we didn't need. A church could have a special program and offering to help another with less funds be able to start a church library.

Janet Jordan, in an article for *Media* magazine, describes a project in which a church in Mississippi started a "little sister" church library in Montana.

13. Buder, p. 15; Towns and Barber, p. 25.
14. Buder, p. 15; Towns and Barber, pp. 25-26.
15. Towns and Barber, p. 26.
16. Ibid., p. 10.
17. Ruth S. Smith, *Publicity for a Church Library*, p. 41.
18. Ibid., p. 30.
19. Ibid., p. 28.

The big sister church donated six hundred books and processing supplies. Two of their members went from Mississippi to Montana to deliver these materials and help get the new library under way.[20]

One denomination sends books free to their small churches and missions starting a library for the first time.[21]

Public libraries had their Andrew Carnegie, whose gifts resulted in the establishment of more than 2,500 public libraries.[22] Perhaps the Lord will give a Christian philanthropist or foundation a vision of what could be accomplished through a church library planting ministry. Many small churches are hesitant to take that first step in starting a library because so many needs cry out for funds. Too often the church library is found at the end of the list of things to be done as money becomes available. But let some outside agency offer to donate shelving and a starting collection, or matching funds, and many churches would suddenly find themselves motivated to get their library going.

A business establishment could encourage churches to start libraries by making materials and equipment available on a time payment plan. Loans to cover the initial investment would help many get started.

TABLE 11

Sources of Income for Church Library

Major Source of Income	Number of Churches	Percentage of Churches
Church budget	109	45%
Gifts and donations	38	16
Memorials	25	10
Fines	18	7
Sunday school budget	14	6
Church subgroups	13	5
Book sales	7	3
Bookstore stamps and coupons	7	3
Book fair	3	1
Other sources*	10	4
Total	244**	100%

*Other sources reported include paper sales, cash refunds, card sales, poster sales, library donation day receipts, special offerings, personal support of librarians, and birthday offerings.
**Since some churches reported more than one primary source of funds, the total exceeds the number of churches surveyed.

20. Janet Jordan, "A Big Sister Can Help," *Media* 5 (January, February, March, 1975): 29.
21. "Yes, a Small Church Needs (and can have) a Library," *The Quarterly Review* 31 (April, May, June, 1971): 27.
22. William Hugh Carlson, *In a Grand and Awful Time*, p. 48.

SURVEY RESULTS

In response to our questionnaire, churches indicated the sources listed in Table 11 as their primary sources of income for the library.

SUMMARY

This chapter has given some starter ideas for financing a new or continuing church library. Use your imagination in developing plans that fit your own situation. Let your first objective be the inclusion of the library on the regular church budget. But, as Christine Buder has written, "The library must keep pace with growing needs and new methods and it is often necessary to find ways to supplement the budget allowance to assure its continual growth."[23]

23. Buder, p. 14.

11

HOUSING AND EQUIPPING THE LIBRARY AS A RESOURCE CENTER

The plans of the diligent lead surely to advantage,
But everyone who is hasty comes surely to poverty (Proverbs 21:5).

THIS CHAPTER deals with how to do your best with what you have, as well as how to plan for ideal facilities. Let yourself indulge in a little dreaming here. Just suppose your church is planning to build a new church plant. The building committee has had a chance to see how well your library has done in spite of poor facilities; but they recognize that you might do even better in a good location. They have put you on the building committee or at least asked for your suggestions. What do you suggest? We hope the ideas found here will give you needed information (and ammunition, if you will) should such a situation arise. We also hope those who must work with very limited facilities will find some helpful ideas for best use of the resources available.

THE ROOM

The room, its location, and what is done with the room all are very important. Sometimes what is done in spite of the room is, of necessity, the important thing.

LOCATION

The preferred location of a resource center in most churches is just off the foyer near the main entrance into the sanctuary. If this can be near the church offices and the education wing, fine; but it is usually more important to be near the sanctuary. In spite of all the varied programs of the church, almost everyone gets to the sanctuary at some time. The library located near the main auditorium will be in the best place to minister to young people and adults, especially. Children and church workers are more willing to go out of their way, if necessary, for library material.

Make your library collection as visible as possible, with some glass between the foyer and library so anyone passing will be aware of the library and its services. This can be accomplished by using a window or just some glass in the door to make it possible for people to look in. Drapes can be pulled across such openings during work sessions, story hours, and other times when privacy may be desirable.

Plan for the future when choosing the location for a library. If possible, have a room next to it that could be converted into additional library space in the future. It's difficult to convert a kitchen or rest room, but a classroom could readily become additional library space.

We recognize that not every church library can have this ideal location. While dreaming of what might be someday, use what you have now to best advantage. Don't give up because your facilities are far from ideal. The library in our church is in the most out-of-the-way basement location I can imagine. Yet we have a very active program, although I feel sure we could do more with a better location.

I have personally witnessed successful libraries operating from open hallways, fold-up shelves, corners of rooms shared with other programs, top floors, and basements, and even in separate buildings. While I don't recommend any of these, my advice is that, if that's what is available, use it for the glory of the Lord.

As seen in Table 12, our survey results show that the most common, as well

TABLE 12

Location of Church Library

Location of Library	Number of Churches	Percentage of Churches
Near narthex, foyer, or lobby	69	47%
Basement	16	11
Educational wing	15	10
Off central hallway	13	9
In or near church office	8	5
Second floor	6	4
Other locations*	21	14
Total	148	100%

*Other locations include adjoining building, Sunday school room, fellowship hall, overflow room, cloak room, mobile unit, and near the pastor's study.

Church Libraries with Varied Shapes, Sizes, and Equipment

as the preferred, location for libraries in responding churches is just off the narthex or foyer leading to the main sanctuary. A few libraries are in the foyer itself or in a lounge near the sanctuary. The second preferred location is in a room off a central hallway on the main floor.

Other churches have libraries in educational wings, in separate buildings, in or near the church office, in the basement, on the second floor or balcony, in a Sunday school room, near the back door, in a cloak room, in a mobile unit, and near the pastor's study.

WINDOWS

A library on an outside wall near a main entrance can attract visitors by displaying books on window shelving. I have seen libraries whose contents can be viewed clearly through large windows as one approaches the main door. This certainly serves as a constant reminder of the library's services.

Keep in mind, however, that window space cuts down on available shelf space. You may not be able to afford the luxury of an entire wall of windows. Balance your needs for shelving and other equipment with your need for visibility.

DISPLAY WINDOW

One of the most helpful features in promoting library use is a display window opening from the back into the library and visible in front from a busy hallway or foyer. The back of the display window can be glass to provide a view into the library or wooden doors that can be opened for arranging displays. The top of this window should be even with the top of the door into the library and the bottom about three feet above the floor. Inside the library, space underneath the display case can be used for storage.

ROOM LOCK

One criterion for an ideal library is the ability to lock it. Many good libraries get along without this, and some prefer to have the library open and available at all times. If the library can be kept open without much loss or mishandling of materials, it may be fine. After visiting some good libraries that are always open, I feel less dogmatic on this subject than I used to; but I still recommend having a room that can be locked when not in supervised use.

ROOM SIZE

I have yet to hear of a church library that felt it had the problem of too much space. You always need more display space and room for growth. And yet we must recognize that the library is one of several church agencies that must work together in the use of all church resources, including that of space.

An ideal arrangement allows separate areas for children, young people, and adults. It provides space, either in an adjoining room or large closet, for storage of audiovisual equipment. And there should be work space to use when processing library materials. These various functions can be served in separate adjoining rooms or in one room, using bookshelves as room dividers.

Respondents to our library survey have an average size library of about 240 square feet, or a room on the order of twelve feet by twenty feet. But, as seen in Table 13, some are over 1,500 and some less than 100 square feet.

A minimum of 250 square feet is recommended for a church library, with at least one square foot per member for churches with more than 250 members. This does not include space for audiovisual materials, Christian education literature, or work space.[1]

HEATING

The library should be heated or air-conditioned, depending on weather conditions, whenever it is open for use. A cold, hot, or stuffy room will discourage use. If possible, the library should be on the same heating system as the church offices to allow for use during the week.

Be sure heat outlets are not covered by furniture. Placement of ducts and registers in relationship to bookshelves and other furniture should receive special consideration when new facilities are planned.

TABLE 13

Size of Library Room

Size in Square Feet	Number of Churches	Percentage of Churches
Less than 100 sq. ft.	20	14%
100 - 199	41	29
200 - 299	21	15
300 - 399	13	9
400 - 499	11	8
500 - 999	18	13
1,000 - 1,499	11	8
1,500 and up	5	4
Total	140	100%

NOTE: The average size library room is 243 square feet. The largest reported is 4,200 square feet.

1. Sunday School Board of the Southern Baptist Convention, *The Church Library Development Plan, Stage 3, Lesson 2: How to Administer a Church Library*, p. 9.

FLOORING

It is helpful, but not essential, to have carpeted flooring in the library, as carpeting is quiet, attractive, and reasonably easy to care for. Asphalt or vinyl floor tile or hardwood flooring can also be used satisfactorily.

WALLS AND CEILING

Plaster or dry wall material painted in light colors and acoustical ceiling material with good light reflection qualities are the best choices for walls and ceiling. Draperies over all windows will add to the attractiveness and quietness of the library, besides assuring privacy when desired.

LIGHTING

A dark, dingy room discourages use. In addition to having good natural lighting from windows and soft, light colors on walls and ceilings, the library needs adequate artificial lighting, such as flourescent ceiling fixtures so users can read titles, shelf markers, and catalog cards comfortably. Reading areas should be well lighted, using floor or table lamps, if needed. Additional light might be needed on the librarian's desk. The display case should be lighted, and bulletin boards should have separate lights if overhead lighting in the area is inadequate.

Electrical outlets should be placed in convenient locations, especially where any extra light might be needed, audiovisual materials used, or an electric typewriter plugged in. Outlets should be placed in locations that won't need to be covered by bookshelves.

SHARED USE OF THE ROOM

You may disagree, but I would rather see a library in a poor location than have it share space with a Sunday school class in a better location. It is sometimes hard to convince church officials of this, but stop and think about the problems created when the library is used as a classroom.

When do people use the library the most? Usually it is before Sunday school and between Sunday school and church. Well, you say, that still leaves time for a class to meet. But have you ever looked into a combination library-classroom just before Sunday school time? If so, you have probably changed your mind about going in. Chairs are set up all around the room, blocking access to shelves. People gather early and visit until class starts. They linger afterwards, while people from other classes are waiting to use the library.

The library that can stay open during Sunday school will have teachers coming for something to fill an unexpected need, classes coming to get acquainted with the library, departmental superintendents coming after their duties are completed to get next week's materials lined up, and early arrivals for church coming to browse and talk, hopefully leaving with helpful counsel and material.

If all these activities haven't kept library workers busy through Sunday school, there may be some time for them to shelve materials brought in before Sunday school so they will be available for checking out later that morning.

If your library has always been used as a Sunday school room, you just don't know the opportunities for service that have been missed. But, if that is the way it is, do the best you can under the circumstances, while working toward a change so your library doesn't stay under those circumstances any longer than necessary.

There are, however, some nonlibrary uses that can be made of a library without hindering its normal use. They may even promote use by bringing people that aren't regular users into the room. Many libraries are ideal places for small committees and planning groups to meet during the week. Pastors and Christian education workers can often meet with small groups in the library more easily than in their offices. Teacher training and other study groups can meet in the library, using its reference facilities, as long as this use does not conflict with a time the library should be available for everyone. Sunday evening meetings, for instance, are all right if the group agrees to vacate the room in time for pre-service library users.

Libraries are often convenient rooms for ushers to use for brief Sunday morning activities that need to be taken care of during church, such as counting the offering and recording attendance. The library, the same as other church spaces, should be programmed for use in the way that will contribute the most to the spiritual ministry of the church.

LIBRARY FURNISHINGS

The way a room is furnished can be just as important as its location and size. Use of attractive, efficient, and appropriate furniture will overcome many deficiencies in the room itself.

CHECKOUT DESK OR COUNTER

If users of all ages check out books from one place, the checkout facility should be desk height so children can reach it. If there are separate checkout places for children and adults, a counter can be used for adults. It is a good idea to have room for two to work at the checkout unit, with accessible drawer space for supplies used most frequently. Comfortable padded chairs or stools should be available for librarians to use when checking out materials.

Be sure to leave at least six feet of free space in front of the checkout desk or counter to allow adequate room for borrowers waiting to sign out materials.

COLLECTION BOXES

The main book return should be on or near the checkout desk or counter. There should also be designated return locations other places in the church as needed for convenience of users. In addition, library users should be able to return material when the library is locked, and even when the church is locked. There should be a collection box built into the library door or on a wall near the door, and another near an outside entrance to the church. Openings should be large enough for usual library materials, but too small for a hand and arm to reach into. The bottom of the box can be cushioned with foam rubber.

SHELVING

Freestanding shelving is preferable, as it can be moved around as needed, even in back-to-back arrangements for better space utilization. Attractive, uniformly finished shelving, whether painted or varnished, adds a great deal to the appeal of your library.

Shelving should be adjustable for varied heights between shelves so changes can be made as needed. Eleven inches between shelves provides for most books, with taller books placed in a special location or on their spines in regular shelves. Shelves should be eight to ten inches deep. Wooden shelves need supports every few feet to prevent sagging.

The use of metal brackets and clips makes adjustment easy. This type of hardware can also be used in such a way that some of the shelves can be set with the back higher than the front for displaying books face out. This is

Courtesy of Demco Educational Corp.

Different Kinds of Shelving

especially important for children's picture books and current periodicals. A strip of wood across the front of the angled shelf keeps books from sliding off.

If bookshelves are built in standard three-foot widths, they can be readily interchanged. In determining the amount of shelving needed, remember that you can place about eight or ten average-size hardbound books or about thirty small paperbacks on a running foot of shelving. Be sure to allow room for expansion. A collection of one thousand books would require about five sections of shelves.

Put little-used items, such as older periodicals, on low and high shelves. Keep the regular collections on middle shelves as much as possible. The nearer things are to eye level, the more they will be used. Remember, too, that eye level is quite different for children than for adults. Children need separate shelving and furniture.

MAGAZINE RACKS

Racks to hold magazines should have slanted shelves twelve inches deep for displaying current magazines, with flat shelves underneath each slanted shelf to store recent back issues; or pockets that hold magazines in such a way that their titles can be seen clearly. A small library with only a few periodicals may want to keep current issues on a reading table.

READING TABLES

There should be at least one reading table for adults and one for children, with appropriate chairs for each. You'll find the library will be used much more if people can sit at a table and look over materials.

Many will find the library a good place to wait for members of the family who are engaged in activities in other parts of the church. While waiting in the library, adults can read current periodicals, examine material from the vertical file, or look over several books before choosing one or more to take home. Children enjoy looking at picture books while parents visit after services. Tables of the right height for children can be made by cutting down adult tables.

CARRELS

Carrels are individual stations that can be used for study, for listening to records and cassettes, or for previewing films. They should be supplied with headphones, electrical outlets, and good lighting. Small libraries may not have any use for carrels, while large ones will use several. They are most useful in libraries that are open more than a short time on Sunday.

Carrel

SEATING

Depending on room size and arrangement, you may be able to have some seating in addition to appropriate chairs at reading tables and carrels. Upholstered window seats with storage underneath, bean bag or regular lounge chairs, and large floor cushions all add interesting seating arrangements.

PAPERBACK RACKS

You may want to place some of your paperbacks in special racks. Metal racks are available, or wooden ones can be built for this purpose. If you are interested in designs for racks to hold paperbacks, whether in the form of pegboard racks, pocket shelves, revolving racks, or mobile racks, write to Educational Facilities Laboratory, 477 Madison Avenue, New York, N.Y. 10022, for their booklet, *Design for Paperbacks: A How-To Report on Furniture for Fingertip Access.*

CARD CATALOG

It is possible to use metal card file drawers to hold your beginning card catalog; but as soon as you can, acquire a wooden card file designed for library use. Units from a library supply house can be matched and added to as your library grows. Each drawer holds 1,000 cards conveniently or about 1,200 when packed full. Since you usually have three to five cards for each book, you will need at least three drawers for each thousand items in your library, and possibly as many as five for a complete card catalog. Drawers can be placed on top of a two-drawer file cabinet or storage unit to conserve space; or they can be mounted on matching cabinets available from library supply houses.

Courtesy of Bro-Dart, Inc.

Card Catalog

DICTIONARY STAND

A dictionary stand to hold a large dictionary or concordance is a helpful, but not essential, addition to a church library.

FILES

A library needs to have at least one two-drawer and preferably at least two two-drawer cabinets or one four-drawer filing cabinet for use as a vertical file, holding such things as pictures, catalogs, missionary information, and small pamphlets.

Legal-sized files are preferable, as they hold larger pictures, maps, and other materials. Two-drawer files have the advantage of providing extra desk-height surface, which can be aligned with the desk or used to hold card catalog drawers or book displays. Be sure, though, that any such combination allows for adequate access to needed materials at any time. For example, if catalog drawers are placed on top of vertical files, try facing them in opposite directions so different people can be using both at the same time.

BOOK TRUCK

You'll find it helpful to have one or more book carts or trucks, preferably with slanting shelves, for use when shelving books, processing new books, or taking books to other locations in the church. These can be built by church carpenters or purchased from library supply houses.

Courtesy of Bro-Dart, Inc.   Courtesy of Bro-Dart, Inc.

Book Truck   "Kik-Step" Stool

STEP STOOL

Both librarian and customer will at times need to use a small step stool to reach things above normal arm's reach. Some styles can also be used for a seat when working with materials on low shelves. A "Kik-Step" stool is about the safest and most convenient, as it rolls on casters when you kick it and grabs the floor when you step on it. This style is available in varied colors from library supply houses.

CABINETS FOR AUDIOVISUAL MATERIALS

There are specially built cabinets and containers for every type of visual aid. Catalogs from library supply houses show what is available for purchase; they also give ideas for adaptation by your own local carpenters. Pegboard racks can be used for some materials. Consideration should be given to humidity and temperature requirements mentioned on containers, especially for films and tapes.

The following suggestions for storing the various types of audiovisual materials mentioned in chapters 5 and 8 are adapted for the most part from the book used as a guide for processing these materials for circulation, *AV Cataloging and Processing Simplified.*[2]

Cassette tapes can be stored in metal drawers made for that purpose or in some other type of cabinet. For our church's tape library we built small wood

Courtesy of Demco Educational Corp.

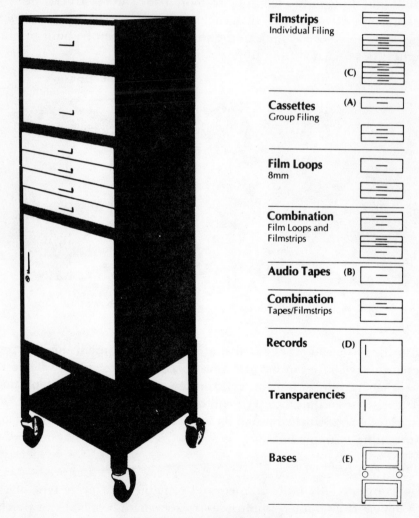

Filmstrips
Individual Filing

(C)

Cassettes   (A)
Group Filing

Film Loops
8mm

Combination
Film Loops and
Filmstrips

Audio Tapes   (B)

Combination
Tapes/Filmstrips

Records   (D)

Transparencies

Bases   (E)

Cabinets for Audiovisuals

2. Jean Thornton John et al., *AV Cataloging and Processing Simplified.*

Drawing by David Culbertson

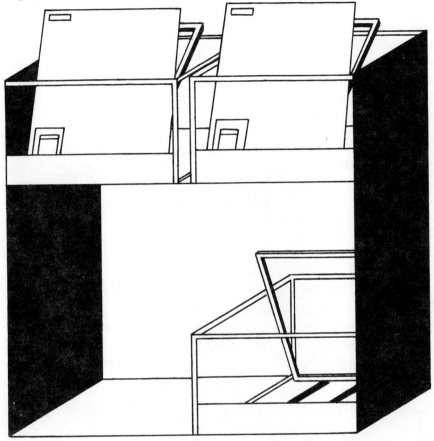

Record Browser Racks

boxes that each hold a single row of about twenty cassettes. We keep these filled with tapes and stacked in file drawers during the week. On Sunday the boxes are spread out on a long table near the sanctuary. This system works well for us right now, but we will need more efficient storage and display equipment as the tape library expands.

Records should be stored vertically to prevent warping and undue amounts of pressure. Browser boxes such as used in record shops are the most convenient for users. If there isn't room for these, put vertical dividers about every two inches on regular shelves so records can be placed upright on them in small groups.

Reel-to-reel tapes should be in boxes stored vertically on shelves with vertical dividers for convenience of handling. Regular shelving should be adjusted to the height of tapes for efficient space utilization.

Slides should be organized in sets and stored in trays that can be used with the type of projectors available in the church. These trays should be stored in closed cupboards for protection from dust and unnecessary handling.

Filmstrips in their cylindrical containers should be kept in drawers, cabinets, or racks designed for this purpose. If this is not feasible, they can be stored in inexpensive clear plastic boxes purchased from a library supply house. Filmstrips that come in boxes with script and/or sound can often be stored in their original containers.

Transparencies should be mounted and kept in envelopes, as mentioned in chapter 8. These envelopes should also contain any instructions or guides to the use of the transparencies. The envelopes can then be stored in a vertical file.

Motion picture films can be stored in their containers in racks designed to hold them. However, since churches usually own very few of these, drawer or cupboard space shared with other audiovisuals is often adequate.

Videotapes should be kept in their containers and stored on shelves or in cupboards designed for their shape. Video cassettes can be stored similarly to other cassettes and video discs can be stored in the same manner as records.

Microforms should be stored in special filing cabinets appropriate for each type of microform. They should be protected from unnecessary handling.

Multimedia kits should be stored in boxes holding the various items of the set together and placed on shelves or in cupboards. Sets made up of some type of film and sound combination will usually be housed according to the type of sound media used.

Nonprojected visual aids include a wide variety of materials with various

Courtesy of Demco Educational Corp.

Map and Picture Cabinet

housing needs. Some maps can be folded and placed in a filing cabinet, while mounted maps need wide, but shallow drawers or shelves and maps on rollers should be kept on a map case. Globes should be kept in cupboards or covered with plastic covers. Small mounted pictures can go in envelopes or folders in the vertical file, while larger ones will need large flat shelves or drawers. Framed pictures can be stored vertically in cabinets.

Objects such as missionary curios need to be kept in dust-free cupboards unless each item is stored in a suitable container and put on shelves. Glass-door cabinets are useful for protecting many objects, while allowing them to be displayed. Drawers that hold maps and large pictures can also be used to store large charts and graphs. Flash cards and games can be kept in boxes on shelves. Other visual aids should be stored with materials of similar size and use, as much as possible.

Storage of Audiovisual Equipment

A large cupboard or closet should be used for audiovisual equipment such as projectors, screens, and recorders. Keep this area locked when not in use. Items should be returned only when a librarian or other authorized person is on duty to check them in and put them away immediately.

Workroom Furniture

The ideal resource center has a small adjoining room or at least a separate area of the library where processing work can be done. This area ideally includes a sink with hot and cold water, a counter with storage cupboards above and below, a work table, chairs, and a typing table. A workroom of this type could also be used as a film previewing room.

Courtesy of Demco Educational Corp.

Dater Stamp   Book Easel

OTHER LIBRARY EQUIPMENT AND SUPPLIES

The library will have use for many smaller items of equipment. These include a typewriter, pencil sharpener, stamp pads, dater stamps, church or library stamp, charging tray, and bulletin boards. Pegboard, a fan or air-conditioner, possibly a heater, some book easels, book supports, tract rack, and shelf files are other items that may or may not be needed in an individual library.

Drawing by David Culbertson

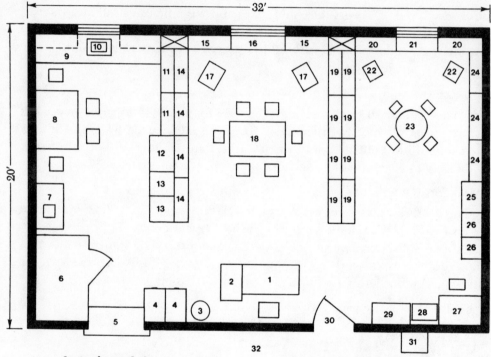

1 circulation desk	17 lounge chair
2 book truck and book deposit	18 reading table
3 "Kik-Step" stool	19 low bookshelves
4 vertical file	20 tall display shelves
5 display window	21 low shelves for picture books
6 audiovisual supply closet	22 floor cushions
7 typing stand	23 children's reading table
8 work table	24 tall shelves
9 counter and cupboards	25 double-bin record browser
10 sink	26 cassette tape cabinet
11 storage shelves	27 carrel
12 map and art cabinet	28 dictionary stand
13 media cabinet	29 card catalog
14 tall bookshelves	30 door with window
15 tall display cases	31 book deposit
16 magazine rack	32 central hallway near sanctuary

Plan for a Well-Equipped Resource Center

FURNITURE ARRANGEMENT

The way the furniture is arranged is an important factor in library use. Areas can be separated by bookshelf units rather than by permanent walls. The walls of the library should be lined with tall bookshelves as much as possible, taking care not to cover heat outlets. Lower bookshelves can be used back-to-back as dividers to separate areas for small children, older children, young people, and adults. Reading areas, work areas, and an audio-visual center can also be defined by careful furniture placement when separate, connecting rooms are not available.

SUMMARY

People build churches; but once the buildings are constructed, the buildings tend to control the activities of the people. Location, size, and arrangement of a library are strong factors in determining the effectiveness of its ministry. If you are handicapped with poor facilities, do your best with what you have, while praying, planning, and working for improvements.

12

LOOKING TO THE FUTURE

Is there anything of which one might say, "See this, it is new"? (Ecclesiastes 1:10).

THE CHURCH LIBRARIAN can never sit down and say, "Now the work is done. The library is well established and operating smoothly. We can just rest on our laurels and enjoy the rewards of our efforts." There is constant need not only to keep up with current activities but to improve and update the library as well.

Changes in society affect everything we do, even the way we operate church libraries. Rapidly developing technologies bring new opportunities and challenges, as well as a need to evaluate current procedures.

Something new isn't always better than something old; but neither should we shut our minds to all that's new. Some of us tend to resist change, fearing the unknown and our own ability to adapt. Others of us, hoping for a new solution to old problems, are too quick to embrace anything novel. As church librarians we need to find a healthy balance between these two extremes. We must examine our needs and determine what will meet those needs best within realistic limits of cost, space, and personnel.

In this chapter we will consider some of the innovations and trends that are affecting or can be expected to affect church libraries. Not every church library will be influenced by these trends, but we might be surprised how much impact new technology will have on our library operations in the years ahead.

COMPUTERS AND THE CHURCH LIBRARY

We will consider first one of the most rapidly developing technological changes in our society. It may or may not be having much effect on your library just yet. But there's a strong likelihood that it will make a difference not many years down the road.

COMPUTER DEVELOPMENT

Although computers have been with us for many years, they have changed considerably. Unlike the cheap, compact models available today, early ones were very large and expensive, making it difficult for a small institution to own one. Thus terminals were linked to central computing facilities, usually located on university campuses or at other research centers. Later, telecommunications improvements made it possible for terminals to be linked to computers many miles away through simple telephone hookups.

Next came minicomputers, smaller and less expensive. Some church libraries got their own minicomputers, usually to handle circulation and other record-keeping functions.

Development of the metal-on-silicon microchip brought on a computer revolution. One microprocessor can fit on a chip smaller than a postage stamp. Small microcomputers can store large amounts of data and perform many operations. New developments have made possible computers with more capabilities, smaller size, and lower price.[1]

Computers can be purchased with their own viewing monitors or can be attached to regular television sets. It is no longer necessary to learn a difficult programming language in order to operate the machine. Simple instructions are entered on a typewriterlike keyboard and the computer does the rest.

With microcomputers available for the price of a good television set, it is not surprising that so many individuals, families, small businesses, churches, and libraries have one or more of them. Some schools are providing one for each faculty member. Church libraries are not at the cutting edge of the microcomputer revolution. But it would probably be safe to say that most public libraries, some school libraries, and a few church libraries now use computers in their operations, and the number of libraries using computers can be expected to increase dramatically in the next few years.

A church library that doesn't have a computer just for the library may have access to one owned by the church. Smaller size makes it possible to move one from the church office to the library or to a classroom with relative ease.

COMPUTER EQUIPMENT

Computer equipment, usually referred to as *hardware,* is changing so rapidly that any specific information given here is likely to be obsolete by the time the book is in print. However, we will mention some general principles to keep in mind.

Look for flexibility and expandability. Instead of getting a computer that is designed for one function only, get one that can perform several operations and can be expanded later.

1. Howard Fosdick, "The Microcomputer Revolution," *Library Journal* 105 (July 1980): 1467-70.

Get advice from other computer users, particularly those in libraries and churches. Talk to computer salesmen about various makes and models available and about services they provide.

There are three major types of microcomputer systems available for libraries. One is called a "turnkey" system, because it is put together by a vendor who provides the necessary hardware, software, installation, and training in one ready-to-use package. A second type, the library-developed system, is simply any system developed by a given library with components of its choice. Another library adapts this system, purchasing its own components. The third type is a microcomputer system designed by the manufacturer specifically for libraries.[2]

COMPUTER PROGRAMS

Before deciding on a computer, determine what *software* you need and which computer will best use that software. *Software* is simply a term for programs to be used with your computer to enable it to do the things you want it to do. You may be fortunate enough to have people in your church that can develop programs, but there are some programs and will be more already available for use with your computer.

There are still many problems of compatibility which are likely to be with us for some time. Not all computers accept all peripheral equipment and all software, so one must plan ahead; technology is developing faster than programs. We will discuss some uses of computers for church libraries that should be kept in mind when making inquiries about computer capabilities.

If your church has a computer, it is probably already using it to keep up-to-date records of such things as membership, contributions, expenses, and attendance. The computer can be programmed to print reports, handle payroll, and match lists of members with certain skills to lists of jobs that need to be done. Some of these same functions can be adapted for library records.

Churches also use computers with word processors to save a great deal of time otherwise spent typing. Letters can be personalized without being typed individually. Bulletins and newsletters can be printed rapidly. One can make corrections and changes quickly, even adding or deleting whole paragraphs or pages. Margins are aligned automatically. Any material that might be used again is stored easily for future use. Libraries can use such equipment for developing mailing lists to promote library use, to let people with specific interests know what is available, and to notify users of overdue material.

Word processors are invaluable for church personnel who write curriculum material. Pastors are also finding them useful for sermon preparation, for there is no need to type several drafts, since changes can be made easily and viewed

2. Joseph R. Matthews, "The Automated Library System Marketplace, 1982," *Library Journal* 108 (March 15, 1983): 547-53.

on the screen at any stage. Thus more of these materials can be produced in an appealing format and circulated through the church library.[3]

Small libraries can use computers to handle circulation just as large libraries do. It is also possible to store all card-catalog information in a computer and produce information quickly on the screen. Large libraries will need several viewing monitors for use by library patrons if card catalogs are transferred to computer. Most libraries planning to do this expect to keep the card catalog operating for at least several months after transferral to be sure the system will work well.

For those libraries retaining their card catalog—and I would be very cautious about giving it up—the computer can still be a great timesaver. With the proper software and printing equipment, the computer can be programmed to print all the catalog cards once the basic information usually entered on the shelf-list or main entry card is entered in the computer.[4]

Computers can keep track of periodical subscriptions. They are helpful in scheduling use of audiovisual equipment. They alphabetize rapidly and take care of many filing jobs. They also can be used to find out where a book is located at any given time. They can generate all kinds of lists, such as all books written by a certain author. Computers will help keep an inventory of holdings.[5]

When calculating the time that can be saved by using computers, one must be realistic and recognize that much time must be spent at the beginning to feed the necessary data into computers. Many hours of keyboard typing are needed to put mailing lists, catalog information, and financial information, along with the necessary coding instructions, into computer storage. Once the initial work is done, updating is required to keep information current. Programs must be written or purchased to instruct the computer how to rearrange and analyze data. A particularly useful capability of the computer is production of lists of all library material on given subjects. Can you imagine how helpful this would be for teachers and group leaders?

COMPUTER INSTRUCTION

We all know there are computer games available for use with home computers. Now there are Bible games, quizzes, home Bible studies, and other learning programs that church libraries could make available for checkout, whether the library has a computer or not. If the library does have a computer compatible with such material, the programs could also be used in the church by individuals or groups.

3. William Proctor, "Should You Invite a Computer to Church?" 28-30, 35-36.
4. David A. Twiest, "Closing the Card Catalogue," *The Christian Librarian* 24 (November 1980): 11-12, 14.
5. David A. Twiest, "Computer Technology: Bane or Blessing," *The Christian Librarian* 24 (May 1981): 53-55.

Libraries that serve Christian day schools will be especially interested in computer-assisted instruction materials that allow students to progress at their own rates.

COMPUTER NETWORKS

Another way that church librarians may use computers is to obtain information from other sources through the computerized bibliographic search services of a research library.[6] Christian bookstores can also supply titles and sources of available books from their computers.

Church libraries can also be hooked up by telephone to other computer services. You can have access to large data bases on almost any subject through your home or church computer by telephone. You may be charged for this service, but it is expected that more free or inexpensive "online searching" of external data bases will be available in the future.[7] Sometimes a few churches form a computer-sharing cooperative, in which one church houses the computer and the others are connected by telephone.

Some sources for computer hardware and software are listed in the directory of suppliers in Appendix 2. However, the field is developing so rapidly that it is best to keep informed about current products through Christian, library, and computer periodicals. Local Christian bookstores should be able to help with software developed especially for use in churches and Christian homes.

Some people are afraid that computers will depersonalize library services. The truth is that they can free workers to spend more of their time helping library users. They also enable workers to provide services that wouldn't otherwise be available.

A computer in the church library will give the librarian one more task—that of training helpers and patrons in its use. This will be no problem for children and young people who have used computers in school or for those who have them in their homes and businesses. Others might need more orientation.

VIDEOTAPES

Whether we like it or not, we have become a television-oriented society. Most of our church families have at least one TV set and spend many hours each week watching it. While there are some worthwhile programs, there are many more that are a waste of time at best and debasing at worst.

Since it is the programs we see on our sets and not the sets themselves that influence our lives, there are ways the church library can help improve that influence. Videotapes and computers hold the key to better use of television

6. Robert Suderman, Carol Hansen, and James Sheldon, "Networks and Sharing of Resources," *The Christian Librarian* 24 (May 1981): 56-58.
7. Richard De Gennaro, "Library Automation & Networking Perspectives on Three Decades," *Library Journal* 108 (April 1, 1983): 629-35.

sets. As is true of computerized Bible games and instructional programs, it is possible to use videotapes to present Christian material.

EQUIPMENT

Videotapes, recorders, and players are available in various types and price ranges. Now that they have become reasonably affordable, more than one million homes in our country have video players. As with computers, basic types— there are two—are not compatible with one another. While it appeared a few years ago that video disc players would have the most potential for library and home use for economical reasons, equipment using video cassettes has become much more popular.

Video cassettes themselves are of two major types, *Beta* and *VHS*. It is necessary to use each type with a machine made to play that kind. Video cassettes produced for the Christian market and sold or rented directly to the consumer or through Christian bookstores and audiovisual outlets are mostly VHS, since that matches most home players. Beta cassettes are available from many companies by special order.[8]

Large churches may want to invest in industrial-grade equipment, which is usually sold directly to churches by franchised dealers. Smaller churches will usually start with the equipment sold in retail outlets.

A home television set serves adequately as a display, although a video monitor may give a better picture. The most economical combination is a player and a television set. A recorder would combine ability to play with ability to record material. We currently recommend getting a VHS player/recorder, since most programs being developed for the use of churches and Christian families are on half-inch cassette tapes compatible with VHS equipment.

Very large screens are also very expensive, so if your video equipment will be used by large groups, you may need three or four TV sets which can all be hooked up to one player.[9]

CARE OF EQUIPMENT

Video equipment is expensive and needs to be cared for properly. The following are some suggestions for prolonging its usefulness.[10]

1. Keep video equipment covered when not in use, but allow air to circulate when it is in use.
2. Avoid exposing video equipment to extreme temperatures.
3. Let video equipment warm up before use. Never expose it to continual dampness.

8. Christopher J. Hayward, "Video Cassettes—New AV Tool," *Librarian's World* 12 (second quarter 1982): 6, 28.
9. John Hack, "Getting Started in Video," *Media* 13 (April, May, June 1983): 6-7.
10. John Hack, "Ten Tips on Maintaining Video Equipment," *Media* 13 (January, February, March 1983): 28-29.

4. Store video equipment out of the reach of children and away from zealous but unqualified "mechanics." Find a secure and reasonably convenient place for storage.
5. Be careful not to bump or drop video equipment. Insist that people who use the equipment be trained in its operation.
6. Follow the manufacturer's instructions in cleaning and adjusting equipment. Have the equipment serviced by professionals when needed.
7. Treat cords gently and check them regularly.

PROGRAM SOURCES

When the first edition of this book was published, there were just a few Bible-related videotapes available. Now there are hundreds of them. Both machine and tape prices have been lowered considerably in that time.

Church libraries should consider having a supply of video cassettes to check out for home viewing by those who have their own players. By doing so they can provide wholesome and profitable material for individual and family viewing. Some libraries also check out video players, but the players are still rather expensive, and few churches can afford to do this. Most libraries require a deposit for the use of equipment and charge for the use of a video cassette.

Many Christian video cassettes can be rented from Christian bookstores. Church libraries will need to make their own arrangements for these, or they may direct patrons to stores that rent cassettes directly.

You will find a list of videotape suppliers in Appendix 2. Since new companies are entering this field constantly, it is best to look in Christian periodicals for current announcements and advertisements of new products.

PROGRAM SUBJECTS

Video cassettes are available covering many subjects of interest to church library users. Just by looking through recent issues of Christian magazines and bookstore trade journals, I found mention of video cassettes on the following subjects: Bible-book expositions, Bible stories for children, Bible studies of many types for individuals or groups, children's Bible lessons using puppets, Christian education, church leadership, counseling, creation-science debates and lectures, documentaries, dramatized stories for children, exercise programs, family entertainment, films, gospel music, New Testament Greek, prophecy, seminary and Bible-college classroom lectures, sex education, spiritual growth, study of modern foreign languages, teacher training, and teaching aids to supplement classroom teaching.

CRITERIA FOR SELECTION OF PROGRAMS

Video cassettes should be carefully selected. If at all possible, preview them. Some questions to ask yourself when previewing a tape are the following.[11]

11. T. M. Moore, "Using Video in the Local Church," 112-13.

1. Is there good lighting, lack of glare, sharpness of picture, and good color?
2. Does the tape get the message across effectively?
3. Are good teaching techniques used? Video is an ideal medium for including visual aids such as charts and maps, yet many tapes show just a speaker lecturing.
4. Is the subject matter what you want?
5. Will your prospective viewers by interested in it and benefited by watching it?
6. Is the tape length appropriate for your use?
7. Are there accompanying materials that will enhance the use of the video program?

VIDEOTAPING

If your church wants to make some of its own videotapes, you will need access to a good video camera and accessories such as microphones, cords, and lighting equipment. Before deciding to invest in this equipment, see if there is someone in the church who already has a video camera and would be interested in operating it for you. This would get you started and give you some experience that would help you decide what your long-term needs are. More sophisticated equipment could be added later if needed.

Many churches are videotaping their services now rather than just soundtaping them. Shut-ins are very appreciative when someone comes to show them the services from their own church, usually bringing church equipment to attach to their home television set. When shut-ins have their own video players, a relative or neighbor can check out a video cassette to take to them. People who miss a service for any reason, as well as those who want to invite someone to their home to see a particular service, can check cassettes out of the library for home viewing. Videotapes can also be shown in prisons, nursing homes, and hospitals.

Many people enjoy making their own videotapes of special programs. Staff members of some church libraries have produced videotapes that train library workers in library procedures and that show patrons how to use the library. One denomination has produced videotapes for new member orientation; it also has tapes for use at retreats and at special church events.

Lessons taught by some of the more capable Bible teachers of the church will be available to more people over a longer period of time if they are videotaped. Seminars can be taped and used many times. Church events should be recorded visually and kept as part of the church's historical records.

Library staff may or may not be involved in producing videotapes, but they should provide a place for the storage of the special cameras and peripheral equipment used in production. They should also have equipment and a place for individual or small-group viewing of both locally produced and commercially obtained video cassettes.

AUDIO CASSETTES

Church librarians report increasing interest in audio cassettes. They tell us that their patrons today are doing less reading and more listening. Because of the versatility of cassettes and the increase in their use, libraries should expand their cassette holdings. Some are still producing only cassettes of Sunday services and passing up much good material now available. There are cassettes of messages by well-known Bible teachers and evangelists, Bible stories for children, Scripture readings in almost every popular version, and a wide variety of music available in handy cassette form for use with inexpensive players.

While video cassettes are newer and more appealing in many ways, audio cassettes have several advantages. They are much less expensive, so a library can afford to have a good variety. They can be enjoyed while one is doing other things such as driving a car or doing housework. Many more homes have audio cassette players than video players. Cassettes can be mailed easily to former members or to missionaries. Obviously there is no reason to expect audio cassettes to be replaced by video cassettes.

We suggested several uses for audio cassettes in chapter 5. The most significant changes in church libraries' uses of cassettes in recent years have been in the numbers of churches handling cassettes and the numbers of cassettes circulating among library users. Several libraries have reported that they check out more cassettes than books each week. I have also noticed, while visiting libraries, that those using makeshift storage and display equipment a few years ago have invested in more durable and practical forms of storage. They now seem convinced that a cassette ministry is a permanent feature of their library and not just a fad.

MICROFORMS

New microforms, providing more storage in less space, have become available in recent years. Viewers are now less expensive and therefore used more widely. Churches are finding uses for microfilms of periodicals, business records, and historical records. A viewer, the only equipment required, provides access to any information stored in this manner. Patrons of school and public libraries are accustomed to operating this equipment. Sometimes computers can be programmed to produce output on microfilm.[12] We can expect to see greater use of microforms in the future.

PUPPETS

Puppets are another audiovisual aid that has grown in favor in recent years. Teachers use them with their classes. Children and young people develop programs to present to others, sometimes making their own puppets. More ready-

---

12. Ralph J. Folcarelli, Arthur Tannenbaum, and Ralph C. Ferragamo, *The Microform Connection*, p. 163.

made puppets and scripts are now available. Librarians should be able to store and check out puppets and related material.

Library Operations

As I was visiting recently with a seminary librarian who has a special interest in church libraries, we came to the conclusion that "good" church libraries were getting better and "poor" ones were either at a standstill or getting worse.

Improvements

There are many encouraging reports of libraries expanding their ministries, involving more people both in the use of the libraries and in their operation. As more people get involved, still more become interested.

Church governing boards have indicated their recognition of the value of library services by giving them a regular place on the church budget, by fitting them into the organizational framework of the church, and by providing prime locations. Church building planners are realizing that libraries usually function best when located in very visible rooms near the main sanctuary.

Needs

But not all is well in the church library scene. When a library is not active, the greatest need is usually for one or more individuals with the interest, time, and commitment to keep working at it. Such individuals also need encouragement and support. Most of this must come from the local congregation, but some can come from external sources.

Denominational Help

Denominational publications can help by publishing articles about successful libraries and by supplying helpful information for librarians.

Workshops

Local and regional library workshops help keep enthusiasm alive in a ministry that is sometimes lonesome and often unappreciated. You will need to keep prodding officials to include library workshops in Sunday school conventions and denominational conferences.

Associations

I am more convinced than ever of the value of affiliating with a good library association. These associations have been growing in recent years, and they are able to provide more help. Their publications include reviews of new books and audiovisual materials, problem-solving suggestions for library management, information about new technologies and suppliers, promotional materials, and announcements about opportunities for librarians to get together to share ideas and resources. The Evangelical Church Library Association has a rental slide-and-tape presentation called "Booker's Quest," designed to acquaint churches with the library ministry.

Among the listings of church library associations found in Appendix 2, you will find international, national, and some active regional associations. In addition check in your area for regional branches of national associations and local groups of librarians that have formed their own organizations. There are also denominational library support groups that provide an increasing array of helpful programs. Some bookstores have organized local associations of church libraries, arranging a location for them to meet and keeping them informed about possible acquisitions.

TRAINING

One of the obstacles preventing some people from helping in the library has been the reluctance people have to serve in an area where they feel unqualified. Churches have been finding some new ways to train workers. One method that is proving useful is to assign each new worker to an experienced worker who will explain procedures and more or less provide apprenticeship training. New training helps, such as cassettes, slides, videotapes, and printed materials, are also available. And the University of Utah even offers a correspondence course for church librarians.[13]

Seminaries are taking a new interest in training pastors and Christian education workers in church library work. Some now offer courses in it, and others include units on it as part of other courses. Some seminaries also offer extension classes open to current and prospective church library workers.[14] This author has visited several seminary libraries since the first edition of this book came out, and has been pleased to find not only that a copy of her book is in the library's collection, but that it is showing evidence of frequent use. All of this seems to indicate that more people are aware of library potential and knowledgeable about library operation.

BINDERIES

When church libraries become better funded and more professional, they make better use of professional library services. One such service is that furnished by binderies, to protect and prolong the life of the many paperback books and booklets finding their way into our libraries. Binderies also put new covers on valuable but worn copies of hardback books and bind copies of periodicals into volumes. The names of local binderies can be obtained from your public library or from The Library Binding Institute, 160 State Street, Boston, Massachusetts 02109.

13. Nancy Dick, "Library Correspondence Course," *Librarian's World* 9 (third quarter 1979): 7.
14. Ronald F. Deering, "Seminaries and Church Media Centers," *Media* 9 (October, November, December 1978): 26-27.

CATALOGING HELPS

Many Christian books are now published with cataloging information. You can obtain either Dewey or Library of Congress classification numbers and other cataloging information from the copyright page of such books. This information is referred to as Cataloging in Publications, or CIP, and is furnished to the publisher by the Library of Congress in Washington, D.C. It saves individual librarians a great deal of time and effort.[15]

INSURANCE

For some reason churches tend to forget their libraries when considering insurance. But even a small library would cost a great deal to replace.

Although a church librarian isn't responsible for purchasing insurance, she should work with church authorities on assessing needs. In the event of fire, flood, wind, or other damage the librarian would be called on to help determine the extent of damages and cost of repairs and replacement.

There are two things the librarian can do to ensure adequate protection. One is to supply church officials with information regarding monetary value of library holdings, equipment, and furnishings. This should be updated annually, probably at the time the annual report is being prepared. The second precaution that should be taken is to see that a duplicate record of library holdings is kept in a safe place outside the church where it wouldn't be destroyed in the event of a major disaster. Such records should be kept with other important church papers in a bank vault. If this isn't possible, the librarian may keep duplicate copies of information in her home. Large libraries will want to consider microfilm or computer-tape storage of this information to save space.

Another responsibility of the librarian is risk prevention. Don't store oily rags or flammable fluids in library closets or drawers. Use metal files for vertical file material and storage of other loose paper items. Be sure electrical cords and equipment are in good condition. Unplug those that are not in use whenever possible.

LOCATION OF LIBRARY SERVICES

CHILDREN'S LIBRARIES

Some churches are developing separate facilities for children's libraries, furnishing and decorating them in appealing fashion. Ideally, such a room adjoins the other library facilities. But whether combined in one room or housed separately, such facilities reflect the attempt to interest entire families in using the library.

15. Jacqulyn Anderson, "Using Classification and Cataloging Aids Wisely," *Media* 6 (January, February, March 1976): 23.

BRANCH COLLECTIONS

Churches are also experimenting in taking library materials to the users. One librarian has prepared an attractive "book box" for small children. It is left in one Sunday-school room for a month and then moved to another room for the next month. She finds teachers very cooperative and children excited about their "box."

HOME SERVICE

Some churches provide home library service for shut-ins by bringing materials for them to choose from. It is best for the visitor to go when one isn't in a hurry to get away, as the visit may be more important to them than the materials left with them.

SERVICES FOR THE HANDICAPPED

As the general public becomes more sensitive to the needs of the handicapped, church builders and librarians will become more concerned with providing for those needs in the library. This concern should be reflected in improvements in library facilities, holdings, and services.

The library should be accessible to people in wheelchairs and should be arranged in a way that allows wheelchairs to get into all parts of the room. Small items should not be left where they would be a hazard to the visually impaired or those with walking difficulties.

Library collections should include large-print materials for the visually handicapped and cassettes for the blind. Video cassettes are appreciated by those with hearing deficiencies.

It would be good for librarians to get some training or obtain the services of others in the congregation already trained in the use of sign language for the deaf. It is also useful to have some knowledge of current speech-reading practices. It will help those who read lips if you enunciate clearly, speak somewhat slowly, and be sure the light is on your face when communicating with anyone relying on speech-reading techniques. Body gestures are also important.

Librarians need to be aware of how best to help retarded children, retarded adults, and others with special needs. Offer help, but don't ask personal questions about disabilities or force unwanted assistance on anyone. With our schools "mainstreaming" more children with special needs, we are also having more opportunities to minister to them, and to be ministered to by them, in our churches.

Emphasize people's abilities rather than their disabilities. Be sure to talk with the person that will use the library materials, not just to the one who is accompanying him. If possible, sit down when talking with someone in a wheelchair.

Your library can be enriched by the help of people with disabilities. People in wheelchairs can work at a circulation desk or process books. One man in a wheelchair provides a valuable ministry in operating cassette duplicating equipment.[16] Other tasks include typing at home and reviewing books for the church newsletter.

CHANGES IN READING INTERESTS

If you have been working in a church library for a few years, you no doubt have observed changes in reading interests over those years. Some things go in cycles. For years romantic novels like those written so many years ago by Grace Livingston Hill were favorites. Then we went through a period where only nonfiction books were in demand, especially "how-to" books on almost any subject. Then books on marriage and family relationships became popular.

We currently are seeing a renewal of interest in light romantic, but spiritually inspirational, novels. Several publishers who had been rejecting fiction manuscripts are now coming out with whole series of this type of book. Others are actively looking for new manuscripts to meet the demand. Fantasy novels are popular, especially among juveniles. There is also new interest in old Christian classics.

While interest in prophecy seems to be waning, interest in more general but in-depth Bible study is growing. More people are asking for Bible study aids to use in personal study and in small-group study.[17]

Churches, as well as individuals, seem to be motivated to explore their roots. Church libraries are encouraging this interest by keeping scrapbooks of historical events in the life of the church. The library may also set up church archives, where official records of church business and activities are kept.

Autobiographical stories are still popular, but readers' interests are moving from the general to accounts of how Christians are dealing with specific problems. We have become more aware of the needs of people with various kinds of disabilities. Many books have been written by and about the disabled, and library patrons are showing a definite interest in these books.

SUMMARY

The church librarian must be open to new things, while preserving what is best from our heritage. The emphasis in this concluding chapter has been on new ways of doing things, but this doesn't mean there is no value in the old ways.

Basic objectives of church libraries have not changed. The same needs and problems are still with us. For the most part, the same library procedures are still being used. The necessity of keeping one's congregation informed and excited about the library has not diminished. The challenge to enlarge and expand the library's ministry is as strong as ever. And, yes, books are here to stay and

16. Ida M. Clark, "Tape Ministry from a Wheelchair," *Media* 9 (July, August, September 1979): 9.
17. "Is There a New Road Ahead for Books?" 22-25.

will not be neglected in spite of our interest in new and exciting technological developments.

Home entertainment centers with their television sets, stereos, cassette players, and videotape machines have changed our ways of learning and relaxing. Our society is becoming more and more oriented toward use of audiovisuals, often in place of books and other printed matter.

It is time for church librarians to help patrons redirect the use of the home television screen for wholesome and profitable viewing. It is also time for librarians to so develop their libraries as to help other Christian education workers present spiritual truths in the most effective manner possible.

I would like to conclude this final chapter by repeating the Bible verse used at the beginning of the first chapter, for I believe it is our great privilege and responsibility as church librarians to help others apply this verse in their lives.

> *Finally, brethren, whatever is true, whatever is honorable, whatever is right, whatever is pure, whatever is lovely, whatever is of good repute, if there is any excellence and if anything worthy of praise, let your mind dwell on these things* (Philippians 4:8).

Courtesy of Demco Educational Corp.

Audio Visual Cabinets

APPENDIX 1

SAMPLE QUESTIONNAIRE FROM LIBRARY SURVEY

THE QUESTIONNAIRE that follows was sent to more than four hundred church librarians. About half of them responded with completed or partially completed questionnaires. Their responses are summarized in Tables 1 through 13, scattered throughout the book.

Many of the librarians sent sample materials and descriptions of their promotional programs, financing methods, staffing organization, and room arrangements. These contributed greatly to the content of this book.

It was thrilling to read letters from church librarians who wrote of blessings they had received in this ministry and blessings others had received because of the ministry of their church libraries.

Librarians also wrote of discouragements and problems. Too often they were not receiving the church support needed for effective service. Many times they wrote of their desire to serve, but lack of knowledge of how to go about it. The problems reported through the survey responses also affected the writing of this book, as they revealed needs and interests of church librarians in varied circumstances.

Dear Church Librarian:

Your participation in the following survey will be greatly appreciated. Results will be used in magazine articles, a book about church libraries, and other means of promoting church library ministries.

1 Name of church _____

2 Address _____

3 Denomination _____

4 Average Sunday school attendance _____ church membership _____

5 Name of librarian _____

6 Address _____

7 Librarian is: paid _____ unpaid _____ professional _____ nonprofessional _____

8 **Number of library workers in addition to head librarian** _____

9 Approximate number of books _____ periodical titles _____ cassettes _____

  records _____ filmstrips _____ slides _____ other _____

10 Describe other audiovisual material and equipment, and location if other

  than library _____

11 **Average number of books checked out each week** _____

12 Who uses your library the most? children _____ young people _____ adults _____

13 When is the library open (days and hours)? _____

14 Are books checked out on a self-serve basis? always ___ sometimes ___ never ___

15 Approximate dimensions of the library _____

16 Describe library's location in the church _____

17 Describe any other location library books are kept or taken to _____

18 Primary sources of income for library _____

19 Approximate annual expenditures for library _____

20 What percent of books were obtained as used books? _____

21 Do you purchase new books primarily from: local bookstore (s) _____ denomi-

  national supplier _____ publisher _____ book club _____ other _____

22 Year that your church library was established _____

23 Pictures, sample promotional materials, and any information concerning the
   following subjects will be appreciated: (1) promotional ideas; (2) blessings re-
   received by individuals from library materials; (3) description of facilities;
   (4) operating procedures; (5) book tables and racks; (6) interesting experiences; (7) extension ministries; (8) problems; and (9) suggestions for a book
   for church libraries. Thank you for your cooperation in this survey.

Sincerely,

DIRECTORY OF SUPPLIERS

THIS INFORMATION is provided to help church librarians locate materials useful in operating libraries, as well as to help in selecting materials for library loan. Since it is impossible to list all available sources, a limited number of representative suppliers have been selected. Inclusion should not be construed as endorsement nor should exclusion be taken as disapproval of any company's products.

Church libraries usually will purchase materials through local retail outlets. Names and addresses of manufacturers and publishers are provided for information and to facilitate correspondence regarding availability of products. For the convenience of Canadian readers, addresses of Canadian suppliers are furnished wherever possible.

This directory consists of supplier listings for the following categories: library supply, equipment, and furniture companies; periodicals relating to church library operation; library organizations; book publishers; denominational affiliations of selected publishers; magazines; suppliers of audiovisual materials.

LIBRARY SUPPLY, EQUIPMENT, AND FURNITURE COMPANIES

GENERAL LIBRARY SUPPLIES, EQUIPMENT, AND FURNITURE

Broadman Press
127 Ninth Avenue, North, Nashville, Tennessee 37234

Bro-dart, Inc.
1609 Memorial Avenue, Williamsport, Pennsylvania 17705
Canada: Bro-Dart, Inc., Canadian Division
Box 423, Brantford, Ontario N3T 2G6

DEMCO, Demco Educational Corporation
Box 7488, Madison, Wisconsin 53707

Gaylord Brothers, Inc.
Box 4901, Syracuse, New York 13221

Highsmith Company, Inc.
Box 800, Highway 106 East, Fort Atkinson, Wisconsin 53538

BOOKPLATES AND BOOKMARKS

Abingdon Press
201 Eighth Avenue, South, Nashville, Tennessee 37202
Canada: G. R. Welch Company, Ltd.
960 Gateway, Burlington, Ontario L7L 5K7

Antioch Publishing Company
888 Dayton Street, Yellow Springs, Ohio 45387

Augsburg Publishing House
Box 1209, Minneapolis, Minnesota 55440
Canada: Concord Canada
806 Edmonton Trail, N.E., Calgary, Alberta T2E 3J7

PROMOTIONAL MATERIALS

The Bethany Press
Box 179, St. Louis, Missouri 63166
Canada: G.R. Welch Company, Ltd.
960 Gateway, Burlington, Ontario L7L 5K7

Ann Marie's Workshop
Box 948, Burnsville, Minnesota 55337

Michael M. Murphy Company
Box 1108, St. Cloud, Minnesota 56301

Sturgis Library Products
Box 348, Sturgis, Michigan 49091

Upstart Library Promotionals
Box 889, Hagerstown, Maryland 21740
Canada: Pinetree Media, Ltd.
Box 1070, Station B, Mississauga, Ontario L4Y 3W4

LIBRARY FURNITURE

Claridge Products and Equipment, Inc.
Box 910, Harrison, Arkansas 72601

Fordham Equipment, Inc.
3308 Edson Avenue, Bronx, New York 10469

Library Bureau
801 Park Avenue, Bronx, New York 13350

G. T. Luscombe Company, Inc.
Box 622, Frankfort, Illinois 60423

R. A. Newhouse, Inc.
110 Liberty Avenue, Mineola, New York 11501

Stein Furniture & Fixture Company
Box 31, Fredericksburg, Texas 78624

H. Wilson Company
555 West Taft Drive, South Holland, Illinois 60473

AUDIOVISUAL STORAGE EQUIPMENT

Benchmark Studios
Box 199, Bonner Springs, Kansas 66012

Luxor Corporation
104 Lake View Avenue, Waukegan, Illinois 60085

PERIODICALS RELATING TO CHURCH LIBRARY OPERATION

American Libraries
American Library Association, 50 E. Huron Street, Chicago, Illinois 60611

Christian Bookseller & Librarian
396 East St. Charles Road, Wheaton, Illinois 60187

The Christian Librarian
Association of Christian Librarians, c/o Ron Jordahl, Prairie Bible Institute Library, Three Hills, Alberta T0M 2A0

Christian Periodical Index
c/o Mrs. Ruth G. Butler, Houghton College, Buffalo Campus, 910 Union Road, Seneca, New York 14224

Christian Review
Box 47058, Atlanta, Georgia 30340

Church and Synagogue Libraries
The Church and Synagogue Library Association, Box 1130, Bryn Mawr, Pennsylvania 19010

Librarian's World
Evangelical Church Library Association, Box 353, Glen Ellyn, Illinois, 60137

Library Journal
R. R. Bowker Company, 1180 Avenue of the Americas, New York, New York 10036

Lutheran Libraries
Lutheran Church Library Association, 122 West Franklin Avenue, Minneapolis, Minnesota 55404

Media: Library Service Journal
The Sunday School Board of the Southern Baptist Convention, 127 Ninth Avenue, North, Nashville, Tennessee 37234

Wilson Library Bulletin
The H. W. Wilson Company, 950 University Avenue, Bronx, New York 10452

LIBRARY ORGANIZATIONS

American Library Association
50 East Huron Street, Chicago, Illinois 60611

Association of Christian Librarians
c/o Marcylin Smid, St. Paul Bible College, Bible College, Minnesota 55375

Catholic Library Association—Parish and Community Library Section
461 Lancaster Avenue, Hartford, Pennsylvania 19041

Church and Synagogue Library Association
Box 1130, Bryn Mawr, Pennsylvania 19010

Church Library Council
5406 Quintana Street, Riverdale, Maryland 20840

Congregational Libraries Association of British Columbia
c/o Evelyn Kingston, Box 399, Fort Langley, British Columbia V0X 1J0

Evangelical Church Library Association
Box 353, Glen Ellyn, Illinois 60137

Lutheran Church Library Association
122 West Franklin Avenue, Minneapolis, Minnesota 55404

Pacific Northwest Association of Church Libraries
Box 12379, Seattle, Washington 98111

Addresses of other denominational library associations can be obtained by writing to denominational headquarters.

BOOK PUBLISHERS

AMG Publishers
6815 Shallowford Road, Chattanooga, Tennessee 37421
Canada: Purpose Products
82 Main Street, South, Markham, Ontario L3P 1N4

Abingdon Press
201 Eighth Avenue, South, Nashville, Tennessee 37202
Canada: G. R. Welch Company, Ltd.
960 Gateway, Burlington, Ontario L7L 5K7

Accent Books
Box 15337, Denver, Colorado 80215
Canada: Lawson-Falle, Ltd.
Box 1144, Cambridge (Galt), Ontario N1R 6C9

Aglow
Box 1, Lynnwood, Washington 98036

Augsburg Publishing House
Box 1209, Minneapolis, Minnesota 55440
Canada: Concord Canada
806 Edmonton Trail, N.E., Calgary, Alberta T2E 3J7

Back to the Bible Broadcast
Box 82808, Lincoln, Nebraska 68501
Canada: Back to the Bible Broadcast
Box 10, Winnipeg, Manitoba R3C 2G2

Baker Book House
Box 6287, Grand Rapids, Michigan 49506
Canada: G. R. Welch Company, Ltd.
960 Gateway, Burlington, Ontario L7L 5K7

Banner of Truth
Box 621, Carlisle, Pennsylvania 17013
Canada: Lawson-Falle, Ltd.
Box 1144, Cambridge (Galt), Ontario N1R 6C9

The Benson Company
365 Great Circle Road, Nashville, Tennessee 37228
Canada: Lawson-Falle, Ltd.
Box 1144, Cambridge (Galt), Ontario N1R 6C9

Bethany House Publishers
6820 Auto Club Road, Minneapolis, Minnesota 55438

The Bethany Press
Box 179, St. Louis, Missouri 63166
Canada: G. R. Welch Company, Ltd.
960 Gateway, Burlington, Ontario L7L 5K7

Bethel Publishing
1819 South Main Street, Elkhart, Indiana 46516

Biblical Research Press
1334 Ruswood, Abilene, Texas 79601

The Brethren Press
1451 Dundee Avenue, Elgin, Illinois 60120
Canada: Christ Is the Answer
Box 5167, Station A, Toronto, Ontario M5W 1N5

Broadman Press
127 Ninth Avenue, North, Nashville, Tennessee 37234
Canada: G. R. Welch Company, Ltd.
960 Gateway, Burlington, Ontario L7L 5K7

Child Evangelism Fellowship Press
Box 348, Warrenton, Missouri 63383

Christian Literature Crusade
Box C, Ft. Washington, Pennsylvania 19034

Christian Mother Goose/Decker Press
Box 3838, Grand Junction, Colorado 81502

Christian Publications, Inc.
Box 3404, Harrisburg, Pennsylvania 17105
Canada: Christian Publications, Ltd.
Box 4188, Station C, Calgary, Alberta T2T 5N1

Cicero Bible Press, Inc. (primarily a distributor)
Airport Road, Harrison, Arkansas 72601

Concordia Publishing House
3558 South Jefferson Avenue, St. Louis, Missouri 63118
Canada: Concord Canada
806 Edmonton Trail, N.E., Calgary, Alberta T2E 3J7

David C. Cook Publishing Company
850 North Grove Avenue, Elgin, Illinois 60120
Canada: David C. Cook of Canada
4141 Weston Road, Unit 15, Weston, Ontario M9L 1T4

Creation House
396 East St. Charles Road, Wheaton, Illinois 60187
Canada: Beacon Distributors
104 Consumers Drive, Whitby, Ontario L1N 5T3

Crossway Books (see Good News Publishers)

Doubleday & Company, Inc.
501 Franklin Avenue, Garden City, New York 11530
Canada: Doubleday of Canada
105 Bond Street, Toronto, Ontario M5B 1Y3

Wm. B. Eerdmans Publishing Company
255 Jefferson Avenue, S.E., Grand Rapids, Michigan 49503
Canada: Oxford University Press
70 Wynford Drive, Don Mills, Ontario M3C 1J9

Evangel Press
301 North Elm Street, Nappanee, Indiana 46550
Canada: Evangel of Canada
Box 294, Brantford, Ontario N3T 2G6

Evangelical Teacher Training Association
Box 327, Wheaton, Illinois 60187

Faith and Life Press
Box 347, Newton, Kansas 67114

Fortress Press
2900 Queen Lane, Philadelphia, Pennsylvania 19129
Canada: Box 940, Kitchener, Ontario N2G 4E3

Free Church Press
1515 East 66th Street, Minneapolis, Minnesota 55423

Friendship Press
575 Riverside Drive, New York, New York 10115

General Baptist Press
940 South Highway 67, Poplar Bluff, Missouri 63901

The C. R. Gibson Company
32 Knight Street, Norwalk, Connecticut 06856
Canada: Dawn Distributors
3500 Pharmacy Avenue #9, Scarborough, Ontario M1W 2T6

Good News Publishers
9825 West Roosevelt Road, Westchester, Illinois 60153
Canada: R. G. Mitchell Family Books, Ltd.
565 Gordon Baker Road, Willowdale, Ontario M2H 2W2

Gospel Light Publications
2300 Knoll Drive, Ventura, California 93003
Canada: R. G. Mitchell Family Books, Ltd.
565 Gordon Baker Road, Willowdale, Ontario M2H 2W2

Gospel Publishing House
1445 Boonville, Springfield, Missouri 65802

Grace Publishing Company, Inc.
Box 23385, Tampa, Florida 33622

Canada: Evangel of Canada
Box 294, Brantford, Ontario N3T 2G6

Hammond Publishing Company, Inc.
115 East Wells Street, Milwaukee, Wisconsin 53202

Harper & Row Publishers, Inc., Religious Division
1700 Montgomery Street, San Francisco, California 94111
Canada: Fitzhenry & Whiteside, Ltd.
150 Lesmill Road, Don Mills, Ontario M3B 2T5

Harvest House Publishers
1075 Arrowsmith, Eugene, Oregon 97402
Canada: R. G. Mitchell Family Books, Ltd.
565 Gordon Baker Road, Willowdale, Ontario M2H 2W2

Herald Press
616 Walnut Avenue, Scottdale, Pennsylvania 15683
Canada: Herald Press
117 King Street, West, Kitchener, Ontario N2G 4M5

Here's Life Publishers, Inc.
Box 1576, San Bernardino, California 92402
Canada: R. G. Mitchell Family Books, Ltd.
565 Gordon Baker Road, Willowdale, Ontario M2H 2W2

Higley Publishing Corporation
Box 2470, Jacksonville, Florida 32203

Horizon House Publishers
Box 600, Beaverlodge, Alberta T0H 0C0
United States: Horizon House Publishers
Rose Way, California 94587

Impact Books
137 West Jefferson, Kirkwood, Missouri 63122

Inter-Varsity Press
Box F, Downers Grove, Illinois 60515
Canada: Inter-Varsity Press—Canada
1875 Leslie Street—Unit 10, Don Mills, Ontario M3B 2M5

Jonathan and David, Inc.
801 Monroe, N.W., Grand Rapids, Michigan 49503
Canada: Word of Canada
Box 6900, Vancouver, British Columbia V6B 4B5

Judson Press
Box 851, Valley Forge, Pennsylvania 19482
Canada: G. R. Welch Company, Ltd.
960 Gateway, Burlington, Ontario L7L 5K7

Keats Publishing, Inc.
Box 876, New Canaan, Connecticut 06840

Salem Kirban, Inc.
2117 Kent Road, Huntingdon Valley, Pennsylvania 19006

John Knox Press
341 Ponce de Leon, Atlanta, Georgia 30365

Kregel Publications
Box 2607, Grand Rapids, Michigan 49501
Canada: R. G. Mitchell Family Books, Ltd.
565 Gordon Baker Road, Willowdale, Ontario M2H 2W2

Light and Life Press
999 College Avenue, Winona Lake, Indiana 46590

Living Books
12155 Magnolia Avenue, Building 11-B, Riverside, California 92503

Loizeaux Brother, Inc.
Box 277, Neptune, New Jersey 07753
Canada: R. G. Mitchell Family Books, Ltd.
565 Gordon Baker Road, Willowdale, Ontario M2H 2W2

McGraw Hill Book Company
1221 Avenue of the Americas, New York, New York 10020

The Macmillan Company
866 Third Avenue, New York, New York 10022
Canada: R. G. Mitchell Family Books, Ltd.
565 Gordon Baker Road, Willowdale, Ontario M2H 2W2

Manna Publications
Box 1111, Camas, Washington 98607

Master Book House
Box 983, El Cajon, California 92022

Moody Press
2101 West Howard Street, Chicago, Illinois 60645
Canada: R. G. Mitchell Family Books, Ltd.
565 Gordon Baker Road, Willowdale, Ontario M2H 2W2

Mott Media
1000 East Huron Street, Milford, Michigan 48042

Multnomah Press
10209 S.E. Division Street, Portland, Oregon 97266
Canada: Beacon Distributors
104 Consumers Drive, Whitby, Ontario L1N 5T3

NavPress
Box 6000, Colorado Springs, Colorado 80934
Canada: The Navigators
Unit 12, 270 Esna Park Road, Markham, Ontario L3R 1H3

Thomas Nelson, Inc., Publishers
Box 946, Nashville, Tennessee 37203
Canada: Lawson-Falle, Ltd.
Box 1144, Cambridge (Galt), Ontario NlR 6C9

New Leaf Press, Inc.
Box 1045, Harrison, Arkansas 72601
Canada: Evangel of Canada
Box 294, Brantford, Ontario N3T 2G6

Oxford University Press
200 Madison Avenue, New York, New York 10016
Canada: Oxford University Press
70 Wynford Drive, Don Mills, Ontario M3C 1J9

Personal Christianity
Box 549, Baldwin Park, California 91706

Pilgrim Publications
Box 66, Pasadena, Texas 77501

Prentice-Hall, Inc.
Box 500, Englewood Cliffs, New Jersey 07632
Canada: Prentice-Hall of Canada, Ltd.
1870 Birchmont Road, Scarborough, Ontario M1P 2E7

Quality Publications
Box 1060, Abilene, Texas 79604

Regal Books
2300 Knoll Drive, Ventura, California 93003
Canada: R. G. Mitchell Family Books, Ltd.
565 Gordon Baker Road, Willowdale, Ontario M2H 2W2

Fleming H. Revell Company
184 Central Avenue, Old Tappan, New Jersey 07675
Canada: G. R. Welch Company, Ltd.
960 Gateway, Burlington, Ontario L7L 5K7

Rose Publishing Company
4676 Morningside Drive S.E., Grand Rapids, Michigan 49508

Rusthoi Soul Winning Publications
Box 595, Montrose, California 91020

Scripture Press Publications, Inc.
1825 College Avenue, Wheaton, Illinois 60187
Canada: Scripture Publications, Ltd.
104 Consumers Drive, Whitby, Ontario L1N 5T3

The Seabury Press
815 Second Avenue, New York, New York 10017
Canada: McGraw-Hill/Ryerson, Ltd.
330 Progress Avenue, Scarborough, Ontario M1P 2Z5

Servant Publications
Box 8617, Ann Arbor, Michigan 48107

Harold Shaw Publishers
Box 567, Wheaton, Illinois 60187
Canada: R. G. Mitchell Family Books, Ltd.
565 Gordon Baker Road, Willowdale, Ontario M2H 2W2

Spring Arbor Distributors
Box 985, Ann Arbor, Michigan 48106

Standard Publishing
8121 Hamilton Avenue, Cincinnati, Ohio 45231
Canada: Dawn Distributors
3500 Pharmacy Avenue, #9, Scarborough, Ontario M1W 2T6

Success with Youth Publications
Box 261129, San Diego, California 92126

Sweet Publishing Company
Box 4055, Austin, Texas 78765
Canada: Son Rise Products
Box 336, Cambridge CG, Ontario N1R 4G7

Sword of the Lord Publishers
Box 1099, Murfreesboro, Tennessee 37130
Canada: Evangel of Canada
Box 294, Brantford, Ontario N3T 2G6

Tyndale House Publishers
336 Gundersen Drive, Wheaton, Illinois 60187
Canada: R. G. Mitchell Family Books, Ltd.
565 Gordon Baker Road, Willowdale, Ontario M2H 2W2

Vision House Publishers
2300 Knoll Drive, Ventura, California 93003
Canada: G. R. Welch Company, Ltd.
960 Gateway, Burlington, Ontario L7L 5K7

Walterick Publishers
Box 2216, Kansas City, Kansas 66110

Warner Press/Publishers
Box 2499, Anderson, Indiana 46011
Canada: G. R. Welch Company Ltd.
960 Gateway, Burlington, Ontario L7L 5K7

The Westminster Press
925 Chestnut Street, Philadelphia, Pennsylvania 19107
Canada: McGraw-Hill/Ryerson, Ltd.
330 Progress Avenue, Scarborough, Ontario MlP 2Z5

Whitaker House
Pittsburgh and Colfax Streets, Springdale, Pennsylvania 15144
Canada: Lawson-Falle, Ltd.
Box 1144, Cambridge (Galt), Ontario NlR 6C9

Word, Inc.
4800 West Waco Drive, Waco, Texas 76796
Canada: Word of Canada
Box 6900, Vancouver, British Columbia V6B 4B5

World Wide Publications
1303 Hennepin Avenue, Minneapolis, Minnesota 55403
Canada: Lawson-Falle, Ltd.
Box 1144, Cambridge (Galt), Ontario NlR 6C9

Zondervan Publishing House
1415 Lake Drive S.E., Grand Rapids, Michigan 49506
Canada: R. G. Mitchell Family Books, Ltd.
565 Gordon Baker Road, Willowdale, Ontario M2H 2W2

DENOMINATIONAL AFFILIATIONS OF SELECTED PUBLISHERS

Abingdon Press	United Methodist
Augsburg Publishing House	Lutheran
Bethany Press	Disciples of Christ
Biblical Research Press	Church of Christ
Brethren Press	Church of the Brethren
Broadman Press	Southern Baptist
Christian Publications, Inc.	Christian and Missionary Alliance
Concordia Publishing House	Lutheran
Evangel Press	Brethren in Christ
Faith and Life Press	Mennonite

Fortress Press	Lutheran
Free Church Press	Evangelical Free
General Baptist Press	General Baptist
Gospel Publishing House	Assemblies of God
Herald Press	Mennonite
Judson Press	American Baptist
John Knox Press	Presbyterian
Light and Life Press	Free Methodist
Pilgrim Publications	Baptist
Quality Publications	Churches of Christ
Rose Publishing Company	Reformed Church in America
Seabury Press	Episcopal
Sweet Publishing Company	Church of Christ
Warner Press/Publishers	Church of God
Westminster Press	Presbyterian

MAGAZINES

Athletes in Action
Box 1576, San Bernardino, California 92402

Campus Life
Box 2720, Boulder, Colorado 80302

Christian Herald
40 Overlook Drive, Chappaqua, New York 10514

Christian Life
396 East St. Charles Road, Wheaton, Illinois 60187

Christian Reader
Box 1913, Marion, Ohio 43302

Christianity Today
465 Gundersen Drive, Carol Stream, Illinois 60187

Decision
The Billy Graham Evangelistic Association, Box 779, Minneapolis, Minnesota 55440
Canada: Box 841, Winnipeg, Manitoba R3C 2R3

Eternity
1716 Spruce Street, Philadelphia, Pennsylvania 19103

Evangelizing Today's Child
Box 348, Warrenton, Missouri 63383

Faith and Inspiration
Box 547, Pleasantville, New York 10570

Family Life Today
2300 Knoll Drive, Ventura, California 93003

Good News Broadcaster
Back to the Bible Broadcast, Box 82808, Lincoln, Nebraska 68501
Canada: Box 10, Winnipeg, Manitoba R3C 2G2

Guideposts
Carmel, New York 10512

HIS
5206 Main Street, Downers Grove, Illinois 60515

Leadership
Box 1916, Marion, Ohio 43302

Moody Monthly Magazine
2101 West Howard Street, Chicago, Illinois 60645

Today's Christian Woman
184 Central Avenue, Old Tappan, New Jersey 07675

United Evangelical Action
National Association of Evangelicals, Box 28, Wheaton, Illinois 60187

Worldwide Challenge
2700 Little Mountain Road, San Bernardino, California 92414

Young Ambassador
Back to the Bible Broadcast, Box 82808, Lincoln, Nebraska 68501
Canada: Box 10, Winnipeg, Manitoba R3C 2G2

Contact denominational headquarters for other titles. See "Periodicals Relating to Church Library Operation" for addresses of magazines published primarily for librarians.

SUPPLIERS OF AUDIOVISUAL MATERIALS AND EQUIPMENT

CASSETTE TAPES

This section lists dealers of cassettes of Bible readings and other speaking. For suppliers of music cassettes, see "Records, Music Cassettes, and Cartridges."

Abingdon Press
201 Eighth Avenue, South, Nashville, Tennessee 37202
Canada: G. R. Welch Company, Ltd.
960 Gateway, Burlington, Ontario L7L 5K7

Ken Anderson Films
Box 618, Winona Lake, Indiana 46590

Augsburg Publishing House
Box 1209, Minneapolis, Minnesota 55440
Canada: Concord Canada
806 Edmonton Trail, N.E., Calgary, Alberta T2E 3J7

Back to the Bible Broadcast
Box 82808, Lincoln, Nebraska 68501
Canada: Back to the Bible Broadcast
Box 10, Winnipeg, Manitoba R3C 2G2

Berg Christian Enterprises
Box 66066, Portland, Oregon 97266

Bethel Publishing
1819 South Main Street, Elkhart, Indiana 46516

Bible Believers' Evangelistic Association, Inc.
Route 3, Box 92, Sherman, Texas 75090

Broadman Press
127 Ninth Avenue, North, Nashville, Tennessee 37234

C.E.I. Publishing Company
Box 858, Athens, Alabama 35611

Christian Duplications International, Inc.
1710 Lee Road, Orlando, Florida 32810
Canada: Lawson-Falle, Ltd.
Box 1144, Cambridge (Galt), Ontario N1R 6C9

Christian Mother Goose/Decker Press
Box 3838, Grand Junction, Colorado 81502

Christian Publications, Inc.
Box 3404, Harrisburg, Pennsylvania 17105
Canada: Box 4188, Station C, Calgary, Alberta T2T 5N1

Cicero Bible Press
1901 Airport Road, Harrison, Arkansas 72601

Concordia Publishing House
3558 South Jefferson, St. Louis, Missouri 63118
Canada: Concord Canada
806 Edmonton Trail, N.E., Calgary, Alberta T2E 3J7

Gospel Light Publications
2300 Knoll Drive, Ventura, California 93003
Canada: R.G. Mitchell Family Books, Ltd.
565 Gordon Baker Road, Willowdale, Ontario M2H 2W2

Harvest House Publishers
1075 Arrowsmith, Eugene, Oregon 97402

Impact Books, Inc.
137 West Jefferson, Kirkwood, Missouri 63122

International Cassette Corporation
Box 1928, Greenville, Texas 75401

King Foundation, Inc.
156 West Main Street, Mesa, Arizona 85201

Living Books, Inc.
12155 Magnolia Avenue, Building 11-B, Riverside, California 92503
Canada: R. G. Mitchell Family Books, Ltd.
565 Gordon Baker Road, Willowdale, Ontario M2H 2W2

Master Book House
Box 983, El Cajon, California 92022

Master Productions
Box 66, Cozad, Nebraska 69130

Moody Press
2101 West Howard Street, Chicago, Illinois 60645
Canada: R. G. Mitchell Family Books, Ltd.
565 Gordon Baker Road, Willowdale, Ontario M2H 2W2

Multnomah Press
10209 S.E. Division Street, Portland, Oregon 97266
Canada: Beacon Distributors
104 Consumers Drive, Whitby, Ontario L1N 5T3

NavPress
Box 6000, Colorado Springs, Colorado 80934
Canada: The Navigators
Unit 12, 270 Esna Park Road, Markham, Ontario L3R 1H3

One Way/Uni-Tape
31 North Vernon Avenue, Newark, Ohio 43055

Personal Christianity
Box 549, Baldwin Park, California 91706

Praise Industries Corporation
6979 Curragh Avenue, Burnaby, British Columbia V5J 4V6
United States: 1308 Meador Street, Unit C-5, Bellingham, Washington 98225

Fleming H. Revell Company
184 Central Avenue, Old Tappan, New Jersey 07675
Canada: G. R. Welch Company, Ltd.
960 Gateway, Burlington, Ontario L7L 5K7

Scripture Press Publications, Inc.
1825 College Avenue, Wheaton, Illinois 60187
Canada: Scripture Press Publications, Ltd.
104 Consumers Drive, Whitby, Ontario L1N 5T3

Servant Publications
Box 8617, Ann Arbor, Michigan 48107

Success With Youth Publications
Box 261129, San Diego, California 92126

Tyndale House Publishers
336 Gundersen Drive, Wheaton, Illinois 60187

Vision House Publishers, Inc.
2300 Knoll Drive, Ventura, California 93003
Canada: G. R. Welch Company, Ltd.
960 Gateway, Burlington, Ontario L7L 5K7

Whitaker House
Pittsburgh and Colfax Streets, Springdale, Pennsylvania 15144
Canada: Lawson-Falle, Ltd.
Box 1144, Cambridge (Galt), Ontario N1R 6C9

H. Wilson Company
555 West Taft Drive, South Holland, Illinois 60473

Word, Inc.
4800 West Waco Drive, Waco, Texas 76796
Canada: Word of Canada
Box 6900, Vancouver, British Columbia V6B 4B5

World Bible Society
Box 495, Brentwood, Tennessee 37027

World Wide Publications
1303 Hennepin Avenue, Minneapolis, Minnesota 55403
Canada: Lawson-Falle, Ltd.
Box 1144, Cambridge (Galt), Ontario N1R 6C9

Zondervan Publishing House
1415 Lake Drive S.E., Grand Rapids, Michigan 49506
Canada: R. G. Mitchell Family Books, Ltd.
565 Gordon Baker Road, Willowdale, Ontario M2H 2W2

CHARTS

Back to the Bible Broadcast
Box 82808, Lincoln, Nebraska 68501
Canada: Back to the Bible Broadcast
Box 10, Winnipeg, Manitoba R3C 2G2

Bible Believers' Evangelistic Association, Inc.
Route 3, Box 92, Sherman, Texas 75090

C.E.I. Publishing Company
Box 858, Athens, Alabama 35611

Cicero Bible Press
1901 Airport Road, Harrison, Arkansas 72601

R. G. Mitchell Family Books, Ltd.
565 Gordon Baker Road, Willowdale, Ontario, Canada M2H 2W2

Moody Press
2101 West Howard Street, Chicago, Illinois 60645
Canada: R. G. Mitchell Family Books, Ltd.
565 Gordon Baker Road, Willowdale, Ontario M2H 2W2

Standard Publishing
8121 Hamilton Avenue, Cincinnati, Ohio 45231
Canada: Dawn Distributors
3500 Pharmacy Avenue, #9, Scarborough, Ontario M1W 2T6

COMPUTER SYSTEMS AND PROGRAMS

AGC Corporation
The Church Systems Group, 170 North Ocoee Street, Cleveland, Tennessee 37311

Christian Administration Information Systems
2797 Alton Lane, Santa Rosa, California 95401

Gaylord Library Systems
Box 61, Syracuse, New York 13201

Genesis Computer Systems, Inc.
676 Third Avenue, Chula Vista, California 92010

Ministry Management Systems
1430 Koll Circle, Suite 107, San Jose, California 95112

Personal Computer Management Corporation
Home Computer Software Division, 1171 Sonora Court, Sunnyvale, California 94086

Small Library Computing
837 Twining Road, Dresher, Pennsylvania 19025

FILMSTRIPS

Argus Communications
Box 5000, Allen, Texas 75002

Augsburg Publishing House
Box 1209, Minneapolis, Minnesota 55440
Canada: Concord Canada
806 Edmonton Trail, N.E., Calgary, Alberta T2E 3J7

Broadman Press
127 Ninth Avenue, North, Nashville, Tennessee 37234

Cathedral Films, Inc.
Box 4029, Westlake Village, California 91359

Child Evangelism Fellowship Press
Box 348, Warrenton, Missouri 63383

Concordia Film Service
3558 South Jefferson, St. Louis, Missouri 63118
Canada: Concord Canada
806 Edmonton Trail, N.E., Calgary, Alberta T2E 3J7

Creation Filmstrip Center, Inc.
Route 1, Haviland, Kansas 67059

Family Films
14622 Lanark Street, Panorama City, California 91402

Gospel Light Publications
2300 Knoll Drive, Ventura, California 93003
Canada: R. G. Mitchell Family Books, Ltd.
565 Gordon Baker Road, Willowdale, Ontario M2H 2W2

Bill Hovey Visuals
5730 Duluth Street, Minneapolis, Minnesota 55422

Master Book House
Box 983, El Cajon, California 92022

R. G. Mitchell Family Books, Ltd.
565 Gordon Baker Road, Willowdale, Ontario, Canada M2H 2W2

Moody Institute of Science
12000 East Washington Boulevard, Whittier, California 90606

FLANNELGRAPH LESSONS, MATERIALS, AND EQUIPMENT

A & M Markus Wholesale Sales
1201 West 190th Street, Gardena, California 90248

Augsburg Publishing House
Box 1209, Minneapolis, Minnesota 55440
Canada: Concord Canada
806 Edmonton Trail, N.E., Calgary, Alberta T2E 3J7

Broadman Press
127 Ninth Avenue, North, Nashville, Tennessee 37234

C.E.I. Publishing Company
Box 858, Athens, Alabama 35611

Child Evangelism Fellowship Press
Box 348, Warrenton, Missouri 63383

Christian Publications, Inc.
Box 3404, Harrisburg, Pennsylvania 17105
Canada: Box 4188, Station C, Calgary, Alberta T2T 5N1

David C. Cook Publishing Company
850 North Grove Avenue, Elgin, Illinois 60120
Canada: David C. Cook Publishing
4141 Weston Road, Unit 15, Weston, Ontario M9L 1T4

Hammond Publishing Company, Inc.
115 East Wells Street, Milwaukee, Wisconsin 53202

Higley Publishing Corporation
Box 2470, Jacksonville, Florida 32203

Living Stories, Inc.
114 Whiting Street, Milford, Kansas 66514
Canada: Evangel of Canada
Box 294, Brantford, Ontario N3T 2G6

Betty Lukens
Box 178, Angwin, California 94508

Scripture Press Publications, Inc.
1825 College Avenue, Wheaton, Illinois 60187
Canada: Scripture Press Publications, Ltd.
104 Consumers Drive, Whitby, Ontario LIN 5T3

Standard Publishing
8121 Hamilton Avenue, Cincinnati, Ohio 45231
Canada: Dawn Distributors
3500 Pharmacy Avenue, #9, Scarborough, Ontario M1W 2T6

Union Gospel Press Division
Box 6059, Cleveland, Ohio 44101

FLASH CARDS

Child Evangelism Fellowship Press
Box 348, Warrenton, Missouri 63383

Christian Publications, Inc.
Box 3404, Harrisburg, Pennsylvania 17105
Canada: Box 4188, Station C, Calgary, Alberta T2T 5N1

Living Stories, Inc.
114 Whiting Street, Milford, Kansas 66514

Standard Publishing
8121 Hamilton Avenue, Cincinnati, Ohio 45231
Canada: Dawn Distributors
3500 Pharmacy Avenue, #9, Scarborough, Ontario M1W 2T6

GAMES

Augsburg Publishing House
Box 1209, Minneapolis, Minnesota 55440

C.E.I. Publishing Company
Box 858, Athens, Alabama 35611

Hammond Publishing Company, Inc.
115 East Wells Street, Milwaukee, Wisconsin 53202

Living Books
12155 Magnolia Avenue, Building 11-B, Riverside, California 92503

R. G. Mitchell Family Books, Ltd.
565 Gordon Baker Road, Willowdale, Ontario, Canada M2H 2W2

Palestine Products
Box 605, Calimesa Plaza, Calimesa, California 92320

Standard Publishing
8121 Hamilton Avenue, Cincinnati, Ohio 45231
Canada: Dawn Distributors
3500 Pharmacy Avenue, #9, Scarborough, Ontario M1W 2T6

Word, Inc.
4800 West Waco Drive, Waco, Texas 76796
Canada: Word of Canada
Box 6900, Vancouver, British Columbia V6B 4B5

Zondervan Publishing House
1415 Lake Drive, S.E., Grand Rapids, Michigan 49506
Canada: R. G. Mitchell Family Books, Ltd.
565 Gordon Baker Road, Willowdale, Ontario M2H 2W2

GLOBES

The George F. Cram Company, Inc.
Box 426, Indianapolis, Indiana 46206
Canada: L. H. Whitton Co.
Box 176, Station "D," Toronto, Ontario M6P 3J8

Rand McNally & Company
Box 7600, Chicago, Illinois 60680
Canada: Thomas Allen & Son, Ltd.
250 Steelcase Road, East Markham, Ontario L3R 2S3

Replogle Globes, Inc.
1901 North Narragansett Avenue, Chicago, Illinois 60639

MAPS

Abingdon Press
201 Eighth Avenue, South, Nashville, Tennessee 37202
Canada: G. R. Welch Company, Ltd.
960 Gateway, Burlington, Ontario L7L 5K7

Faith Venture Visuals, Inc.
Box 423, Lititz, Pennsylvania 17543

Gospel Light Publications
2300 Knoll Drive, Ventura, California 93003
Canada: R. G. Mitchell Family Books, Ltd.
565 Gordon Baker Road, Willowdale, Ontario M2H 2W2

Hammond Publishing Company, Inc.
115 East Wells Street, Milwaukee, Wisconsin 53202

Replogle Globes, Inc.
1901 North Narragansett Avenue, Chicago, Illinois 60639

Scripture Press Publications, Inc.
1825 College Avenue, Wheaton, Illinois 60187
Canada: Scripture Press Publications, Ltd.
104 Consumers Drive, Whitby, Ontario L1N 5T3

Standard Publishing
8121 Hamilton Avenue, Cincinnati, Ohio 45231
Canada: Dawn Distributors
3500 Pharmacy Avenue, #9, Scarborough, Ontario M1W 2T6

Winnfield House Publishers
Box 25129, Colorado Springs, Colorado 80936

MOTION PICTURES

Ken Anderson Films
Box 618, Winona Lake, Indiana 46590

Broadman Films
127 Ninth Avenue, North, Nashville, Tennessee 37234

Cathedral Films, Inc.
Box 4029, Westlake Village, California 91359

Concordia Film Service
3558 South Jefferson, St. Louis, Missouri 63118

Family Films
14622 Lanark Street, Panorama City, California 91402

Films for Christ Association
North Eden Road, Elmwood, Illinois 61529

Gospel Films
Box 455, Muskegon, Michigan 49443

Master Book House
Box 983, El Cajon, California 92022

Moody Institute of Science
12000 East Washington Boulevard, Whittier, California 90606

Word, Inc.
4800 West Waco Drive, Waco, Texas 76796

PUPPETS AND PUPPET SCRIPTS

Accent Books
Box 15337, Denver, Colorado 80215

Broadman Press
127 Ninth Avenue, North, Nashville, Tennessee 37234

David C. Cook Publishing Company
850 North Grove Avenue, Elgin, Illinois 60120
Canada: David C. Cook Publishing
4141 Weston Road, Unit 15, Weston, Ontario M9L 1T4

Gospel Publishing House
1445 Boonville, Springfield, Missouri 65802

Higley Publishing Corporation
Box 2470, Jacksonville, Florida 32203

Puppet Pals
100 Belhaven, Los Gatos, California 95030

Puppets from One Way Street
Box 2398, Littleton, Colorado 80161

Puppets, Puppets
Box 2128, Dallas, Texas 75221

Scripture Press Publications, Inc.
1825 College Avenue, Wheaton, Illinois 60187

Standard Publishing
8121 Hamilton Avenue, Cincinnati, Ohio 45231

Sweet Publishing Company
Box 4055, Austin, Texas 78765

RECORDS, MUSIC CASSETTES, AND CARTRIDGES

Back to the Bible Broadcast
Box 82808, Lincoln, Nebraska 68501
Canada: Box 10, Winnipeg, Manitoba R3C 2G2

The Benson Company
365 Great Circle Road, Nashville, Tennessee 37228
Canada: Lawson-Falle, Ltd.
Box 1144, Cambridge (Galt), Ontario N1R 6C9

Bethany House Publishers
6820 Auto Club Road, Minneapolis, Minnesota 55438

Calvary Records, Inc.
142 8th Avenue, North, Nashville, Tennessee 37203

Concordia Publishing House
3558 South Jefferson, St. Louis, Missouri 63118
Canada: Concord Canada
806 Edmonton Trail, N.E., Calgary, Alberta T2E 3J7

Destiny Records
Box 545, Corona del Mar, California 92625

Dynamic Media
718 Sixth Avenue South, Nashville, Tennessee 37203

Faith and Life Press
Box 347, Newton, Kansas 67114

Gospel Light Publications
2300 Knoll Drive, Ventura, California 93003
Canada: R. G. Mitchell Family Books, Ltd.
565 Gordon Baker Road, Willowdale, Ontario M2H 2W2

Manna Music, Inc. & Manna Records
2111 Kenmere Avenue, Burbank, California 91504

Praise Industries
6979 Curragh Avenue, Burnaby, British Columbia V5J 4V6
United States: 1308 Meador Street, Unit C-5, Bellingham, Washington 98225

Scripture Press Publications, Inc.
1825 College Avenue, Wheaton, Illinois 60187
Canada: Scripture Press Publications, Ltd.
104 Consumers Drive, Whitby, Ontario L1N 5T3

Servant Publications
Box 8617, Ann Arbor, Michigan 48107

Singspiration Music & Records
1415 Lake Drive, S.E., Grand Rapids, Michigan 49506
Canada: R. G. Mitchell Family Books, Ltd.
565 Gordon Baker Road, Willowdale, Ontario M2H 2W2

Standard Publishing
8121 Hamilton Avenue, Cincinnati, Ohio 45231
Canada: Dawn Distributors
3500 Pharmacy Avenue, #9, Scarborough, Ontario M1W 2T6

H. Wilson Company
555 West Taft Drive, South Holland, Illinois 60473

Windy Distributor Company
13624 East Highway 350, Kansas City, Missouri 64138

Word, Inc.
4800 West Waco Drive, Waco, Texas 76796
Canada: Word of Canada
Box 6900, Vancouver, British Columbia V6B 4B5

REEL-TO-REEL TAPES

The Benson Company
365 Great Circle Road, Nashville, Tennessee 37228

Canada: Lawson-Falle, Ltd.
Box 1144, Cambridge (Galt), Ontario N1R 6C9

Dynamic Media
718 Sixth Avenue, South, Nashville, Tennessee 37203

R. G. Mitchell Family Books, Ltd.
565 Gordon Baker Road, Willowdale, Ontario, Canada M2H 2W2

H. Wilson Company
555 West Taft Drive, South Holland, Illinois 60473

SLIDES

Augsburg Publishing House
Box 1209, Minneapolis, Minnesota 55440
Canada: Concord Canada
806 Edmonton Trail, N.E., Calgary, Alberta T2E 3J7

Bible Believers' Evangelistic Association, Inc.
Route 3, Box 92, Sherman, Texas 75090

Concordia Publishing House
3558 South Jefferson Avenue, St. Louis, Missouri 63118
Canada: Concord Canada
806 Edmonton Trail, N.E., Calgary, Alberta T2E 3J7

Master Book House
Box 983, El Cajon, California 92022

TEACHING PICTURES

Augsburg Publishing House
Box 1209, Minneapolis, Minnesota 55440
Canada: Concord Canada
806 Edmonton Trail, N.E., Calgary, Alberta T2E 3J7

David C. Cook Publishing Company
850 North Grove Avenue, Elgin, Illinois 60120
Canada: David C. Cook Publishing
4141 Weston Road, Unit 15, Weston, Ontario M9L 1T4

Higley Publishing Corporation
Box 2470, Jacksonville, Florida 32203

Scripture Press Publications, Inc.
1825 College Avenue, Wheaton, Illinois 60187
Canada: Scripture Press Publications, Ltd.
104 Consumers Drive, Whitby, Ontario L1N 5T3

Standard Publishing
8121 Hamilton Avenue, Cincinnati, Ohio 45231
Canada: Dawn Distributors
3500 Pharmacy Avenue, #9, Scarborough, Ontario M1W 2T6

Sweet Publishing Company
Box 4055, Austin, Texas 78765
Canada: Son Rise Products
Box 336, Cambridge CG, Ontario N1R 4G7

Union Gospel Press Division
Box 6059, Cleveland, Ohio 44101

TRANSPARENCIES FOR OVERHEAD PROJECTORS

Bible Believers' Evangelistic Association, Inc.
Route 3, Box 92, Sherman, Texas 75090

David C. Cook Publishing Company
850 North Grove Avenue, Elgin, Illinois 60120
Canada: David C. Cook Publishing
4141 Weston Road, Unit 15, Weston, Ontario M9L 1T4

Dynamic Media
718 Sixth Avenue, South, Nashville, Tennessee 37203

Faith Venture Visuals, Inc.
Box 423, Lititz, Pennsylvania 17543

General Audio Visual Company
333 West Merrick Road, Valley Stream, New York 11580

Bill Hovey Visuals
5730 Duluth Street, Minneapolis, Minnesota 55422

R. G. Mitchell Family Books, Ltd.
565 Gordon Baker Road, Willowdale, Ontario, Canada M2H 2W2

Moody Press
2101 West Howard Street, Chicago, Illinois 60645
Canada: R. G. Mitchell Family Books, Ltd.
565 Gordon Baker Road, Willowdale, Ontario M2H 2W2

3M Company
3M Center, St. Paul, Minnesota 55101

H. Wilson Company
555 West Taft Drive, South Holland, Illinois 60473

VIDEO CASSETTES

Agape Ministries
Box 6006, Titusville, Florida 32780

The Benson Company
365 Great Circle Drive, Nashville, Tennessee 37228

Bible Believers' Evangelistic Association, Inc.
Route 3, Box 92, Sherman, Texas 75090

Bible Study Hour Video Cassettes
1716 Spruce Street, Philadelphia, Pennsylvania 19103

CLP Video
Box 983, El Cajon, California 92022

Cathedral Films, Inc.
Box 4029, Westlake Village, California 91359

Christian Mother Goose Publishers/Decker Press, Inc.
Box 3838, Grand Junction, Colorado 81502

David C. Cook Publishers
850 North Grove Avenue, Elgin, Illinois 60120

Covenant Video
3200 West Foster Avenue, Chicago, Illinois 60625

Crown Video Service, Inc.
Box 844, Wheaton, Illinois 60189

Family Video Center
Development Services, Spring Arbor Distributors
5600 N.E. Hassalo Street, Portland, Oregon 97213

George Fox College Television Center
Newberg, Oregon 97132

Gospel Light Publications—G. L. Media
2300 Knoll Drive, Ventura, California 93003

See-Hear Industries
Box 4529, Carson, California 90749

Standard Publishing
8121 Hamilton Avenue, Cincinnati, Ohio 45231

Tyndale Christian Video
336 Gundersen Drive, Wheaton, Illinois 60187

VCI Home Video
6535 East Skelly Drive, Tulsa, Oklahoma 74145

Video Bible Library, Inc.
Box 17515, Portland, Oregon 97217

Video Dynamics
Box 20330, Jackson, Mississippi 39209

Video Equipping Ministries
Box 1619, Morristown, Tennessee 37814

Video Ministries, Inc.
Box 5886, Tacoma, Washington 98405

Video Outreach
5159 Cahuenga Boulevard, North Hollywood, California 91601

Vision Video
2030 Wentz Church Road, Worcester, Pennsylvania 19490

Word Home Video Unit
4800 West Waco Drive, Waco, Texas 76796

World Wide Pictures
1201 Hennepin Avenue, Minneapolis, Minnesota 55403

EQUIPMENT FOR USE WITH AUDIOVISUAL MATERIALS

Cassette Recorders, Players, and Duplicators

Broadman Press
127 Ninth Avenue, North, Nashville, Tennessee 37234

Christian Duplications International, Inc.
1710 Lee Road, Orlando, Florida 32810
Canada: Lawson-Falle, Ltd.
Box 1144, Cambridge (Galt), Ontario N1R 6C9

Dukane Corporation
2900 Dukane Drive, St. Charles, Illinois 60174

General Audio Visual Company
333 West Merrick Road, Valley Stream, New York 11580

Long's Electronics
Box 11347, Birmingham, Alabama 35202

One Way/Uni-Tape
31 North Vernon Avenue, Newark, Ohio 43055

Praise Industries
6979 Curragh Avenue, Burnaby, British Columbia V5J 4V6
United States: 1308 Meador Street, Unit C-5, Bellingham, Washington 98225

Recordex Corporation
1935 Delk Industrial Boulevard, Marietta, Georgia 30067

H. Wilson Company
555 West Taft Drive, South Holland, Illinois 60473

Display Boards and Chalkboards

A & M Markus Wholesale
1201 West 190th Street, Gardena, California 90248

C.E.I. Publishing Company
Box 858, Athens, Alabama 35611

Claridge Products and Equipment, Inc.
Box 910, Harrison, Arkansas 72601

Hammond Publishing Company, Inc.
115 East Wells Street, Milwaukee, Wisconsin 53202

Palestine Products
Box 605, Calimesa Plaza, Calimesa, California 92320

Standard Publishing
8121 Hamilton Avenue, Cincinnati, Ohio 45231
Canada: Dawn Distributors
3500 Pharmacy Avenue, #9, Scarborough, Ontario M1W 2T6

Universal Bulletin Board Company, Inc.
920 Broadway, New York, New York 10010

Projectors

Bell & Howell
Audio Visual Products Division
7100 McCormick Road, Chicago, Illinois 60645

C.E.I. Publishing Company
Box 858, Athens, Alabama 35611

David C. Cook Publishing Company
850 North Grove Avenue, Elgin, Illinois 60120
Canada: David C. Cook Publishing
4141 Weston Road, Unit 15, Weston, Ontario M9L 1T4

Audio Visual Division, Dukane Corporation
2900 Dukane Drive, St. Charles, Illinois 60174

Faith Venture Visuals, Inc.
Box 423, Lititz, Pennsylvania 17543

General Audio Visual Company
333 West Merrick Road, Valley Stream, New York 11580

G. T. Luscombe Company
Box 622, Frankfort, Illinois 60423

3M Company
3M Center, St. Paul, Minnesota 55101

H. Wilson Company
555 West Taft Drive, South Holland, Illinois 60473

Screens

Broadman Press
127 Ninth Avenue, North, Nashville, Tennessee 37234

C.E.I. Publishing Company
Box 858, Athens, Alabama 35611

Dynamic Media
718 Sixth Avenue, South, Nashville, Tennessee 37203

General Audio Visual Company
333 West Merrick Road, Valley Stream, New York 11580

G. T. Luscombe Company
Box 622, Frankfort, Illinois 60423

APPENDIX 3

CLASSIFICATION SYSTEM FOR CHURCH LIBRARIES

THE CLASSIFICATION NUMBERS given in this appendix are those selected from the eighteenth edition of the Dewey system as being most appropriate for church libraries. Each library should make its own adaptations by crossing off unneeded numbers, adding others (using a public library copy, if necessary), changing wording where desirable, expanding sections as needed.

Before using the numbers listed in this appendix, be sure to read the discussion of classification in chapter 7, especially its explanation of the Dewey system and how to use standard subdivisions and the area table.

Since church libraries often have some materials that fall outside the 200 series, Dewey's "Second Summary," with 100 divisions of the entire system, is reprinted here. If these numbers don't provide all you need, choose others from schedules in the latest *Dewey Decimal Classification and Relative Index* or from an abridged edition.

The 200 series is broken down into more subdivisions, since most church library materials fall within these numbers. An area table, with notations to be used with other numbers, follows the list selected from the 200 series.

SECOND SUMMARY

THE 100 DIVISIONS

000   Generalities
010   Bibliographies & catalogs
020   Library & information sciences
030   General encyclopedic works
040
050   General serial publications

Reprinted with permission from *Edition 18 Dewey Decimal Classification and Relative Index,* volume 1: *Introduction. Tables,* p. 450.

060	General organizations & museology
070	Journalism, publishing, newspapers
080	General collections
090	Manuscripts & book rarities
100	Philosophy & related disciplines
110	Metaphysics
120	Knowledge, cause, purpose, man
130	Popular & parapsychology, occultism
140	Specific philosophical viewpoints
150	Psychology
160	Logic
170	Ethics (Moral philosophy)
180	Ancient, medieval, Oriental
190	Modern Western philosophy
200	Religion
210	Natural religion
220	Bible
230	Christian doctrinal theology
240	Christian moral & devotional
250	Local church & religious orders
260	Social & ecclesiastical theology
270	History & geography of church
280	Christian denominations & sects
290	Other religions & comparative
300	The social sciences
310	Statistics
320	Political science
330	Economics
340	Law
350	Public administration
360	Social pathology & services
370	Education
380	Commerce
390	Customs & folklore
400	Language
410	Linguistics
420	English & Anglo-Saxon languages

430	Germanic languages	German
440	Romance languages	French
450	Italian, Romanian, Rhaeto-Romanic
460	Spanish & Portuguese languages
470	Italic languages	Latin
480	Hellenic	Classical	Greek
490	Other languages

500	Pure sciences
510	Mathematics
520	Astronomy & allied sciences
530	Physics
540	Chemistry & allied sciences
550	Sciences of earth & other worlds
560	Paleontology
570	Life sciences
580	Botanical sciences
590	Zoological sciences

600	Technology (Applied sciences)
610	Medical sciences
620	Engineering & allied operations
630	Agriculture & related
640	Domestic arts & sciences
650	Managerial services
660	Chemical & related technologies
670	Manufactures
680	Miscellaneous manufactures
690	Buildings

700	The arts
710	Civic & landscape art
720	Architecture
730	Plastic arts	Sculpture
740	Drawing, decorative & minor arts
750	Painting & paintings
760	Graphic arts	Prints
770	Photography & photographs
780	Music
790	Recreational & performing arts

800	Literature (Belles-lettres)
810	American literature in English
820	English & Anglo-Saxon literatures
830	Literatures of Germanic languages
840	Literatures of Romance languages
850	Italian, Romanian, Rhaeto-Romanic
860	Spanish & Portuguese literatures
870	Italic languages literatures Latin
880	Hellenic languages literatures
890	Literatures of other languages

900	General geography & history
910	General geography Travel
920	General biography & genealogy
930	General history of ancient world
940	General history of Europe
950	General history of Asia
960	General history of Africa
970	General history of North America
980	General history of South America
990	General history of other areas

SELECTED DEWEY CLASSIFICATION NUMBERS IN THE 200 (RELIGION) SERIES

Some of the classification numbers listed are included for information purposes rather than for actual use. Usually these are headings under which are also listed subheadings that may be used in place of the headings. In some cases, the higher level is omitted entirely. For example the Dewey system assigns 222.3 to the books of Judges and Ruth, but a church librarian will usually use the next level which assigns 222.32 to Judges and 222.35 to Ruth. Thus, the 222.3 level is omitted. In the case of the first five books of the Old Testament, 222.1 is left in as it can be used for general books dealing with the entire Pentateuch, while 222.11 would be used for a book dealing with Genesis alone. Thus, both levels are included.

Suggestions for individualized adaptations of this list appear at the end of the 200 series listing.

200	Religion
201	Philosophy and theory of Christanity
202	Miscellany of Christianity
203	Dictionaries, encyclopedias, concordances of Christianity
204	General special

205	Serial publications of Christianity
206	Organizations of Christianity
207	Study and teaching of Christianity
207.1	Schools and courses
207.11	Colleges and universities
207.12	Secondary schools
207.3	Other educational aspects
208	Collections of Christianity
209	Historical and geographical treatment of Christianity and Christian thought
210	Natural religion
211	God
212	Nature of God
213	Creation
214	Theodicy
215	Science and religion
215.2	Astronomy
215.7	Life sciences
215.72	Anthropology and ethnology
215.74	Biology and natural history
215.8	Archeology
215.9	Technology
216	Good and evil
217	Worship and prayer
218	Man
219	Analogy
220	Bible (study) ⟶ 220.09 History of
220.1	Origins and authenticity
220.12	Canon
220.13	Inspiration
220.14	Authorship
220.15	Prophetic message
220.2	Concordances and indexes
220.3	Dictionaries and encyclopedias
220.4	Original texts and early versions
220.5	Modern versions
220.6	Interpretation and criticism
220.7	Commentaries
220.8	Special subjects treated in Bible
220.9	Geography, history, chronology of Bible lands in Bible times
221	Old Testament

220.91 Women of Bible
220.92 Couples
220.93 Men of the Bible
220.95 Bible Stories

222	Historical books of Old Testament
222.1	Pentateuch
✓222.11	Genesis
222.12	Exodus
✓222.13	Leviticus
222.14	Numbers
✓222.15	Deuteronomy
222.16	Ten Commandments
222.2	Joshua
222.32	Judges
222.35	Ruth
222.43	Samuel 1
222.44	Samuel 2
222.53	Kings 1
222.54	Kings 2
222.63	Chronicles 1
222.64	Chronicles 2
✓222.7	Ezra
222.8	Nehemiah
222.9	Esther
223	Poetic books of Old Testament
✓223.1	Job
223.2	Psalms
✓223.7	Proverbs
223.8	Ecclesiastes
✓223.9	Song of Solomon
224	Prophetic books of Old Testament
✓224.1	Isaiah
✓224.2	Jeremiah
224.3	Lamentations
224.4	Ezekiel
224.5	Daniel
224.6	Hosea
224.7	Joel
224.8	Amos
✓224.9	Minor prophets
224.91	Obadiah
224.92	Jonah
224.93	Micah
224.94	Nahum
✓224.95	Habakkuk

224.96   Zephaniah
224.97   Haggai
224.98   Zechariah
✓224.99 Malachi
✓225   New Testament → 225.1 *Apostle Lives*
226   Gospels and Acts   225.7 *Dictionary of NT*
✓226.1   Harmonies of the Gospels
226.2   Matthew
✓226.3   Mark
✓226.4   Luke
226.5   John
✓226.6   Acts of Apostles
226.7   Miracles
✓226.8   Parables
✓226.9   Sermon on Mount
226.93   Beatitudes
226.96   Lord's Prayer
227   Epistles
✓227.1   Romans
✓227.2   Corinthians 1
227.3   Corinthians 2
✓227.4   Galatians
227.5   Ephesians
✓227.6   Philippians
227.7   Colossians
227.81   Thessalonians 1
227.82   Thessalonians 2
✓227.83 Timothy 1
227.84   Timothy 2
227.85   Titus
227.86   Philemon
✓227.87 Hebrews
227.91   James
✓227.92 Peter 1
227.93   Peter 2
227.94   John 1
227.95   John 2
227.96   John 3
227.97   Jude
✓228   Revelation
229   Apocrypha, pseudepigrapha, deuterocanonical works

230   Christian doctrinal theology
231   God, Trinity, Godhead
231.1   God the Father, Creator
231.2   God the Son, Redeemer
231.3   God the Holy ~~Ghost~~ Spirit
231.4   Attributes
231.5   Providence — will of God
231.6   Love and wisdom
231.7   Sovereignty
231.73 Miracles — Healing
231.74 Revelation
231.8   Justice and goodness
232   Jesus Christ and his family   Christology
232.1   Incarnation and messiahship of Christ
232.2   Christ as Logos
232.3   Atonement of Christ
232.4   Sacrifice of Christ
232.5   Resurrection of Christ
232.6   Second coming of Christ
232.7   Judgment of Christ
232.8   Natures of Christ
232.9   Doctrines on family and life of Jesus — commitment
232.91 Mary, mother of Jesus
232.92 Infancy of Jesus
232.93 Mary's husband and parents
232.94 John the Baptist
232.95 Public life of Jesus
232.96 Passion and death of Jesus
232.97 Resurrection, appearances, ascension of Jesus
233   Man
233.1   Creation and fall
233.2   Sin
234   Salvation
234.1   Grace
234.2   Faith
234.3   Redemption
234.4   Regeneration
234.5   Repentance and forgiveness
234.6   Obedience
234.7   Justification
234.8   Sanctification

234.9   Predestination and free will
235   Spiritual beings
235.3   Celestial hierarchy
235.4   Devils
235.47   Satan
236   Eschatology
236.1   Death
236.2   Future state of man
236.24   Heaven
236.25   Hell
236.3   Millennium
236.8   Resurrection of the dead
236.9   Last judgment
237   [Unassigned]   *famous women*
238   Creeds, confessions of faith, covenants, catechisms
239   Apologetics and polemics
240   Christian <u>moral</u> and devotional theology
241   Moral theology
242   Devotional literature
242.1   Classics of meditation and contemplation
242.2   For daily use
242.3   For religious occasions
242.33   Advent and Christmas
242.34   Lent
242.35   Holy Week
242.36   Easter
242.37   Other feast and fast days
242.4   For consolation in times of illness, troubles, bereavement
242.7   Specific prayers and groups of prayers
242.8   Collections of prayers
243   Evangelistic writings for individuals and families
244   [Unassigned]
245   Hymns without music
246   Art in Christianity
247   Church furnishings and related articles
248   Practice of religion in personal and family life   **Personal religion**
248.2   Religious experience
248.24   Converts and conversion
248.273 Fasting and abstinence
248.29   Other, including stigmata, speaking in tongues (glossolalia), pil-
         grimages

248.3   Private worship, prayer, meditation, contemplation
248.4   Guides to conduct of Christian life
248.5   Witness bearing - Evangelism
248.6   Stewardship   248.84 women   248.85 men
249   Christian worship in family life   (Family Worship) 264
250   Local Christian church and Christian religious orders
251   Preaching - helps
252   Texts of sermons
253   Secular clergymen and pastoral duties 253.5 counseling
254   Parish government and administration
254.3   Radio and television work - communication
254.4   Public relations and publicity
254.5   Membership
254.6   Programs
254.7   Buildings, equipment, grounds
254.8   Finance
255   Religious congregations and orders
256   [Unassigned]
257   [Unassigned]
259   Parochial activities by parishes and religious orders
260   Christian social and ecclesiastical theology
261   Social theology
261.1   Role of Christian church in society
261.5   Christianity and intellectual development 261.56 media
261.7   Christianity and civil government
261.72   Religious freedom
261.8   Christianity and socioeconomic problems
261.83   Social problems
261.833 Crime
261.873 War and peace
262.1   Governing leaders + leadeship in church
262.2   Parishes and religious orders in church organization
262.4   Government and organization of systems governed by election
262.7   Nature of the church
262.8   Church and ministerial authority and its denial
262.9   Church law and discipline
263   Days, times, places of religious observance
263.1   Biblical Sabbath
263.2   Observance of seventh day
263.3   Sunday
263.4   Sunday observance

263.9   Other days and times
264   Public worship
264.1   Prayer
264.2   Music
264.7   Prayer meetings
265   Other rites, ceremonies, ordinances   Sacraments
265.1   Baptism
265.2   Confirmation
265.3   Eucharist, Holy Communion, Lord's Supper
265.5   Matrimony
265.8   Rites in illness and death
265.9   Other acts
✓266   Missions
266.022 Home ⎤
266.023 Foreign ⎬ 266.02
266.025 Medical ⎦
✓266.09 Missionary stories
267   Associations for religious work
267.1   Of both men and women
267.2   Of men
267.4   Of women
267.6   Of young adults
267.7   Of boys
267.8   Of girls   *C. E. section*
✓268   Religious training and instruction — Discipleship
268.1   Administration
268.2   Buildings and equipment
268.3   Personnel
✓268.4   Teaching departments and divisions
268.432 Children's division
268.433 Young people's division
268.434 Adult division
268.435 Home departments
268.5   Records and rules
✓268.6   Methods of instruction and study
268.635 Audiovisual methods — *How to manuels: clowns etc.*
268.7   Services *Christian Service*
268.8   Specific denominations and sects
✓269   Organized spiritual renewal
269.2   Revivals and camp meetings
269.6   Retreats

270 Historical and geographical treatment of organized Christian church
271 Religious congregations and orders in church history
272 Persecutions in general church history
273 Doctrinal controversies and heresies in general church history
274 Christian church in Europe
275 Christian church in Asia
276 Christian church in Africa
277 Christian church in North America
278 Christian church in South America
279 Christian church in other parts of world
280 Denominations and sects of Christian church
281 Primitive and Oriental churches
282 Roman Catholic church
283 Anglican churches
284 Protestant denominations of Continental origin
285 Presbyterian, American Reformed, Congregational churches
286 Baptist, Disciples of Christ, Adventist churches
287 Methodist churches
288 Unitarianism
289 Other denominations and sects
290 Other religions and comparative religion
291 Comparative religion
292 Classical religion
293 Germanic religion
294 Religions of Indic origin
294.3 Buddhism
294.5 Hinduism
295 Zoroastrianism
296 Judaism
297 Islam and religions derived from it
298 [Permanently unassigned]
299 Other religions
299.1 *unification church*

List in the following space additional classification numbers for use in your library.
299.2 *7th day adventist*

305.2 *culture - young people*

306.8 *Family - marriage*
306.81 *sexual education*

92 - *Biography*
920 - *Biography Collections*

Fic - *fiction*

Some suggestions for applying the 200 series classifications in individual church libraries are as follows:

1. Use the permanently unassigned number, 298, and decimal subdivisions of 298 for subjects that cannot be adequately classified elsewhere.
2. If there are still subjects not covered in the 200 series, use the currently unassigned numbers—237, 244, 256, and 257.
3. For the exact classification number of your denomination or other specific denominations whose material you have in quantity, check in the 280 series in an unabridged copy of the Eighteenth Edition of *Dewey Decimal Classification* at your public library.
4. If you wish to expand classification of general Old Testament and New Testament works, add the decimals used for such expansion in the 220's to the 221's and 225's.
5. The numbers following 28 in 281 through 289 can be added to numbers 230 and 268.8, to indicate doctrines and religious training, respectively, for specific denominations.

Selected Area Notations from Table 2

(Refer to instructions in chapter 7 for use of these area notations, which are never used alone, but combined with other classification numbers.)

—1 Areas, regions, places in general
—2 Persons regardless of area, region, place
—3 The ancient world

Selected from *Dewey Decimal Classification and Relative Index*, edition 18, volume 1: *Introduction. Tables*, pp. 123-369.

—4 Europe
 —41 Scotland and Ireland
 —42 British Isles England
 —43 Central Europe Germany
 —44 France and Monaco
 —45 Italy and adjacent territories
 —46 Iberian Peninsula and adjacent islands Spain
 —47 Eastern Europe Union of Soviet Socialist Republics (Soviet Union)
 —48 Northern Europe Scandinavia
 —49 Other parts of Europe
—5 Asia Orient Far East
 —51 China and adjacent areas
 —52 Japan and adjacent islands
 —53 Arabian Peninsula and adjacent areas
 —54 South Asia India
 —55 Iran (Persia)
 —56 Middle East (Near East)
 —57 Siberia (Asiatic Russia)
 —58 Central Asia
 —59 Southeast Asia
—6 Africa
 —61 North Africa
 —62 Countries of the Nile Egypt
 —63 Ethiopia (Abyssinia)
 —64 Northwest African coast and offshore islands Morocco
 —65 Algeria
 —66 West Africa and offshore islands
 —67 Central Africa and offshore islands East Africa
 —68 South Africa Republic of South Africa
 —69 South Indian Ocean islands
—7 North America
 —71 Canada
 —72 Middle America Mexico
 —73 United States
 —74 Northeastern United States (New England and Middle Atlantic states)
 —75 Southeastern United States (South Atlantic states)
 —76 South central United States Gulf Coast states
 —77 North central United States Lake states
 —78 Western United States

  —79 Great Basin and Pacific Slope region of United States
     Pacific Coast states

—8 South America
  —81 Brazil
  —82 Argentina
  —83 Chile
  —84 Bolivia
  —85 Peru
  —86 Northwestern South America and Panama
  —87 Venezuela
  —88 Guianas
  —89 Other parts of South America

—9 Other parts of world and extraterrestrial worlds Pacific Ocean
  islands (oceania)
  —93 New Zealand and Melanesia
  —94 Australia
  —95 New Guinea (Papua)
  —96 Other parts of Pacific Polynesia
  —97 Atlantic Ocean islands
  —98 Arctic islands and Antarctica
  —99 Extraterrestrial worlds

APPENDIX 4

SUBJECT HEADINGS FOR CHURCH LIBRARIES

THE SECTION IN CHAPTER 7 that deals with subject headings should be read for an explanation of how to use the subject headings listed in this appendix. Headings for inclusion here have been chosen for their applicability to church cataloging. It is not a list that has been officially adopted by any library group. It consists of the author's suggestions of headings believed to be particularly useful for church libraries and resource centers. Headings are shown in capital letters since that is the way they are to be typed on catalog cards. (See chapter 7 for typing instructions.)

You will not need to use all the headings given but should choose those most appropriate for your library. As suggested in chapter 7, you may want to make a check mark (√) in front of each heading the first time you use it in your catalog and cross off headings you decide against ever using. Add headings you find you need. Replace ones whose terminology you don't like with ones worded more appropriately for your library.

NAMES AS HEADINGS

You will need to add names of many types to the list given here. A recent almanac will supply names from which to select, in categories such as countries and schools. Make up your own list of names that are appropriate for the subject matter in your library, allowing space to add names as needed. This list can be kept in your library notebook if it is too long to write into this book. The following are some of the categories of types of names you may need:

Names of individuals, including Bible characters
Books of the Bible
Groupings of Bible books (e.g., Gospels, Epistles)
Family names
Countries

States
Geographical areas
Cities
Nationalities
Indian tribes
Denominations
Clubs, societies, and organizations within and outside the local church
Schools
Animals or other specific items with names needed as subject headings

CROSS REFERENCES

Whenever you find a *see* reference, it follows a subject heading under which someone may look for information and leads the catalog user to the subject heading under which your library actually gives this information. A *see also* reference indicates additional subject headings under which a user may wish to look for related information. Instructions for typing cross reference catalog cards are given in chapter 7.

LIST OF SUBJECT HEADINGS

ABOLITION. *See* SLAVERY
ABORIGINES. *See also* ETHNOLOGY
ABORTION. *See also* FAMILY PLANNING
ABSTINENCE. *See also* ALCOHOLISM; FASTING; TEMPERANCE
ADOLESCENCE. *See also* CHILD STUDY; YOUNG PEOPLE
ADVENTURE
AGED. *See* SENIOR CITIZENS
AGNOSTICISM
ALCOHOLISM. *See also* ABSTINENCE; CASE STUDIES; DRUG
  ABUSE; LIQUOR PROBLEMS: TEMPERANCE
ALLEGORIES. *See also* FABLES; FICTION; PARABLES
AMISH. *See also* RELIGIONS
AMUSEMENTS. *See also* CHURCH ENTERTAINMENTS; GAMES,
  RECREATION
ANCESTOR WORSHIP
ANECDOTES. *See also* HUMOR; ILLUSTRATIONS
ANGELS
ANIMALS. *See also* ANIMALS–STORIES
ANIMALS–STORIES. *See also* ANIMALS
ANNUALS. *See* YEARBOOKS
ANTHROPOLOGY
ANTICHRIST
ANTI-COMMUNIST EFFORTS. *See also* COMMUNISM;
  COMMUNISM AND RELIGION

APOCRYPHA
APOLOGETICS. *See also* CHRISTIANITY—EVIDENCES
APOSTLES. *See also* BIBLE BIOGRAPHY
APOSTLES' CREED. *See also* CREEDS
ARABS AND JEWS. *See* JEWS AND ARABS
ARCHEOLOGY. *See also* ANTHROPOLOGY; BIBLE ARCHEOLOGY;
  CIVILIZATION
ARCHITECTURE, CHURCH
ART. *See also* CHRISTIAN ART
ARTS AND CRAFTS. *See also* ART; FOLK ART
ASSOCIATIONS
ASTROLOGY. *See also* OCCULT PRACTICES
ATHEISM
ATHLETES
ATHLETICS
ATLASES. *See also* MAPS
ATONEMENT. *See* REDEMPTION
AUDIOVISUAL EDUCATION. *See also* AUDIOVISUAL MATERIALS
AUDIOVISUAL MATERIALS. *See also* AUDIOVISUAL EDUCATION
AUTOBIOGRAPHIES. *See also* BIOGRAPHY
BAHAISM. *See also* RELIGIONS
BAPTISM. *See also* SACRAMENTS; THEOLOGY
BEATITUDES
BEAUTY, PERSONAL. *See* GROOMING
BEHAVIOR. *See* ETIQUETTE
BIBLE
BIBLE—OLD TESTAMENT. *See* OLD TESTAMENT
BIBLE—NEW TESTAMENT. *See* NEW TESTAMENT
BIBLE AND SCIENCE. *See* SCIENCE AND THE BIBLE
BIBLE ARCHEOLOGY
BIBLE BIOGRAPHY
BIBLE CANON
BIBLE CATECHISMS. *See* CATECHISMS
BIBLE COMMENTARIES
BIBLE CONCORDANCES
BIBLE CRITICISM AND INTERPRETATION. *See also*
  HERMENEUTICS
BIBLE DICTIONARIES
BIBLE DOCTRINE. *See* THEOLOGY
BIBLE ENCYCLOPEDIAS
BIBLE EVIDENCES
BIBLE FESTIVALS
BIBLE GEOGRAPHY
BIBLE HISTORICAL EVENTS

BIBLE HISTORY
BIBLE IN LITERATURE. *See also* CHRISTIAN LITERATURE
BIBLE INSPIRATION
BIBLE INTRODUCTION
BIBLE LANDS
BIBLE MANUSCRIPTS
BIBLE MAPS
BIBLE MIRACLES
BIBLE NATURAL HISTORY
BIBLE PLAYS. *See* PLAYS AND PAGEANTS
BIBLE PROPHECIES. *See also* PROPHECY
BIBLE READING
BIBLE STORIES
BIBLE STUDY
BIBLE SURVEY
BIBLE VERSIONS
BIBLE WOMEN. *See* BIBLE BIOGRAPHY
BIOGRAPHY. *See also* BIBLE BIOGRAPHY; BIOGRAPHY
BIOGRAPHY, MISSIONARY. *See* BIOGRAPHY
BIOGRAPHY, SCRIPTURAL. *See* BIBLE BIOGRAPHY
BIRTH CONTROL. *See* FAMILY PLANNING
BLACKS. *See also* BIOGRAPHY; CIVIL RIGHTS; RELIGION;
   SEGREGATION
BLIND, MINISTRIES AND MATERIALS FOR THE
BOOK REVIEWS
BOOKS, LARGE PRINT. *See* BLIND, MINISTRIES AND MATERIALS
   FOR THE
BOOKS, TALKING. *See* BLIND, MINISTRIES AND MATERIALS
   FOR THE
BOOKS AND READING. *See* CHRISTIAN LITERATURE
BOYS' CLUBS
BUDDHISM
BURIAL CUSTOMS. *See also* FUNERALS
CALVARY
CALVINISM. *See also* RELIGIONS
CAMPING. *See also* OUTDOOR COOKERY; OUTDOOR
   RECREATION
CAMPS
CANON. *See* BIBLE CANON
CAPITAL PUNISHMENT
CAREERS. *See also* VOCATIONAL GUIDANCE
CARTOONS. *See also* COMIC BOOKS
CASE STUDIES
CATALOGS

CATECHISMS
CATHOLIC CHURCH. *See* ROMAN CATHOLIC CHURCH
CEMETERIES
CHALK TALKS. *See also* AUDIOVISUAL EDUCATION; AUDIOVISUAL
  MATERIALS; CHRISTIAN EDUCATION; TEACHING AIDS
CHAPLAINS
CHARACTER. *See* CHRISTIAN LIFE
CHARITIES
CHARTS
CHILD STUDY
CHILDREN. *See* CHILD STUDY
CHILDREN, EXCEPTIONAL
CHILDREN, INSTITUTIONS FOR. *See* CHILDREN'S HOMES
CHILDREN IN OTHER LANDS
CHILDREN'S CHRISTIAN LIFE
CHILDREN'S HOMES. *See also* INSTITUTIONAL CARE
CHILDREN'S SONGS
CHILDREN'S STORIES
CHOIRS. *See also* CHURCH MUSIC
CHORAL SPEAKING
CHRIST. *See* JESUS CHRIST
CHRISTIAN ART
CHRISTIAN BIOGRAPHY. *See* BIBLE BIOGRAPHY; BIOGRAPHY
CHRISTIAN CHARACTER
CHRISTIAN CONDUCT. *See also* CHRISTIAN LIFE
CHRISTIAN DOCTRINE. *See* THEOLOGY
CHRISTIAN EDUCATION. *See also* AUDIOVISUAL EDUCATION;
  OBJECT LESSONS
CHRISTIAN EDUCATION FOR ADULTS
CHRISTIAN EDUCATION FOR CHILDREN
CHRISTIAN EDUCATION FOR COLLEGE AGE
CHRISTIAN EDUCATION FOR FAMILIES
CHRISTIAN EDUCATION FOR THE MENTALLY RETARDED. *See
  also* CHILDREN, EXCEPTIONAL
CHRISTIAN EDUCATION FOR PRESCHOOL CHILDREN
CHRISTIAN EDUCATION FOR YOUNG PEOPLE
CHRISTIAN ETHICS. *See also* CHRISTIAN LIFE
CHRISTIAN LIFE
CHRISTIAN LITERATURE
CHRISTIAN SCIENCE
CHRISTIANITY. *See also* APOLOGETICS; CHRISTIAN LIFE;
  CHURCH HISTORY
CHRISTIANITY AND ECONOMICS. *See also* CHRISTIAN ETHICS
CHRISTIANITY AND EDUCATION. *See also* SCIENCE AND THE
  BIBLE

CHRISTIANITY AND OTHER RELIGIONS. *See also* COMPARATIVE RELIGION

CHRISTIANITY AND POLITICS. *See* CHURCH AND STATE

CHRISTIANITY AND SCIENCE. *See* SCIENCE AND THE BIBLE

CHRISTIANITY AND THE WORLD

CHRISTIANITY AND WAR

CHRISTOLOGY. *See* JESUS CHRIST

CHRISTMAS. *See also* NATIVITY OF JESUS CHRIST

CHRISTMAS PROGRAMS

CHURCH

CHURCH ADMINISTRATION

CHURCH AND EDUCATION. *See* CHRISTIAN EDUCATION

CHURCH AND LABOR. *See* CHRISTIANITY AND ECONOMICS

CHURCH AND RACE PROBLEMS. *See* RACE PROBLEMS

CHURCH AND SOCIAL PROBLEMS. *See* SOCIAL PROBLEMS

CHURCH AND STATE

CHURCH AND WAR. *See* CHRISTIANITY AND WAR

CHURCH ARCHITECTURE. *See* ARCHITECTURE, CHURCH

CHURCH ATTENDANCE. *See* PUBLIC WORSHIP

CHURCH BIOGRAPHY. *See* BIBLE BIOGRAPHY; BIOGRAPHY

CHURCH DISCIPLINE

CHURCH ENTERTAINMENTS. *See also* AMUSEMENTS; GAMES; PARTIES

CHURCH FATHERS. *See* BIOGRAPHY; CHURCH HISTORY

CHURCH FINANCE

CHURCH FURNITURE

CHURCH HISTORY. *See also* HISTORY

CHURCH LAW

CHURCH LIBRARIES

CHURCH MUSIC. *See* SACRED MUSIC

CHURCH PUBLICITY

CHURCH SCHOOLS. *See* CHRISTIAN EDUCATION; SUNDAY SCHOOLS

CHURCH SOCIABLES. *See* CHURCH ENTERTAINMENTS

CHURCH WORK. *See also* LAY MINISTRY; PASTORAL WORK

CHURCHES. *See also* ARCHITECTURE, CHURCH; CITY AND SUBURBAN CHURCHES; COMMUNITY CHURCHES; RURAL CHURCHES

CITY AND SUBURBAN CHURCHES

CIVIL RIGHTS. *See also* BLACKS; MINORITIES; RACE PROBLEMS; SOCIAL PROBLEMS

CIVILIZATION. *See also* ANTHROPOLOGY; ETHNOLOGY; SOCIOLOGY

CLERGY. *See also* PASTORAL WORK; PASTORS

CLERGYMEN'S WIVES. *See* PASTOR'S WIVES

CLIPPINGS

COLLEGES AND UNIVERSITIES. *See also* SCHOOLS

COMIC BOOKS

COMMUNISM. *See also* ANTI-COMMUNIST EFFORTS; COMMUNISM AND RELIGION

COMMUNISM AND RELIGION. *See also* ANTI-COMMUNIST EFFORTS; COMMUNISM

COMMUNITY CHURCHES

COMPARATIVE RELIGION. *See also* RELIGIONS

CONFIRMATION. *See also* RITES AND CEREMONIES; SACRAMENTS

CONGREGATIONALISM. *See also* CHURCH ADMINISTRATION

CONSCIENCE. *See also* CHRISTIAN ETHICS

CONSOLATION

CONSTITUTIONS. *See also* CHURCH ADMINISTRATION

CONVERSION. *See also* CHRISTIAN LIFE; THEOLOGY

CONVICTS. *See* CRIME AND CRIMINALS

COOKERY. *See also* COOKERY FOR INSTITUTIONS; OUTDOOR COOKERY

COOKERY, OUTDOOR. *See* OUTDOOR COOKERY

COOKERY FOR INSTITUTIONS. *See also* COOKERY

COOPERATIVE PROGRAMS

CORRESPONDENCE SCHOOLS AND COURSES

COUNCILS AND SYNODS. *See also* CHURCH ADMINISTRATION

COUNSELING. *See also* PSYCHOLOGY, PASTORAL

COURTESY. *See* ETIQUETTE

COURTSHIP. *See* DATING

CRAFTS. *See* ARTS AND CRAFTS

CREATION. *See also* EVOLUTION; SCIENCE AND THE BIBLE

CREEDS. *See also* CHURCH HISTORY; THEOLOGY

CRIME AND CRIMINALS. *See also* JUVENILE DELINQUENCY; SOCIAL PROBLEMS

CRIME PREVENTION. *See also* CRIME AND CRIMINALS

CRIMINALS. *See* CRIME AND CRIMINALS

CRIMINOLOGY. *See* CRIME AND CRIMINALS

CROSSWORD PUZZLES. *See also* PUZZLES

CRUCIFIXION

CULTS

CURRENT EVENTS

CUSTOMS. *See* MANNERS AND CUSTOMS

DAILY VACATION BIBLE CHOOL. *See* VACATION BIBLE SCHOOL

DANCING. *See also* AMUSEMENTS

DARWINISM. *See* EVOLUTION

DATING. *See also* ETIQUETTE; MARRIAGE

DEACONS AND DEACONESSES

DEAD SEA SCROLLS

DEATH. *See also* CONSOLATION; FUNERALS; THEOLOGY

DECORATIVE ART. *See* ART

DELINQUENTS. *See* CRIME AND CRIMINALS

DELUGE. *See* FLOOD

DEMOCRACY

DEMONOLOGY. *See also* DEMONS; OCCULT PRACTICES

DEMONS. *See also* ANGELS

DENOMINATIONS

DEVIL. *See also* DEMONS; SATAN

DEVOTIONS. *See also* FAMILY DEVOTIONS; PRAYER; WORSHIP

DIARIES. *See* AUTOBIOGRAPHIES

DICTIONARIES. *See* ENCYCLOPEDIAS AND DICTIONARIES

DIRECTORIES

DISASTER RELIEF

DISCIPLES, TWELVE. *See* APOSTLES

DISPENSATIONS. *See also* THEOLOGY

DIVINE HEALING

DIVINITY OF CHRIST

DIVORCE. *See also* FAMILY; MARRIAGE; SOCIAL PROBLEMS

DOCTRINES. *See* THEOLOGY

DRAMA, RELIGIOUS. *See* PLAYS AND PAGEANTS

DRUG ABUSE. *See also* DRUGS AND YOUTH

DRUG ADDICTION. *See* DRUG ABUSE

DRUGS AND YOUTH. *See also* DRUG ABUSE

DRUNKENNESS. *See* ALCOHOLISM

EARTH SCIENCES

EASTER. *See also* LENT; RESURRECTION

EASTERN CHURCHES. *See also* ORTHODOX EASTERN CHURCH; RELIGIONS

ECCLESIASTICAL LAW. *See* CHURCH LAW

ECOLOGY

ECONOMICS AND CHRISTIANITY. *See* CHRISTIANITY AND ECONOMICS

ELECTION. *See* PREDESTINATION

ENCYCLOPEDIAS AND DICTIONARIES. *See also* BIBLE DICTION-ARIES; BIBLE ENCYCLOPEDIAS; REFERENCE BOOKS

ENVIRONMENT. *See* ECOLOGY

EPITAPHS. *See* BURIAL CUSTOMS; CEMETERIES

ESCHATOLOGY. *See also* PROPHECY; THEOLOGY

ESSAYS

ETERNAL LIFE. *See also* FUTURE LIFE; THEOLOGY

ETERNITY. *See also* FUTURE LIFE

ETHICS. *See also* CHRISTIAN ETHICS; PHILOSOPHY; POLITICAL ETHICS; SEXUAL ETHICS; SOCIAL ETHICS

ETHNOLOGY. *See also* ANTHROPOLOGY; CIVILIZATION
ETIQUETTE
EVANGELISM. *See also* PERSONAL WORK; REVIVALS
EVENING SCHOOLS. *See* SCHOOLS
EVIL. *See* THEOLOGY
EVIL SPIRITS. *See* DEMONS
EVOLUTION. *See also* CREATION; SCIENCE AND THE BIBLE
EXCEPTIONAL CHILDREN. *See* CHILDREN, EXCEPTIONAL
EXISTENTIALISM
EXORCISM
EXPLORERS. *See also* HEROES
FABLES. *See also* ALLEGORIES; FOLKLORE
FAITH. *See also* CHRISTIAN LIFE; THEOLOGY
FAITH CURE. *See* DIVINE HEALING
FALL OF MAN. *See also* THEOLOGY
FAMILY. *See also* FAMILY PLANNING; FAMILY WORSHIP;
  MARRIAGE
FAMILY ALTAR. *See* FAMILY WORSHIP
FAMILY DEVOTIONS. *See* FAMILY WORSHIP
FAMILY PLANNING. *See also* SEX INSTRUCTION; SEXUAL ETHICS
FAMILY WORSHIP
FAMINES
FASTING
FATHERS. *See* FAMILY
FEAR
FEASTS. *See also* BIBLE FESTIVALS; RITES AND CEREMONIES
FESTIVAL. *See also* BIBLE FESTIVALS; MANNERS AND CUSTOMS
FICTION
FILMSTRIPS. *See also* AUDIOVISUAL MATERIALS
FINANCE, CHURCH. *See* CHURCH FINANCE
FINANCE, PERSONAL. *See* PERSONAL FINANCE
FIRST AID
FLAGS. *See also* AUDIOVISUAL MATERIALS
FLOOD
FLOWER ARRANGEMENT. *See* ARTS AND CRAFTS
FOLK MUSIC. *See* MUSIC
FOLKLORE
FOREIGN MISSIONS. *See also* MISSIONS
FORGIVENESS
FORTUNE TELLING. *See* OCCULT PRACTICES
FOSTER HOMES. *See* CHILDREN'S HOMES
FREE WILL. *See* THEOLOGY
FREEDOM OF RELIGION
FREEDOM OF WORSHIP. *See* FREEDOM OF RELIGION

FUND RAISING
FUNDAMENTALISM. *See also* RELIGIONS
FUNERALS. *See also* BURIAL CUSTOMS; MANNERS AND CUSTOMS;
    RITES AND CEREMONIES
FUTURE LIFE. *See also* ESCHATOLOGY; HEAVEN; HELL
FUTURE PUNISHMENT. *See* FUTURE LIFE
GAMES. *See also* AMUSEMENTS; ATHLETICS; RECREATION;
    SPORTS
GEOGRAPHY. *See also* BIBLE GEOGRAPHY
GEOGRAPHY, BIBLICAL. *See* BIBLE GEOGRAPHY
GERONTOLOGY. *See* SENIOR CITIZENS
GIRLS' CLUBS
GLOBES. *See also* AUDIOVISUAL MATERIALS
GLOSSOLALIA. *See* TONGUES SPEAKING
GOD. *See also* THEOLOGY; TRINITY
GOOD AND EVIL. *See* THEOLOGY
GRACE. *See also* THEOLOGY
GRAVES. *See* BURIAL CUSTOMS
GREEK CHURCH. *See* ORTHODOX EASTERN CHURCH
GREEK LANGUAGE
GRIEF. *See* CONSOLATION
GROOMING
GUIDANCE. *See* COUNSELING
HALLOWEEN. *See also* OCCULT PRACTICES
HANDICAPPED
HANDICRAFT. *See* ARTS AND CRAFTS
HAPPINESS. *See also* CHRISTIAN LIFE
HEALING, DIVINE. *See* DIVINE HEALING
HEALTH
HEATHENISM. *See also* MISSIONS; RELIGIONS
HEAVEN. *See also* ESCHATOLOGY; FUTURE LIFE
HEBREW LANGUAGE
HEBREW LITERATURE. *See* JEWISH LITERATURE
HEBREWS. *See* JEWS
HELL. *See also* ESCHATOLOGY; FUTURE LIFE
HERESIES
HERMENEUTICS. *See also* BIBLE CRITICISM AND
    INTERPRETATION
HEROES AND HEROINES
HINDUISM
HIPPIES
HISTORY. *See also* BIBLE HISTORY; CHURCH HISTORY
HISTORY, CHURCH. *See* CHURCH HISTORY
HOLIDAYS. *See also* CHRISTMAS; EASTER; FESTIVALS

HOLINESS
HOLY BIBLE. *See* BIBLE
HOLY DAYS. *See* FESTIVALS; HOLIDAYS; MANNERS AND
  CUSTOMS
HOLY SPIRIT
HOME. *See* FAMILY
HOME LIFE. *See* FAMILY
HOME MISSIONS. *See also* MISSIONS
HOMILETICS. *See* PREACHING
HOMOSEXUALITY. *See* SEXUAL ETHICS
HOROSCOPE. *See* ASTROLOGY; OCCULT PRACTICES
HOSPITALS. *See also* INSTITUTIONAL CARE
HUMILITY
HUMOR. *See also* CARTOONS
HYMN STORIES
HYMNS. *See also* HYMN STORIES; SACRED MUSIC
ILLITERACY. *See* LITERACY
ILLUSTRATIONS
IMMORTALITY. *See* FUTURE LIFE; THEOLOGY
INDIANS
INFANTS. *See* CHILD STUDY
INSPIRATION, BIBLICAL. *See* BIBLE INSPIRATION
INSTITUTIONAL CARE. *See also* CHILDREN'S HOMES; HOSPITALS
INSTITUTIONS. *See* INSTITUTIONAL CARE
INSTRUMENTAL MUSIC. *See also* SACRED MUSIC
INTEMPERANCE. *See* ALCOHOLISM
INTERFAITH MARRIAGE
ISLAM. *See also* RELIGIONS
ISRAEL-ARAB RELATIONS. *See* JEWS AND ARABS
ISRAELITES. *See* JEWS
JESUS CHRIST. *See also* BIOGRAPHY, SCRIPTURAL; CHRISTI-
  ANITY; CRUCIFIXION; DIVINITY OF CHRIST; GOD; MESSIAH;
  NATIVITY OF JESUS CHRIST; PARABLES; PASSION OF JESUS
  CHRIST; PROPHECY; REDEMPTION; RESURRECTION; SECOND
  COMING; TEACHINGS OF JESUS; THEOLOGY; TRINITY
JESUS PEOPLE. *See* HIPPIES
JEWISH FESTIVALS. *See* FESTIVALS
JEWISH LITERATURE
JEWS. *See also* JEWS AND ARABS; JUDAISM
JEWS AND ARABS
JOBS. *See* CAREERS
JOKES. *See* HUMOR
JUDAISM. *See also* JEWS; RELIGIONS
JUSTIFICATION. *See also* REDEMPTION; THEOLOGY

MIGRANT LABOR

MILLENNIUM. *See also* ESCHATOLOGY; SECOND COMING

MINISTERS OF THE GOSPEL. *See* PASTORS

MINISTRY. *See* PASTORAL WORK

MINORITIES. *See also* BLACKS; RACE PROBLEMS; SOCIAL
  PROBLEMS

MIRACLES. *See also* BIBLE MIRACLES; DIVINE HEALING

MISSIONARIES. *See also* BIOGRAPHY

MISSIONARY STORIES

MISSIONS. *See also* HOME MISSIONS; FOREIGN MISSIONS

MISSIONS, MEDICAL. *See also* FOREIGN MISSIONS; HOME
  MISSIONS; MISSIONS

MIXED MARRIAGE. *See* INTERFAITH MARRIAGE

MODERNISM. *See also* FUNDAMENTALISM; RELIGION;
  THEOLOGY

MOHAMMEDANISM. *See* ISLAM

MOHAMMEDANS. *See* ISLAM

MORALITY. *See* ETHICS; MORALS

MORALS

MORMONS AND MORMONISM. *See also* RELIGIONS

MORTUARY CUSTOMS. *See* FUNERALS

MOSLEMISM. *See* ISLAM

MOSLEMS. *See* ISLAM

MOTHERS. *See also* FAMILY; WOMEN

MOTION PICTURES. *See* MOVING PICTURES

MOURNING CUSTOMS. *See* FUNERALS

MOVIES. *See* MOVING PICTURES

MOVING PICTURES. *See also* AUDIOVISUAL MATERIALS

MUSIC. *See also* INSTRUMENTAL MUSIC; SACRED MUSIC; VOCAL
  MUSIC

MUSICAL INSTRUMENTS. *See also* INSTRUMENTAL MUSIC

MUSLIMISM. *See* ISLAM

MUSLIMS. *See* ISLAM

MYTHOLOGY

NAMES

NARCOTICS. *See* DRUG ABUSE

NATIVITY OF JESUS CHRIST. *See also* CHRISTMAS

NATURE STUDY

NEGRO SPIRITUALS

NEGROES. *See* BLACKS

NEW BIRTH. *See* REGENERATION

NEW TESTAMENT (Use subdivisions shown under BIBLE)

NEWSPAPER CLIPPINGS. *See* CLIPPINGS

NEWSPAPERS. *See also* CLIPPINGS

NONVIOLENCE. *See also* CHRISTIANITY AND WAR; PACIFISM
OBJECT LESSONS
OCCULT PRACTICES
OCCUPATIONS. *See* CAREERS
OLD AGE. *See* SENIOR CITIZENS
OLD TESTAMENT (Use subdivisions shown under BIBLE)
ORCHESTRAL MUSIC. *See* INSTRUMENTAL MUSIC
ORDINANCES
ORGAN MUSIC. *See* INSTRUMENTAL MUSIC
ORGANIZATIONS. *See* ASSOCIATIONS
ORIGIN OF MAN. *See also* CREATION; EVOLUTION; SCIENCE AND
   THE BIBLE
ORIGIN OF SPECIES. *See also* CREATION; EVOLUTION; SCIENCE
   AND THE BIBLE
ORPHANS AND ORPHANS' HOMES. *See* CHILDREN'S HOMES
ORTHODOX EASTERN CHURCH. *See also* RELIGIONS
OUTDOOR COOKERY. *See also* CAMPING
OUTDOOR LIFE. *See* CAMPING
OUTDOOR RECREATION. *See also* CAMPING; CAMPS;
   RECREATION
PAGANISM. *See* HEATHENISM
PAGEANTS. *See* PLAYS AND PAGEANTS
PAIN. *See* SUFFERING
PAMPHLETS
PAPACY. *See also* ROMAN CATHOLIC CHURCH
PARABLES
PARENTS. *See* FAMILY
PARISH LIBRARIES. *See* CHURCH LIBRARIES
PARLIAMENTARY PRACTICE. *See also* CHURCH
   ADMINISTRATION
PARTIES. *See also* AMUSEMENTS; CHURCH ENTERTAINMENTS
PASSION OF JESUS CHRIST
PASSION PLAYS
PASTORAL WORK
PASTORS. *See also* CLERGY; PASTORAL WORK; PASTORS' WIVES
PASTORS' WIVES
PEACE
PERIODICALS
PERSECUTION. *See also* MARTYRS
PERSONAL APPEARANCE. *See* GROOMING
PERSONAL DEVELOPMENT. *See* SUCCESS
PERSONAL FINANCE
PERSONAL WORK. *See also* EVANGELISM
PERSONALITY

PHILOSOPHY. *See also* ETHICS
PHONOGRAPH RECORDS. *See also* AUDIOVISUAL MATERIALS
PICTURES. *See also* ART; AUDIOVISUAL MATERIALS
PILGRIM FATHERS. *See* CHRISTIAN BIOGRAPHY
PLANNED PARENTHOOD. *See* FAMILY PLANNING
PLAYS, BIBLE. *See* PLAYS AND PAGEANTS
PLAYS AND PAGEANTS
POETRY
POLITICAL ETHICS. *See also* ETHICS
POLITICS AND CHRISTIANITY. *See* CHURCH AND STATE
POLLUTION
POSTERS. *See also* ECOLOGY
PRAYER
PRAYER MEETINGS
PRAYERS
PREACHERS. *See* PASTORS
PREACHING. *See also* PASTORAL WORK; SERMONS
PREDESTINATION. *See also* THEOLOGY
PREVENTION OF CRIME. *See* CRIME PREVENTION
PRIMERS
PROFESSIONS. *See* CAREERS
PROHIBITION. *See also* ALCOHOLISM; LIQUOR PROBLEMS;
  TEMPERANCE
PROJECTORS. *See also* AUDIOVISUAL MATERIALS
PROPHECY. *See also* ESCHATOLOGY; THEOLOGY
PROPHETS. *See also* BIBLE BIOGRAPHY
PROTESTANTISM. *See also* CHRISTIANITY; CHURCH HISTORY;
  RELIGIONS
PSYCHIATRY. *See also* MEDICINE AND RELIGION; PSYCHOLOGY
PSYCHOLOGY. *See also* COUNSELING
PSYCHOLOGY, CHILD. *See* CHILD STUDY
PSYCHOLOGY, PASTORAL. *See also* COUNSELING
PUBLIC RELATIONS
PUBLIC WORSHIP. *See also* WORSHIP
PURITANS. *See also* BIOGRAPHY; CHURCH HISTORY; RELIGIONS
PUZZLES
QUESTIONS AND ANSWERS
QUIZ BOOKS. *See* QUESTIONS AND ANSWERS
QUMRAN TEXTS. *See* DEAD SEA SCROLLS
QUOTATIONS
RACE PROBLEMS. *See also* MINORITIES; SOCIAL PROBLEMS
RACES. *See* ETHNOLOGY
RADIO BROADCASTING
RAPID READING

READING
READINGS AND RECITATIONS
RECORDS, PHONOGRAPH. *See* PHONOGRAPH RECORDS
RECREATION. *See also* AMUSEMENTS; LEISURE; SPORTS
REDEMPTION. *See also* SALVATION; THEOLOGY
REFERENCE BOOKS. *See also* ENCYCLOPEDIAS AND DICTIONARIES
REFORMATION. *See also* CHURCH HISTORY; PROTESTANTISM
REFUGEES
REGENERATION
RELIGION. *See* RELIGIONS; THEOLOGY
RELIGION AND SCIENCE. *See* SCIENCE AND THE BIBLE
RELIGIONS. *See also* CHRISTIANITY AND OTHER RELIGIONS;
  COMPARATIVE RELIGION
RELIGIOUS ART. *See* CHRISTIAN ART
RELIGIOUS BIOGRAPHY. *See* BIBLE BIOGRAPHY; BIOGRAPHY
RELIGIOUS DRAMA. *See* PLAYS AND PAGEANTS
RELIGIOUS EDUCATION. *See also* CHRISTIAN EDUCATION
RELIGIOUS FREEDOM. *See* FREEDOM OF RELIGION
RELIGIOUS LIBERTY. *See* FREEDOM OF RELIGION
RELIGIOUS LITERATURE. *See also* CHRISTIAN LITERATURE
RELIGIOUS POETRY. *See also* CHRISTIAN LITERATURE; POETRY
RESURRECTION. *See also* FUTURE LIFE
RETIREMENT. *See also* LEISURE; SENIOR CITIZENS
REVELATION. *See* BIBLE INSPIRATION; THEOLOGY
REVIVALS. *See also* CHURCH HISTORY; EVANGELISM
RIDDLES. *See also* AMUSEMENTS
RITES AND CEREMONIES. *See also* BIBLE FESTIVALS; FUNERALS;
  MANNERS AND CUSTOMS
ROMAN CATHOLIC CHURCH
RULES OF ORDER. *See* PARLIAMENTARY PRACTICE
RURAL CHURCHES. *See also* CHURCHES
SABBATH
SACRAMENTS. *See also* THEOLOGY
SACRED ART. *See* CHRISTIAN ART
SACRED MUSIC. *See also* HYMNS; INSTRUMENTAL MUSIC; VOCAL
  MUSIC
SACRIFICE. *See also* THEOLOGY; WORSHIP
SAINTS
SALVATION. *See also* REDEMPTION; THEOLOGY
SALVATION ARMY. *See also* MISSIONS
SANCTIFICATION. *See also* THEOLOGY
SATAN
SATIRE. *See also* HUMOR
SCHOOL, PAROCHIAL. *See* CHRISTIAN EDUCATION

SCHOOLS. *See also* CHRISTIAN EDUCATION; COLLEGES AND UNI-
VERSITIES; SEMINARIES
SCIENCE AND THE BIBLE
SECOND COMING. *See also* ESCHATOLOGY
SECTS. *See also* COMPARATIVE RELIGION; CULTS; RELIGIONS
SEMINARIES
SENIOR CITIZENS. *See also* RETIREMENT
SERMON ON THE MOUNT
SERMONS. *See also* PREACHING
SEX INSTRUCTION. *See also* FAMILY PLANNING; SEXUAL ETHICS
SEXUAL EDUCATION. *See* SEX INSTRUCTION
SEXUAL ETHICS. *See also* ABORTION; FAMILY PLANNING;
MORALS
SHORT STORIES
SIN. *See also* CHRISTIAN ETHICS; SALVATION; THEOLOGY
SINGLE WOMEN. *See* WOMEN
SKITS. *See also* PLAYS AND PAGEANTS
SLAVERY
SLIDES. *See also* AUDIOVISUAL MATERIALS
SMOKING. *See also* DRUG ABUSE
SOCIAL ETHICS. *See also* ETHICS
SOCIAL PROBLEMS
SOCIAL SCIENCES
SOCIAL WORK
SOCIALISM
SOCIETIES. *See* ASSOCIATIONS
SOCIOLOGY
SONGBOOKS. *See also* HYMNS; VOCAL MUSIC
SORCERY. *See* OCCULT PRACTICES
SORROW. *See also* CONSOLATION
SOUL. *See also* THEOLOGY
SOUL WINNING. *See* PERSONAL WORK
SPEAKING IN TONGUES. *See* TONGUES SPEAKING
SPEECH MATERIAL
SPIRIT. *See* SOUL
SPIRITISM. *See* SPIRITUALISM
SPIRITS. *See* DEMONOLOGY
SPIRITUALISM. *See* OCCULT PRACTICES
SPORTS. *See* ATHLETICS; GAMES; RECREATION
STEWARDSHIP
STORIES. *See* ANECDOTES; HUMOR; SHORT STORIES;
STORIES, BIBLE; MISSIONARY STORIES; STORIES, RELIG-
IOUS; STORIES IN RHYME
STORIES, BIBLE

STORIES, MISSIONARY. *See* MISSIONARY STORIES
STORIES, RELIGIOUS
STORIES IN RHYME
STORYTELLING
SUCCESS
SUFFERING
SUICIDE. *See also* SOCIAL PROBLEMS
SUMMER CAMPS. *See* CAMPS
SUNDAY
SUNDAY SCHOOL CURRICULA
SUNDAY SCHOOLS. *See also* CHRISTIAN EDUCATION
SYMBOLISM. *See also* CHRISTIAN ART
SYMPATHY. *See* CONSOLATION
SYNAGOGUES. *See* JUDAISM
SYSTEMATIC THEOLOGY. *See* THEOLOGY
TABERNACLE
TALKING BOOKS. *See* BLIND, MINISTRIES AND MATERIALS FOR
  THE; PHONOGRAPH RECORDS
TALMUD. *See* JEWISH LITERATURE
TEACHING. *See* CHRISTIAN EDUCATION
TEACHING AIDS. *See also* AUDIOVISUAL EDUCATION; AUDIO-
  VISUAL MATERIALS; CHRISTIAN EDUCATION
TEACHINGS OF JESUS
TEEN AGE. *See* ADOLESCENCE; YOUNG PEOPLE
TELEVISION AND CHILDREN. *See also* AMUSEMENTS
TEMPERANCE. *See also* ABSTINENCE; ALCOHOLISM; LIQUOR
  PROBLEMS
TEMPLES
TEMPTATION
TEN COMMANDMENTS
THANKSGIVING DAY. *See also* HOLIDAYS
THEOLOGY. *See also* BIBLE DOCTRINE
TITHES. *See also* CHURCH FINANCE; STEWARDSHIP
TOBACCO. *See* SMOKING; DRUG ABUSE
TONGUES SPEAKING
TRAVEL
TRINITY. *See also* THEOLOGY
TRUST. *See* FAITH
TYPOLOGY. *See also* THEOLOGY
UNDERGROUND, ANTI-COMMUNIST. *See* ANTI-COMMUNIST
  EFFORTS
UNISON SPEAKING. *See* CHORAL SPEAKING
UNITARIANISM. *See also* RELIGIONS

UNITED NATIONS
UNIVERSITIES. *See* COLLEGES AND UNIVERSITIES
VACATION BIBLE SCHOOL
VACATION CHURCH SCHOOL. *See* VACATION BIBLE SCHOOL
VIOLENCE
VIRGIN BIRTH. *See also* THEOLOGY
VISITATION. *See also* CHURCH WORK; LAY MINISTRY; PASTORAL
  WORK
VOCAL MUSIC. *See also* HYMNS; MUSIC; SONGBOOKS; VOCAL
  MUSIC
VOCATIONAL GUIDANCE. *See also* CAREERS; COUNSELING
VOCATIONS. *See* CAREERS; VOCATIONAL GUIDANCE
WAR AND RELIGION. *See* CHRISTIANITY AND WAR
WEDDINGS. *See also* ETIQUETTE; MARRIAGE; MARRIAGE CUS-
  TOMS AND RITES
WEEKDAY RELIGIOUS INSTRUCTION
WILL. *See* FREE WILL
WIT AND HUMOR. *See* HUMOR
WITCHCRAFT. *See* OCCULT PRACTICES
WOMAN. *See* WOMEN
WOMEN. *See also* BIOGRAPHY; PSYCHOLOGY; SOCIAL PROBLEMS;
  WOMEN IN THE CHURCH; WOMEN'S LIBERATION MOVEMENT
WOMEN IN THE BIBLE. *See* BIBLE BIOGRAPHY
WOMEN IN THE CHURCH
WOMEN'S LIBERATION MOVEMENT
WORK
WORLD RELIEF
WORSHIP. *See also* THEOLOGY
WORSHIP PROGRAMS
WRITING
YEARBOOKS
YOUNG ADULTS
YOUNG MEN. *See* YOUNG PEOPLE
YOUNG PEOPLE. *See also* YOUTH PROBLEMS
YOUNG WOMEN. *See* YOUNG PEOPLE; WOMEN
YOUTH PROBLEMS
ZEN BUDDHISM. *See also* RELIGIONS
ZIONISM. *See also* JEWS
ZODIAC. *See also* OCCULT PRACTICES

BIBLIOGRAPHY

Akers, Susan Grey. *Simple Library Cataloging.* Chicago: American Library Association, 1954.

Aldrich, Ella V. *Using Theological Books and Libraries.* Englewood Cliffs, New Jersey: Prentice-Hall, 1963.

Althoff, Leona Lavender. *The Church Library Manual.* Nashville: Convention Press, 1955.

American Libraries, all issues (see Appendix 2 for address).

American Library Association. *A. L. A. Rules for Filing Catalog Cards.* 2d ed. Chicago: American Library Association, 1949.

Anderson, Jacqulyn, comp. *The Church Media Center Development Plan.* Nashville: Broadman, 1978.

Anderson, Jacqulyn. *Media Center Techniques* series. Nashville: Broadman, 1978. Set of four cassette tapes. C-60.

Anderson, Margaret. "Make Friends with Books." *Covenant Companion,* February 9, 1968, pp. 14-16.

Arbuthnot, May Hill. *Children and Books.* Rev. ed. Chicago: Scott, Foresman, 1957.

Atherton, Pauline, and Christian, Roger W. *Librarians and Online Services.* White Plains, New York: Knowledge Industry Publications, 1977.

Bahr, Alice Harrison. *Video in Libraries—A Status Report, 1979-80.* 2d ed. White Plains, New York: Knowledge Industry Publications, 1980.

Barshinger, Clark. "Guaranteed Better Reading." *Christian Teacher,* September-October 1971, p. 13.

Bauer, Harry C. *Seasoned to Taste.* Seattle: University of Washington Press, 1961.

Benson, Mary C. *Church Library Manual.* Winona Lake, Indiana: Light & Life, 1967.

Berry, Ronald W. "The Ubiquitous Cassette." *Christian Life,* October 1975, pp. 76-77.

Borgwardt, Stephanie. *Library Display.* 2d ed. Johannesburg: Witwatersrand University Press, 1970.

Brown, Marel. "A Book Becomes a Bridge." *Christian Life,* November 1971, pp. 58-59.

Buder, Christine. *How to Build a Church Library.* St. Louis: Bethany Press, 1955.

Carlson, William Hugh. *In a Grand and Awful Time—Essays from the Librarian's Desk on Twentieth Century Man and His Books.* Corvallis: Oregon State University Press, 1967.

Chernik, Barbara E. *Introduction to Library Services for Library Technicians.* Littleton, Colorado: Libraries Unlimited, 1982.

Christian Librarian, all issues (see Appendix 2 for address).

Christian Periodical Index, all issues (see Appendix 2 for address).

Church and Synagogue Libraries, all issues (see Appendix 2 for address).

Coplan, Kate. *Effective Library Exhibits—How to Prepare and Promote Good Displays.* New York: Oceana, 1958.

Dahlman, Dorothy. "Your Church Needs a Resource Center." *Standard,* April 1, 1975, pp. 25-28.

Daily, Jay E. *Organizing Nonprint Materials—A Guide for Librarians.* New York: Marcel Dekker, 1972.

Dewey, Melvil. *Abridged Dewey Decimal Classification and Relative Index.* 10th ed. rev. Lake Placid Club, New York: Forest Press, 1972.

Dewey, Melvil. *Dewey Decimal Classification and Relative Index.* 18th ed. 3 vols.: vol. 1, *Introduction. Tables;* vol. 2, *Schedules;* vol. 3, *Relative Index.* Lake Placid Club, New York: Forest Press, 1971.

Dick, Nancy. "Blessed Is the Church Librarian." *Success,* Winter 1974-75, pp. 11-12.

Dobbins, Gaines S. *Learning to Lead.* Nashville: Broadman, 1968.

Duff, Annis. *"Bequest of Wings."* New York: Viking, 1944.

Fitch, George Hamlin. *Comfort Found in Good Old Books.* San Francisco: Elder, 1911.

Folcarelli, Ralph J.; Tannenbaum, Arthur; and Ferragamo, Ralph C. *The Microform Connection.* New York: R. R. Bowker, 1982.

Foote, Elizabeth Louisa. *The Church Library, a Manual.* New York: Abingdon, 1931.

Fosdick, Howard. *Computer Basics for Librarians and Information Scientists.* Arlington, Virginia: Information Resources, 1981.

Gangel, Kenneth O. *Competent to Lead—A Guide to Management in Christian Organizations.* Chicago: Moody, 1974.

Getz, Gene A. *Audiovisual Media in Christian Education.* Chicago: Moody, 1972.

Gould, Geraldine N., and Wolfe, Ithmer C. *How to Organize and Maintain the Library Picture/Pamphlet File.* New York: Oceana, 1968.

Guide to Use of Dewey Decimal Classification. Lake Placid Club, New York: Forest Press, 1962.

Haines, Helen E. *Living with Books: The Art of Book Selection.* 2d ed. New York: Columbia University Press, 1950.

Hammack, Mary L. "A Resource Center for Your Church." *Moody Monthly,* October 1971, pp. 46-47.

Hannaford, Claudia, and Smith, Ruth S. *Promotion Planning.* Bryn Mawr, Pennsylvania: Church and Synagogue Library Association, 1975.

Harmon, Robert B. *Simplified Cataloging Manual for Small Libraries and Private Collections.* San Jose: Bibliographic Research Library, 1975.

Harvey, John F., ed. *Church and Synagogue Libraries.* Metuchen, New Jersey: Scarecrow Press, 1980.

Hayward, Christopher. "Captivating! Video Is Today's Medium for Information and Entertainment." *Bookstore Journal,* July 1982, pp. 22-24.

Hendricks, William. "Christian Video—What's Available for the Christian Market." *Bookstore Journal,* July 1982, pp. 41-43.

Hendricks, William. "Video Preview—Keeping Up with the Christian Video Explosion." *Bookstore Journal,* February 1983, pp. 93-96.

Herring, John. "Converting to Computers." *Moody Monthly,* March 1983, pp. 58-59, 93-96.

Hicks, Warren B., and Tillin, Alma M. *Developing Multi-Media Libraries.* New York: Bowker, 1970.

Hillicker, Charles. "Understanding Microcomputers." *Christian Bookseller,* May 1982, pp. 22-24.

Hulley, David A. "The Micros Are Here!" *Christian Bookseller & Librarian,* May 1983, pp. 22-23.

Hunt, Gladys. *Honey for a Child's Heart.* Grand Rapids: Zondervan, 1969.

"Is There a New Road Ahead for Books?" *Christianity Today,* March 4, 1983, pp. 22-25.

John, Erwin E. "A Church Library Needs Good Operating Procedures." *International Journal of Religious Education,* October 1966, p. 12.

John, Erwin E. *The Key to a Successful Church Library.* Minneapolis: Augsburg, 1958.

Johnson, Jean; Franklin, Marietta; McCotter, Margaret; and Warner, Veronica. *AV Cataloging and Processing Simplified.* Raleigh: Audiovisual Catalogers, 1971.

Johnson, Marian S. *Planning and Furnishing the Church Library.* Minneapolis: Augsburg, 1966.

Johnson, Marian S. *Promoting Your Church Library.* Minneapolis: Augsburg, 1968.

Joiner, Lee Marvin; Vensel, George J.; Ross, Jay D.; and Silverstein, Burton J. *Microcomputers in Education.* Holmes Beach, Florida: Learning Publications, 1982.

Kehl, D. G. "Books That Helped Shape Their Lives." *Moody Monthly,* November 1973, p. 38.

Kelts, Helen. "Your Church Library: A Place to Share the Wealth." *Christian Life,* November 1975, pp. 86-89, 97.

Ker, Neil, ed. *The Parochial Libraries of the Church of England.* London: Faith Press, 1959.

Kohl, Rachel, and Rodda, Dorothy, comps. *Church and Synagogue Library Resources.* Bryn Mawr, Pennsylvania: Church and Synagogue Library Association, 1975.

Kroeker, Wally. "The World out of Which Books Grow." *Moody Monthly,* July-August 1974, pp. 37-47.

Landrum, Phil. "Getting in on the Children's Book Boom." *Christian Life,* November 1974, pp. 102-4.

Librarian's World, all issues (see Appendix 2 for address).

Library Journal, all issues (see Appendix 2 for address).

Lindskoog, Kathryn. "Resurrect Those Church Dry Bones—How to Put New Life into Your Church Library." *Eternity,* November 1969, pp. 68-70.

Lutheran Libraries, all issues (see Appendix 2 for address).

Lynn, Edwin Charles. *Tired Dragons—Adapting Church Architecture to Changing Needs.* Boston: Beacon, 1972.

McMichael, Betty. "The Church Library and the Christian Bookstore." *Bookstore Journal,* October 1974, pp. 48-50.

McMichael, Betty. "How Does Your Church Library Compare with Others?" *Evangelical Beacon,* August 20, 1974, pp. 14-15.

McMichael, Betty. "Summer Time Is Reading Time." *Evangelical Beacon,* April 4, 1972, pp. 6-7.

Marks, Harvey. "Those Invaluable Resource Centers." *Christian Life,* March 1974, p. 39.

Martin, Dorothy. "How to Choose the Best Books for Your Children." *Moody Monthly,* November 1972, p. 32.

Media: Library Services Journal, previously published as *Church Library Magazine,* all issues (see Appendix 2 for address).

Meloon, Will. "The Mighty Cassette." *Christian Life,* February 1974, pp. 62-65.

Moore, T. M. "Using Video in the Local Church." *Leadership,* Winter 1982, pp. 112-13.

Moyer, Elgin S. *Building a Minister's Library.* Chicago: Moody, 1944.

Moyer, Elgin S. *The Pastor and His Library.* Chicago: Moody, 1953.

Newton, Charlotte. *Church Library Manual.* Athens, Georgia: Charlotte Newton (892 Prince Avenue, 30606), 1964.

Newton, LaVose. *Church Library Handbook.* Rev. ed. Portland, Oregon: Multnomah, 1972.

Parmelee, Dan. "Devotional Cassettes—Ways to Use Them." *Standard,* January 1, 1974, p. 27.

Piercy, Esther J. *Commonsense Cataloging.* New York: H. W. Wilson, 1965.

Proctor, William. "Should You Invite a Computer to Church?" *Christian Herald,* February 1982, pp. 28-30, 35-36.

Read, E. Anne. *The Cathedral Libraries of England.* Oxford: Oxford Bibliographical Society, 1970.

Reapsome, James W. "Making Church Libraries Come Alive." *Moody Monthly,* November 1969, pp. 44-46.

Robinson, Jack, "You Can Read Faster." *Moody Monthly,* November 1972, p. 26.

Rodda, Dorothy, and Harvey, John, comps. *Directory of Church Libraries.* Philadelphia: Drexel, 1967.

Rorvig, Mark E. *Microcomputers and Libraries: A Guide to Technology, Products and Applications.* White Plains, New York: Knowledge Industry Publications, 1981.

Sanford, A. P., and Schauffler, Robert Haven. *The Magic of Books—An Anthology for Book Week.* New York: Dodd, Mead, 1938.

Saul, Arthur K. *121 Ways Toward a More Effective Church Library.* Wheaton, Illinois: Victor Books/SP Publications, 1980.

Schakelaar, Eva, ed. "Library Lines." *Teach,* Spring 1968—Winter 1974.

Scheer, Gladys E. *The Church Library—Tips and Tools.* St. Louis: Bethany Press, 1973.

Seelye, Tedd F. "The Cassette Explosion." *Moody Monthly,* July-August 1973, pp. 38-41.

Shelley, Marshall. "Ministering Undercover: A Survey of Church Librarians." *Leadership,* Winter 1983, pp. 98-102.

Skanse, Ruth T. "How to Build a Church Library." *Standard,* August 15, 1973, pp. 25-26.

Smith, Jay J. *Minister's Library Handbook.* Boston: Wilde, 1958.

Smith, Ruth S. *Cataloging Made Easy—How to Organize Your Congregation's Library.* New York: Seabury, 1978.

Smith, Ruth S. *Getting the Books off the Shelves.* New York: Hawthorn, 1975.

Smith, Ruth S. *Publicity for a Church Library.* Grand Rapids: Zondervan, 1966.

Smith, Ruth S. *Running a Library.* New York: Seabury, 1982.

Sogaard, Viggo B. *Everything You Need to Know for a Cassette Ministry.* Minneapolis: Bethany Fellowship, 1975.

Stone, Clara Ruth, ed. *Library Manual for Missionaries.* Watertown, Minnesota: Christian Librarians' Fellowship, Inc. (104 Riverside Terrace, 55388), 1979.

Straughan, Alice. *How to Organize Your Church Library.* Westwood, New Jersey: Revell, 1962.

Sunday School Board of the Southern Baptist Convention. *The Church Library Development Plan.* 3 vols. (Stages 1, 2, and 3). Nashville: Convention Press, 1968-69.

Sunday School Board of the Southern Baptist Convention. *Church Library Space, Equipment, and Furnishings.* Nashville: Sunday School Board of the Southern Baptist Convention, 1970.

Swarthout, Arthur W. *Selecting Library Materials.* Bryn Mawr, Pennsylvania: Church and Synagogue Library Association, 1974.

Todd, Wayne E. *Library Services in the Church.* Nashville: Convention Press, 1969.

Towns, Elmer L., and Barber, Cyril J. *Successful Church Libraries.* Grand Rapids: Baker, 1971.

200 (Religion) Class Reprinted from Edition 18 Unabridged Dewey Decimal Classification. Nashville: Broadman, 1971.

Velleman, Ruth A. *Serving Physically Disabled People—An Information Handbook for All Libraries.* New York: R. R. Bowker, 1979.

Westby, Barbara M., ed. *Sears List of Subject Headings.* 10th ed. New York: H. W. Wilson, 1972.

Westing, Harold J. "Right Before Your Eyes—Video Becomes a Viable Christian Education Tool." *Bookstore Journal,* July 1982, pp. 47-48.

White, Joyce. "Church and Synagogue Libraries." *Drexel Library Quarterly,* April 1970, pp. 111-78.

White, Joyce L. "Church Libraries: Unrecognized Resources." *American Libraries,* April 1971, pp. 397-99.

White, Joyce L., and Humeston, E. J., Jr., eds. *Processing of the Second Annual Church Library Conference.* Philadelphia: Drexel, 1964.

Widber, Mildred C., and Ritenour, Scott Turner. *Focus: Building for Christian Education.* Philadelphia: Pilgrim, 1969.

Wilson Library Bulletin, all issues (see Appendix 2 for address).

Witter, Evelyn, "Steps to a Sunday School Library." *Sunday School Times,* February 27, 1965, p. 153.

Wong, Joseph Y. "But How Do I Start a Church Library?" *Good News Broadcaster,* January 1975, pp. 8-13.

INDEX